DRAGONTRAX
CHINA VS US

The Great Strategic Competition
American Enterprise Forms the Front Line

KIM TAYLOR

TGM

Publisher: TGM

Library of Congress Control Number: 2024913029

ISBN: 979-8-9908039-0-9 (hardback)
ISBN: 979-8-9908039-1-6 (paperback)
ISBN: 979-8-9908039-2-3 (ebook)

For Laura
without whom this book
would not have been possible

Contents

Introduction

As I sailed down the Yangtze river on a slow boat *in* China, the idiom on a slow boat *to* China kept coming to mind. I began to realize that both the slow boats in and to China held important lessons in understanding the country. My slow boat making its way down the river pasted swift currents, whirlpools and hidden rocks. Deep recesses and blind bends held obscure dangers. Passing through the Three Gorges Dam demonstrated China's rapid development and technological prowess. The journey embodied both the challenges and opportunities of China.

To avoid dangers and capitalize on the opportunities required knowledge. It also required patience to play the long game. "On a slow boat to China" had originated from a 1948 song and had been adopted by the winning poker player who wanted to put his unlucky opponent on a long slow journey to prolong the contest and maximize his winnings. There can only be one winner, who must have the ability to think long term, see beyond the temporary losses and use strategy to reach the end game. Today, that end game has become winning the "strategic competition" between China and the US.

Bruce Henderson, of Boston Consulting Group, on "The Origin of Strategy", provided an understanding of strategic competition. He proposed that business competition is a clash of economic ideologies in which one dominant economic ideology will emerge to shape the future. In the case of China versus the US, ideological competition pits capitalism and democracy against state capitalism and digitally managed authoritarianism.

Henderson reminds us that competition in nature begins with life itself, starting with one-celled organisms. If resources are adequate, a population can grow and evolve. But he points out, citing Gause's principle of competitive exclusion: "No two species can coexist that make their living in the identical way." Gause's principle concludes "animals of different species could survive and persist together. If they were the same species, they could not."[1]

When a pair of species compete for essential resources, one of them will eventually displace the other—that is, the axiom of the survival of the fittest. In business, however, the struggle may turn out to be more complex. Henderson explained a business strategist could draw upon their imagination and logical reason to speed up the rate of change and effect competition. The strategic effect shortens what would take generations in evolution found in the biological world. Furthermore, the strategist moves the company beyond a simple fight for market share and seeks to define the market, establishing boundaries between itself and rivals removing any equivalency in the customer's consideration.[2] Business competition forces competitive advantage through uniqueness or differentiation.

For over forty years, China and the US have coexisted, simply by not making their living the same way, with the US being the brain and China being the brawn. America provided the innovative breakthroughs; China manufactured the resulting outputs by creating and controlling the world's largest factory floor.

Lucky enough to leave business school and begin my career with an upstart, DirecTV, a video broadcast television provider, I found myself on the ground floor of Henderson's idea of disruption and differentiation. Facing the de facto territorial monopolies of cable television, DirecTV had the advantages of massive bandwidth. DirecTV could broadcast hundreds of channels at fractional costs over their competitors. Carving out unique niches with exclusive sports and foreign programming set this satellite provider apart from decades of cable TV sameness. Beginning my stint, when the company had less than 2 million customers and departing just short of 10 million, had made for an exhilarating rocket ride.

Next came Sony International Television Networks, spanning continents and cultures. Mining Sony's acquisition of Columbia Pictures' video library, new acquisitions and original productions, Sony was launching newly created and branded video channels throughout the world. Two networks standout, as they represented how brands and products are perceived by the intended audience and how dependent a corporate headquarters can be on those in-market, of-culture, employees.

In India, it was SET (Sony Entertainment Television). As the format rights to the *Idol* singing contest had been purchased, *Indian Idol* was rolling out as one of the first reality competition shows in the marketplace. The insight, while Indians may have been quite used to voting for political candidates and the inherent outcome of one loser, voting against fellow countrymen and devastating their dream of fame by kicking them off the show, was a new concept. The marketplace ratings winner went to the Star TV channel and its format show, *Who Wants to Be a Millionaire*, whose social zeitgeist was memorialized in the movie, *Slum Dog Millionaire*.

The other network was Animax, comprised of Japanese-language anime. Its positioning and personality was very much the version of Japan's pastel, soft, round, respectful family fare. In Latin America, the programming chosen for their Animax feed was adult-focused and represented the edgier manga animation available. A clash of color, design and description made it difficult to stay true to a global brand positioning, and yet still serve the needs of the individual marketplace. The flip side to Animax's challenges was in the multiethnic city-state of Singapore, composed mainly of the Chinese Han ethnic group. While programming and product positioning between the Singaporean, Japanese and US offices was rather uncontentious in strategic and tactical execution, a territorial, secretive dynamic was always in play. On one visit to Singapore, I was greeted with the reveal of a new campaign; anime mascots had been developed to represent the channel. There were two little, round, pastel characters; one wore a shirt with a "Q" emblazoned, the other with a "T". Clearly, the development of animated representations of a global brand property, which could be manipulated to put forth any message, was out of bounds. I asked, what are the Q and T meant to represent? The answer became obvious not in verbal response, but in the red flush his face quickly exposed. I answered myself, "you mean you made them on the QT." This was my introduction to the cleverness of an ethnic Han, armed with a perfect understanding of English slang.

Meanwhile, back in the states, cable television was rising to the occasion of competition. Comcast, America's largest cable and internet operator, was evolving and developing products and strategies to take advantage of DirecTV's weaknesses. The disruptor would become the disrupted. Comcast was at the forefront of time-shifted, on demand programming, coupled with internet access, effectively future proofing itself for the day when programming would be accessed via the internet. Arriving at Comcast's headquarters, I first worked on general marketing initiatives. But, as Comcast sought to regain market share, and as their bandwidth increased, niche markets could now be pursued. Soon, I was in pursuit of these untapped market segments for Comcast. The low hanging fruit was the largest segment, Hispanics.

The key insight, immigrants, and first- and second-generation Latin Americans did not seek to assimilate, but rather to acculturate. Often bilingual, carrying unique familial and cultural traits — success would depend on whole of corporate support and knowledge.

It was through my China research shared in this book I discovered why I had struggled to make inroads at Comcast with the American Chinese consumer. Had it been the product? The price? As I had queried a fellow employee as to the why, the retort had been "the Chinese are cheap, they won't buy anything." Actually, our positioning was wrong— Confucian values espouse frugality; our positioning did not speak to a value for money the consumer could justify.

After several years of reflection on power competition, and drawing upon my experience, my gaze turned to China. What would I need to know to be a successful businessperson if dealing with the Chinese marketplace. The quest to increase my own China knowledge was the genesis of this book. I recalled reading Thomas Friedman's *The World Is Flat* in 2005 as I flew from the world's largest democracy, India, to the world's largest communist country, China, and passed through Hong Kong's international airport, on my way to then home, Los Angeles, CA. It was there, descending between skyscrapers, disembarking into the cavernous airport halls, that the China bug bit me. It was the bug of a capitalist that sees a vast, unsaturated marketplace, and it had bitten many around the world for centuries.

I discovered along the way that my lack of knowing China was not particularly unique. China's first Western advertising man, Carl Crow, wrote my favorite description of attempting to crack the code of the seductive Chinese market in 1937. From his *400 Million Customers*:

> I don't suppose there is a proprietary medicine

manufacturer of importance in any part of the world who has not, at one time or another, encouraged his imagination to play with the idea of the prosperous business he might build up, and the wealth he might accumulate, if he could, by some means, convince a reasonable number of Chinese of the efficiency of his remedies. The less the manufacturer knows about China, apart from the population figure, the less restricted are his day-dreams, and, as he usually knows nothing about the country, his fancy is in most cases free to wander into distant and prosperous fields.[3]

To win a competition, you must develop a strategy; to create a winning strategy, you must have knowledge. As stated by University of Hong Kong professor Jean-Pierre Lehmann, "[China's] centrality in our 21st century world makes it imperative that outsiders understand what is shaping its views and decisions...."[4] China's opacity around its business practices, when compared to America's transparency, has created a knowledge and information gap, providing China with a strategic business advantage.

The objective of this book is to provide insights on what and who has and is shaping China's views and decisions since its founding as a Communist country in 1921. The "who" are China's three most powerful leaders, Mao Zedong, Deng Xiaoping and today's president, Xi Jinping. The "what" are the policy decisions each has made to reach China's declared intention to restore the country to greatness and lead the world. How Xi Jinping plans to achieve China's goal is explored through his official "thoughts".

The entanglement of globalized commerce has created a web of resource dependency in raw materials, intellectual property, and digital and physical outputs. This predicament has given rise to a new concept—weaponized interdependency. American enterprise should expect to encounter and compete with China anywhere in the world and within any industry.

Within China, for American enterprise to simply pull up stakes and walk away from physical sunk costs, market share revenue, and future opportunities to build or rebuild elsewhere in the world will in some cases require decades of effort and hefty investment.

The decisions corporations have made to date to compete within China are laid bare within these pages. Laced throughout are anecdotes and examples as well as case studies of multinational corporations' detrimental experiences with China as it seeks to reach its goal of dominance.

In the decade that I have taken to research and write this book, I have watched history unfold. The geopolitical and technical changes in both the US and China are moving at an incredible speed. However, with the foundational knowledge provided within, you will be able to rip the current day headlines regarding China with an understanding of the genesis of the issue and be able to use your logic and imagination to meet the challenge.

American enterprise sits on the front line of this very important strategic competition. We can exercise what we know best—economic competition. The goal should be to channel the wise words of hockey great Wayne Gretzky when anticipating his next puck attack —skate to where the dragon is going. Not where he has been.

PART I

CHAPTER 1

Xi Jinping and His Thoughts for a New Era

Tell China's story well, and do a good job of external propaganda.
—Xi Jinping

China's preeminent leader, Xi Jinping, is the most powerful Chinese ruler since Mao Zedong, who was the father of the Chinese Revolution and autocratic leader of the nation from its founding in 1949 until his death in 1976. Xi is also on track to be China's most transformative and disruptive leader since Deng Xiaoping, who ruled from 1978–1989. Deng instituted China's period of reform and opening, beginning in 1978, which allowed China to rise from internal crisis and generate unprecedented wealth and development.

Xi came to power in 2012. With his second five-year term beginning in 2017, he abolished term limits and declared his reign open-ended. He broke with norms established under Deng that had sought to separate branches of government and ensure peaceful transitions of power. Xi's changes meant that leaders were no longer limited to two consecutive five-year terms.

Xi's paramount leadership positions include general secretary of the CPC, president of the People's Republic of China (PRC), and chairman of the Central Military Commission, placing him at the center of everything that controls China's politics and policy. He has been dubbed by the CPC as the "core" (*hexin*) leader—one who builds a working consensus among all senior acting and retired leaders, even though many may fundamentally disagree with him—and externally by the West as the CEO of Everything.

How did this one man, a member of a political party numbering ninety-six million, rise through the ranks to carry the flag of the Chinese nation and become a torchbearer for today's Chinese Dream?

Westerners frequently describe Chinese politics as opaque. There is much we don't know. However, we do know that Xi is a princeling, as the sons of revolutionaries who worked with Mao are labeled. This gave Xi an advantage to climb the ranks of leadership. Princelings most often make up the nucleus of China's political elite class. Xi's backstory, real and propaganda-enhanced, positions him as a man of the masses who had an aspirational rise and is meant to represent the future China desires.

What is the future China desires? Bluntly stated, it is to be number one in the world. Having a leader with open-ended reign, unquestionable decision-making authority, and a story that appeals to the masses makes charting a course for supremacy much more streamlined and efficient.

The world is in a volatile stage, and to assume its leadership mantle with the perception of a benevolent yet strong leader who also exudes worldly wisdom required opaque construction of a perfect man. The architects of this perfect man—Xi, and how he will meet the goal of global leadership, leads us to several behind-the-scenes thought makers.

In 2009, Liu Mingfu, a military officer, published an important book. Its main title was *The China Dream*, but the subtitle is more important: *Great Power Thinking and Strategic Posture in the Post-American Era*. The cover of the American version of the book quoted Henry Kissinger from *On China*: "In Liu's view, no matter how much China commits to a peaceful rise, a conflict is inherent in US-China relations. The relationship between China and the United States will be a 'marathon contest' and a 'duel of the Century.'"[1]

The ideas, strategies, and pronouncements in Liu's book

spawned paradigm shifts in American thinking about its relationship with China. It fostered changes in the thinking of America's greatest China "doves." The doves are a group of influential Western thinkers and leaders who believed that China's integration into the Western-led international order would shift China's thinking and actions to mirror ours.

In 2017, Liu Mingfu, author of *The China Dream*, and coauthor Wang Zhongyuan, both of the Chinese People's Liberation Army, published an English-language version of *The Thoughts of Xi Jinping: Thoughts Shape the World, Thoughts Shape the Future, Xi's Thoughts Help Better Understanding China and the World*. The accepted and used term to refer to the thoughts of Xi Jinping is Xi Jinping Thought, and for simplicity and efficiency, throughout this book it will be referred to as XJT.

Another convention used throughout this book refers to the Communist Party of China (CPC), which is the official party title, as the Chinese Communist Party (CCP). They are used interchangeably, and even the Chinese switch back and forth. In the official text of XJT, they use CPC. Of note, the author Liu described himself as a "Chinese Communist Party member" in his bio. Maybe Liu committed a Freudian slip, as China's Communist Party barely resembles the theoretical visions of Marx and Engels, but it exhibits a reimagined communism with distinct Chinese characteristics.

Returning to Xi Jinping, one may wonder why this one man was chosen to lead out of a population of 1.4 billion and from among ninety-six million members of the CCP. Liu's *The China Dream* may provide some clues. Liu saw China rising to the top of global leadership not through destructive, conventional war but through what he posited as beneficial economic competition between nations. But in this competition, relying on China's historical emperor and communist leadership models based on a single man, a key helmsman must be identified and groomed.

Liu called for China to develop a national collective will and to rally around the elites, known as princelings or sons of Mao's modern-day emperors. Liu provided the reasoning for and attributes of a strongman leader, stating: "China is on a strategic sprint to become the world's global leader."[2] To achieve this goal, strategic leadership led by the elites is necessary to identify opportunities, provide a road map for strategic innovation and design, and rally the people to its cause. The leader must be able to solve the challenges of society as proof that the country's coordinated, singular vision will serve the country in achieving global leadership. Liu mined the past as proof of the CCP's thinking:

> In the study of the history concerning the rise of great powers, the statesmen, as the elites that lead and command other elites, play a special strategic role. A people without great statesmen cannot rise up. All the great powers have their great statesmen. Their design and establishment of the country, their wisdom, capabilities, struggles and sacrifices, and connection and contact with the public enable them to stand in the vanguard of the era and at the strategic helm to guide and boost the country and its people toward prosperity.[3]

The idea of the Chinese elite is best explained by Evan Osnos in *The New Yorker* article "Born Red." "The Communist Party dedicated itself to a classless society but organized itself into a rigid hierarchy, and Xi started life near the top."[4] Xi was born in 1953, and his father, Xi Zhongxun, was at the time China's propaganda minister. When Xi Jinping was five, his father was promoted to vice premier. Xi Jinping then began to attend an exclusive school nicknamed "cradle of leaders."

Because the Communists had won the revolution and established the PRC in 1949, they believed they and their descendants would own the leadership of the country indefinitely.[5] This claim of leadership for the elites in succession was rooted in the historical experiences of emperors whose eldest sons were chosen as the "sons of heaven" and expected to rule as autocrats of all under Heaven. Mao, as the first supreme leader after the communist revolution, had intended to end the feudal traditions of dynastic rule. His intentions were for China to be ruled by the people of the proletariat, but centuries of experience pulled them back to an inherent Chinese trait—reliance on a single ruler. The solution was to create a hybrid system that distributed power among an elite class, who would then choose a supreme leader from among its own ranks.

In 1962, Xi Jinping, not yet ten years old, saw his father banished from government for supporting a novel that was viewed as critical of Mao. This placed the Xi family in a politically vulnerable situation. After Mao began the Cultural Revolution in 1966, he began a program known as Sent-Down Youth Movement, which exported urban high school and college students to the countryside to be reeducated by the country's peasants. Xi Jinping was sent to an area where his father had connections.[6] Elder Xi may have been a fallen star in Mao's eyes, but personal alliances are the currency of old and new China.

Xi Jinping's ability to point to his experience during the critical time of the Cultural Revolution provided a foundation for Xi as a man of the people. During Xi Jinping's first term as general secretary, Osnos reported on a television cartoon targeting children entitled "'How to Make a Leader," which described Xi, despite his family pedigree, as a symbol of meritocracy: Xi had lived among the villagers in a cave and endured hard labor.[7] Xi's narrative from this sent-down youth experience allowed him to put aside the humiliation his family must have felt from Mao's rebuke, and he was positioned as whole-heartedly embracing the structure and ideology of the communist party.

As we'll see later, in Xi's speeches he references not only his time as a sent-down youth but also the hardships he observed and endured throughout various Chinese provinces as he worked his way up the political hierarchy. These stories helped cement his image as a man of the masses.

Another key Chinese contributor in the making of Xi is Wang Huning, who was dubbed "China's crown theorist" in an article for *Foreign Affairs* written by Ryan Mitchell. Wang ascended to the Politburo Standing Committee in 2017 after a long tenure as head of the CPC's Central Policy Research Office, which directs the party's ideological platform. His current position is chairman of the Chinese People's Political Consultative Conference.

To achieve its desired rise, China needed more than just a charismatic leader. The country also needed a strong ideology designed to bind the will of the people to the party. From Mitchell's China's crown theorist, when the party's Politburo Standing Committee was introduced in 2017, "only one face came as a surprise. . . . [I]t was that of Wang Huning, a long-time party ideologist . . . [who] will have ideological authority second only to that of President Xi Jinping himself."[8]

Per Mitchell, Wang spent his academic career studying, writing, and developing an ideology for China based on "the concept of sovereignty in Western thought."[9] For Wang, the key takeaway of sovereignty was for the party to control the country and provide protection from any internal or external threats. In Wang's study of why the West had risen, based on the concept of sovereignty, he concluded that Western nations had relied on strong-man rule, able to thwart foreign and religious influence, creating loyalty among the masses and

provide periods of stability. These men led a West to dominate the globe.[10]

Mitchell explained what Wang was striving for: a China
whose political system holds the strength to protect the
country from outside influence or physical invasion. Wang's
vision was not to be impeded by modern Western values
of individual liberties, nor held back by ancient Confucian
benevolence, but to structure itself beneath an unquestionable authoritarian leader. This authoritarian leader would
resist the West, and to supplement Wang's view of sovereignty, Xi would need to be more than a man of the Chinese
masses. Xi's stature needed to be elevated to an irreproach-
able, larger-than-life figure and appear to the outside world
as one who could lead the world to a new phase of international discourse. There was a need to project soft power,
a need for acceptance, and the ability to pull both people
and nations to China's cause. Early in Xi's reign, the CCP
invested a great deal of energy in Xi being the face of that
soft power. The reason to create this soft power was to support building a cult of personality. It was justified in the
writings of XJT and endearingly referred to as charisma.

As today's Chinese political elite look back on their post-
revolutionary history, they see Mao as the strongman who
was able to pull the country together with an iron fist. The
elites conveniently disregarded the atrocities that befell their
fellow countrymen, as the check on Mao's power had been
eliminated, but the goal of unification was achieved.

The Chinese political elites are master students of history.
Their study of the rise and fall of the Soviet Union is subject
to continuous scrutiny. As the CCP always fears a disintegration of its hold on power, it has looked to Mao's North Star
in leadership dynamics, Soviet leader Vladimir Lenin, and is
bringing his maxims forward to support its theory of personality construction through Xi Jinping.

Liu cited Lenin's thinking on a ruling party to maintain its power. It cannot be held with force alone, the preexisting condition to keep power required charisma. "With charisma, we can seize power, or else we may lose our own power."[11]

While internal deference to Xi's cult of personality is important to keep people in awe and in support of Xi's goals for the nation, hard power and global vision need to be demonstrated externally. The Chinese elites realize the world is divided between the makers and creators of the world's tangible and intangible goods. To truly lead the world and draw others into its sphere of influence, China must move up the value-add chain. Until recently, China's wealth accumulation was dependent on manufacturing goods that derived from other nations' creative breakthroughs. The world has for decades decried modern China's inability to innovate, calling it a copycat nation. The desire to shed this subservient role led the CCP to prioritize innovation.

Marrying Liu's *The China Dream*, which called for China to rise up and lead without interference, to Wang's theory that to do so requires absolute devotion to a singular figurehead in the leadership position provides us with clarity as to why China chose to break with Deng's desire for peaceful transitional leadership and return to a strongman Mao model of leadership. Liu described this in his introduction to XJT:

> An innovation-based country needs creative statesmen. . . . It is impossible for a country that has no excellent statesmen to stand firm among the nations of the world; a country without great statesmen will never rise above the common herd. The pioneering and innovation-promoting statesmen represent the most powerful soft strength of a country.[12]

International recognition and validation of Xi's rising power is essential to China's efforts to build a cult of personality and a worldly leader. Global validation reassures its people of being led by one who can return them to a place of world dominance and erase their humiliations. Ironically, to bolster proof of Xi's paramount importance and charisma, XJT points to American publications, polls, and a former ambassador to China.

In *TIME* magazine's 2009 list of the world's most influential people, Vice President Xi was named most likely to ascend to the presidency in 2012. Xi remained on *TIME*'s list for several years, and in 2014 his bio was accompanied by the following commentary by Jon Huntsman, former US ambassador to China:

> Xi Jinping has emerged as the most transformational Chinese leader since Deng Xiaoping. His steady style exudes confidence while revealing little, capturing the attention of thought leaders worldwide. . . . Xi will become the first truly global leader to represent a country that for centuries has struggled with cohesion and unity. . . . [I]t will either be a failed effort, which would be catastrophic for the region, or a reformed Middle Kingdom that will become America's greatest challenge and opportunity of the 21st century.[13]

This is instructive of how an American's words were used in XJT to support the image China is constructing and showcases the power of censorship and ability to recast foreign media's coverage of China with impunity. While the ability to reference an internationally recognized people power index established by *TIME* magazine and the accompanying commentary by a respected US politician is useful in establishing

Xi as a formative global leader, Huntsman's original comments were not without reservations to Xi's and China's ability to achieve long-term success.

The authors of XJT, in a chapter on Xi's leadership, recast Huntsman's remarks to make it appear as though he had become convinced that Xi was a leader of global importance and vision and that the US should take notice. In paraphrasing Huntsman's remarks, the authors also recast Huntsman as a dove. Per XJT's telling:

> The charisma and the governing style of Xi Jinping are strongly accepted and supported by the masses, which not only receives good reputation in China, but also exerts impact on the world. . . . Jon Meade Huntsman who proposed taking China down in 2011 (referencing a debate response when Huntsman was running for President), considered in 2014 that Xi Jinping was a Chinese leader with the most distinctive features for transition after Deng Xiaoping. . . . In Huntsman's opinion, Xi Jinping is a leader calm and confident. He continues to lead China to succeed in the fierce competitions in the international market, and has received the attention of leaders worldwide. . . . Xi Jinping will become the first truly global leader of China.[14]

In the CCP's manufacturing of Xi Jinping, XJT tells us in one sentence how it placed all its bets on one man. It is the most comprehensive statement of positioning for Xi and his rule (shorthand added): "It can be seen that Xi Jinping's grand philosophy of political governance [known as XJT] is able to broaden the vision of a ruling party; his rejuvenation [nationalism/Chinese Dream] is able to solve the problems in national progress; and his charisma [cult of personality] has been favored by the people."[15]

In the molding of Xi as China's grand brand ambassador, two American companies, Bloomberg and Disney, ran afoul of the Chinese version of *TIME* magazine's myth in the making. It is important to understand how the construction of a perfect leader will not be jeopardized by outside interference and how China leverages economic coercion in support of this strategy.

As he rose through the ranks, Xi billed himself as a "clean" politician. However, in June 2012, months before Xi's installation as general secretary, *Bloomberg News*, a subsidiary of Bloomberg L.P., ran an article titled, "Xi Jinping Millionaire Relations Reveal Fortunes of Elite." The first two paragraphs read,

> Xi Jinping, the man in line to be China's next president, warned officials on a 2004 antigraft conference call: 'Rein in your spouses, children, relatives, friends and staff, and vow not to use power for personal gain.' As Xi climbed the Communist Party ranks, his extended family expanded their business interests to include minerals, real estate and mobile-phone equipment, according to public documents complied by Bloomberg.[16]

The report did not directly implicate Xi, his wife, or his daughter, but the *Bloomberg News* site was immediately blocked in China, joining a growing list of banned American news and information sites. Bloomberg L.P.'s business is predicated on providing financial information to the financial industry. Its differentiator and competitive advantage lie in its deep sourcing, the user's ability to create custom analysis on the fly, and its split-second access to immediate, dynamic information and data.

Bloomberg News is designed to feed the Bloomberg Terminal as well as a wider consumer audience through branded video and digital and print mediums. Its journalistic output provides color and insight to aid in financial data analysis.

As both mainland China and Hong Kong were becoming more important to international financial markets, the presence of Bloomberg Terminal was proliferating in China's marketplace, with an estimated two thousand machines in use by 2013. For *Bloomberg News* to run a deep dive on the ascendant Xi would naturally be expected by Western audiences. *Bloomberg News* management had not expected that the Xi story would be visible in mainland China. Foreseeing an eventual clash with the Chinese government at some point over an offending article led management to install a censoring device designed to stop reporting at the water's edge. Internally, *Bloomberg News* appended Code 204 to any coverage of Chinese politics and social issues, allowing only financial news to freely flow to China's eyes. It is unknown why the article on Xi was not appended, but the revelation of the censor code led other American journalists to investigate *Bloomberg News* policies. *The New York Times* reported that the use of Code 204 traced back as far as 2011.[17] Interviews with *Bloomberg News* employees show the stance taken was one of adhering to a strict licensing agreement with the Chinese government to provide only financial news.

As Code 204 was reported by other US news organizations, then New York City mayor Mike Bloomberg, founder and owner of Bloomberg L.P., remained mum on the issue. Shortly after, when Bloomberg was no longer a public official, Andrew Ross Sorkin of CNBC queried him about the self-censorship. Bloomberg did not directly address the question but sought to establish a stance whereby the news must comply with Chinese authority and to do so is a cost of market access. In acquiescence to China's ability to control information, Michael Bloomberg stated, "We follow those rules and if you don't follow the rules, you're not in the country."[18] Bloomberg's answer was realpolitik. In Eleanor Randolph's biography of Bloomberg, *The Many Lives of Michael Bloomberg*, she cut to the chase of the financial implications:

> The real problem was that the Bloomberg system [terminals] could not thrive without the best and fastest possible financial data out of China, and the top officials in China knew it. "If you're half a second slower than Reuters, there's trouble," said one former Bloomberg insider. "That was huge leverage over Bloomberg for the Chinese."[19]

The second company, American giant Disney, through no direct action became a victim of Xi's cult construction. In a visit to America in 2013, Xi and President Obama were photographed walking together in California. A meme was created in China that rendered Xi as Winnie the Pooh and Obama as Tigger. All things Pooh seemed to be banned. BBC reported, "It is not only that China's censors will not tolerate ridicule of the country's leader . . . he makes no mistakes and that is why he is above the population and unable to be questioned."[20] To ensure the point was made, in August 2018, Disney's *Christopher Robin* was denied release in China as it prominently featured Pooh.

Xi's brand has been protected behind walls constructed both overtly and through quietly complicit self-censorship, ensuring that the masses will hear no evil of their mighty leader.

Let's turn to the Chinese Dream, which was designed to inspire and unite the people. We'll uncover the promises of the Chinese Dream, knowing that the strategy to achieve the dream is wrapped in a perfect man whose ideology and vision is beyond reproach and underwritten by Liu and Wang.

CHAPTER 2

Chinese Dream

Achieving the rejuvenation of the Chinese nation has been the greatest dream.
—Xi Jinping

Shortly before Xi was to assume the office of president of the PRC on November 12, 2012, American author Thomas Friedman wrote an opinion piece for *The New York Times* entitled "China Needs Its Own Dream." Friedman rhetorically asked, "Does Xi have a 'Chinese Dream' that is different from the 'American Dream'? Because if Xi's dream for China's emerging middle class—300 million people expected to grow to 800 million by 2025—is just like the American Dream (a big car, a big house, and Big Macs for all) then we need another planet."[1] Friedman's observation was intended not so much to hold back China's desire for greater material gains or excuse the excesses of the West but more to acknowledge the unsustainability of the world's current consumption trend. Friedman was stating from his point of view what Xi would be facing when picking up the mantel of the CCP:

> So Xi Jinping has two very different challenges from his predecessor. He needs to ensure that the Communist Party continues to rule—despite awakened citizen pressure for reform—and that requires more high growth to keep the population satisfied with party control. But he also needs to manage all the downsides of that growth—from widening income gaps to mas-

> sive rural-urban migration to choking pollution
> and environmental destruction. The *only* way to
> square all that is with a new Chinese Dream that
> marries people's expectations of prosperity with
> a more sustainable China.[2]

Several books referencing various concepts of a Chinese Dream (besides Liu's) were written prior to Friedman's column, but Friedman had often been viewed in a positive light by the Chinese, and his commentary seemed to hit a chord. His column was translated and widely circulated in Chinese press.

Two weeks after Xi's presidential installation, he visited the National Museum of China in Beijing to view and speak at the exhibition called *The Road to Rejuvenation*. This exhibition covered the mid-nineteenth century to the present, calling out the "Century of Humiliation" at the hands of foreigners and China's recovery brought by the CCP. It was in this setting and his accompanying speech that Xi first officially articulated the dream: "Everyone has an ideal, ambition and dream. We are now all talking about the Chinese Dream. In my opinion, achieving the rejuvenation of the Chinese nation has been the greatest dream of the Chinese people since the advent of modern times. . . . History shows that the future and destiny of each and every one of us are closely linked to those of our country and nation. One can do well only when one's country and nation do well."[3] In this statement Xi hearkened back to Liu's dream construction. The dream is not individual but collective and finds power in expression through patriotism and nationalism.

The official acknowledgement and articulation of the Chinese Dream created a catchphrase and frenzy forever tied to President Xi. *The Economist* explained the importance of a catchphrase's utility in China: "The adoption of a personal slogan—one that conveys a sense of beyond—normal wisdom and vision in a short, memorable and perhaps somewhat opaque phrase—has been a rite of passage for all Chinese leaders since Mao Zedong. Mr. Xi's 'Chinese dream' slogan is exceptional, though. . . . [I]t makes no allusion to ideology or party policy. It chimes, quite possibly deliberately, with a foreign notion—the American dream. But it is calculated in its opacity. . . . The dream seems designed to inspire rather than inform."[4]

This initial vagueness served a great purpose in allowing Xi to continue to develop the CCP's vision of the dream and employ it to solve many of the issues China faces. It is used to wink at the hardline nationalists, motivate the masses to overcome their Century of Humiliation, remind its people of China's cultural history as a cohesive unit, and support the socialist cause for all boats to rise.

By April 2013 Xi placed the dream squarely on the backs of the middle class in another speech, telling them that their dreams will not fall from the sky. He implored the working class to pick up the mantle, to be the builders of socialism with Chinese characteristics in this new era, and to practice the officially sanctioned, still-developing core socialist values (covered in chapter 11). Xi, in creating relevance for the working class, encouraged them to pursue personal dreams and the Chinese Dream. But to be clear, it is not simply an individualistic material orgy; the dream serves a much broader purpose: "To meet our development goals, we must enrich ourselves not only materially but culturally and ethically as well."[5] This dream has the potential to rectify the missing link to a traditionally rich cultural history that was destroyed by the Cultural Revolution, and this dream should revive pride in the civilization's evolution.

The Chinese Dream caught fire and received an incredible level of campaign support from the propaganda machine.

Books were written and surveys were taken that can provide American marketers with great insight into this emerging middle class. Possibly the greatest insight we find is the divide that is hidden within this vast populous—those born before 1978's reform and opening and those born after.

Xi gave us a window into the different experiences between these pre- and post-1978 groups with a speech he gave in Seattle, Washington, in 2015 called, "The Chinese Dream Is the People's Dream." Speaking on the journey of his generation, he told the story of his time as a sent-down youth and how he labored beside the poor and undernourished. He described how the people experienced months without meat in their meals and that his desire was to help rectify this difficult situation. He then pivoted to demonstrate how the party changed these fortunes after 1978. He elaborated on how all the material and infrastructure investments in this impoverished region had completely changed people's lives. The ability to have meat was no longer a distant dream.

Xi's personal observation of the typical Chinese life pre- and postreform leads us to revisit Maslow's hierarchy of needs and to ask how it varies between American and Chinese, or between West and East, cultures (figure 1).

Figure 1: Maslow's hierarchy of needs in the West and East

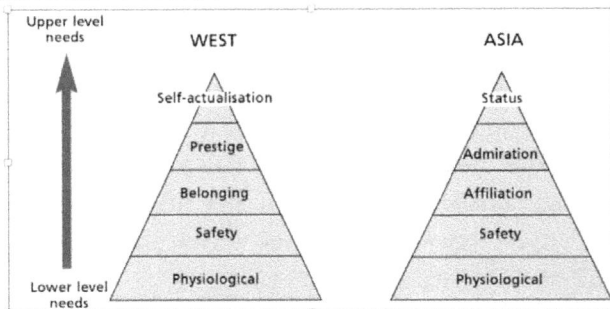

Weng Marc Lim, Ding Hooi Ting, Pei Then Khoo, and Wei Yi Wong, "Understanding Consumer Values and Socialization—a Case of Luxury Products. *Management & Marketing Challenges for the Knowledge Society* 7, No. 2 (2012): 209–220.

After 1978, Western MNCs entered China, bringing along their Western business practices and management theory, and forced a reassessment of Maslow's hierarchy and its relevance to the Chinese consumer.

Maslow's hierarchy of needs stems from a base level of needs necessary for survival and holds that until your primal needs are met, you cannot progress up the ladder to satisfy your higher-level needs. Maslow's theory was first posited in 1943 and was predicated on Western thinking and experience. Since then, many studies and theories have contributed to its reinterpretation and reimagination to incorporate the broader spectrum of civilizational differences.

Brenda Geren provided a strong overview in "Motivation: Chinese Theoretical Perspectives" of how management theories applied to China highlight key West/East differences. Geren explained that when creating a culturally relevant motivational model, a distinction between needs and values must be considered. Maslow showed how base-level needs such as food, shelter, and safety are universal. However, to reach the higher levels of motivation, values become key. The reason for a divergence in this hierarchy between West and East lies in the source of values being learned, not inherent. Within a culture, behaviors are formed by the group and influenced by cultural factors such as philosophy, religion, and customs.

Geren cited Maslow's description of a deficit or a common human need and the ensuing behavior: "for the man that is extremely and dangerously hungry, no other interests exist but food . . . .[S]uch a man may fairly be said to live by bread alone."[6] Xi's personal experience as related to his Seattle audience is a direct example of Maslow's common need throughout humankind.

Geren noted a key difference in values for China stemming from its collective society. Group needs supersede individual needs, leading to the Chinese desiring holistic social and esteem needs, meaning that group harmony is most important. "Some claim that Western society stresses individual behavior, whereas China stresses the collective one, and therefore, one cannot apply the same model to both cultures."[7] She elaborated on a study of the spectrum of individualism vs collectivism across countries that found China had the lowest score on individualism, indicating the most collective country, and the US had the highest score.[8]

The cultural value of group harmony, or the idea of a harmonious society (i.e., stability), is based on Confucius. This lineage is recognized by the CCP and leveraged to foster social stability. China is littered with inside cultural insights, beliefs, and superstitions not always apparent to the uninitiated. For a window into China's collective cohesion and reverence for cosmic alignment with nature, look to the 2008 Beijing Olympics. The opening ceremony was a spectacle of choreographed human performance filled with Chinese people performing in unison with undifferentiated costumes yet flowing in effortless movement to appear as one. As China's hosting of the Olympics brought great national pride, it capitalized on the fortuitous benefit of the summer Olympics falling in August 2008. "The Beijing Olympics opening ceremony began at 8:08 a.m., on the eighth day of the eighth month of 2008. The exact time was picked by organizers because of the meaning of the number eight to the Chinese. It represents luck, prosperity and wealth."[9] "[T]he Olympics in general have painted a picture of the new China: increasingly prosperous, powerful, harmonious and open."[10] What China was saying about the auspiciousness of the number eight was not for the individual but the desire of the nation. The Chinese Dream was further incorporated into this nation's proud moment with the official Olympics motto. "'One World, One Dream' is simple in expressions, but profound in meaning. . . .

It reflects the values of harmony . . . philosophies and ideals of the Chinese people since ancient times . . . harmony among people, building up a harmonious society and achieving harmonious development are the dream and aspirations of the Chinese."[11]

It should be noted that in 2007, Xi was given the job to chair the coordinating committee for the Olympics under extreme circumstances, including financial corruption and overruns in venue building, an uprising in the autonomous region of Tibet, global demonstrations in support of Tibet along the Olympic torch relay route, and an earthquake in Sichuan Province that killed eighty thousand people. Despite worldwide scrutiny, Xi's performance was deemed by the CCP as successful.

Xi's policies and state-led priorities answer Friedman's question: the Chinese Dream is not the same as the American Dream. Yes, Xi will lead the people to move toward an internally based consumption model but not toward a dream fulfillment founded in individualism, personal liberties, and unequal material gains.

If China is a collectivist society, and status is the highest aspiration of the hierarchy of needs, what would satisfy the Chinese Dream? Xi pointed to the rejuvenation of the nation, for China's status to once again be the most powerful nation and one that will never again sacrifice her sovereignty. To galvanize the people and motivate them to fight for this national revival, the CCP use an historical period, covering one hundred years. Within this period, roughly the 1840s through the founding of the PRC in 1949, China fell from the international apex of world power into complete disarray. The CCP branded and effectively uses this Century of Humiliation to stoke nationalism and promote collective cohesion.

Xi gave a speech to Peking University students on May 4, 2014, about the Chinese Dream. The date of the speech was chosen deliberately. The CCP always uses key dates when making specific points about issues or giving directives. With a long history of monumental events, the party can be masterful at using turning points of the past to speak to the current and future. May 4, 1919, was such a moment. It was a student-led uprising against imperialism, as the victors of World War I cleaved away Chinese territory and handed it to Japan as a reward for military alliance. It is viewed in China as the beginning of a distant dream to rise and shake itself of externally induced humiliation. Xi told the university students that since the Opium Wars of the 1840s and 1850s waged on them by the imperial Western nations, it was a long-simmering dream to rejuvenate the nation. Xi explained that prior to Western mercantilist interaction, China was the world's top economic power. Xi described the catalyst to China's change in fortune befalling it from the Opium Wars, citing the critical juncture of the Industrial Revolution as the turning point in the trajectory of the century to come.[12]

During the mid-nineteenth century, as China's control of its nation was disintegrating, Western nations were harnessing new means of production and innovations that were pushing the world into international trade treaties and laws. The changes China was forced to concede broke what had been centuries of national relations relying on managed tributary systems that kept its sphere of influence at the center and the superiority of its values, ethics, and culture unquestioned.[13]

Xi's speech was unique in an acceptance of the truth about what happened to China. When China had the chance under the Qing dynasty, the choice was made to dismiss this technologically induced arc of history. China was the most financially successful nation on Earth. Its value system and codes of conduct were so distinctively different; its hubris, founded in the past, did not allow it to accept that past performance was not indicative of future success. What was not unique about Xi's framing of this one-hundred-year period was a desire to shift this missed opportunity onto the backs of invading "barbarians."

Xi left his audience with an antidote to this perceived national embarrassment by utilizing patriotism. He instilled a sense of confidence by pointing to the success China had achieved under the CCP. China developed, the Chinese were stronger, and their progress created respect once again for the country. He also reminded students of their uniqueness, which derived from their traditional culture with "deep roots in the Chinese people's mentality, influencing their way of thinking and behavior unconsciously."[14]

Xi had drawn a contrast to the humble China of old and the new, party-led modern era. For Chinese continuity, he reached back to its ancient traditional values. Mao tried to destroy China's feudal ways and traditional values as he saw them as an impediment to China's ability to rise. Today, the CCP recognizes that calling on those old virtues provides a natural link to a singular Chinese Dream.

In linking to its historical, innate value system, it is a recognition of the definition of how values are acquired—through learning and repeated application. Mao may have wanted to rid the country of the old customs and way of thinking, but today's CCP seeks to harness and mold them to support pride of nation and provide a familiar system that at times in history provided stability and hierarchy in the Chinese people's world. China's three-thousand-year history embedded these values so deeply that they cannot be mandated as obsolete. The party has accepted this fact and now seeks to tinker around the edges, shaping and nudging some while adding others but critically co-opting the value system to build a powerful, collective nation. We look at the construction of today's core socialist values in chapter 11.

As Xi stamped ownership on the Chinese Dream,

internally there was much questioning of its similarity to the American Dream. In 2013, China's number-one box office film was *American Dreams in China*. Based on a true story and set in the 1980s, the film follows three Peking University students' desire to go to America in search of their dreams. As reform and opening had given Chinese visibility to a broader world from which they had been shielded for decades, and with the potential to immigrate, one of the three students makes his way to New York City.

The *American Dreams* protagonist, though educated, fails to make it in New York City and returns to Beijing to reconnect with his two classmates. Together they form a successful educational company called New Oriental that prepares students for the Test of English as a Foreign Language.

The moral of the story asks Chinese not to view their heritage with shame. While China, in its infancy of reform and opening, looked outward for modern-day instruction in development, dreaming, and living, thirty years later they are smarter, and the answer to these questions lies inward. ChinaFile.com, a China watcher website, concluded in its review of the film: "The Chinese people believe that even if their approach is imperfect and the results deficient, they will still pursue their dreams the Chinese way."[15] Exactly as Xi wishes.

The Chinese Dream is designed to give people confidence in themselves and their nation. They are reexamining their culture and embracing it with a modern twist. The party's ability to authentically pull from the past and marry it with a vision for China's future makes it necessary to better understand the dream in the context of the Chinese people. With the CCP's North Star for the dream set in a rejuvenated, proud nation, the stage is set for a rising, harmonious, collective society.

While underlying values can sustain a nation for

centuries, dreams morph over time. The American Dream did not begin with a house and a two-car garage; that was, from World War II until recently, the common person's definition. The American Dream began with ideas of freedom through religion and personal agency. Further ideas of self-determination and equality pushed the dream expansively. The Chinese Dream in the modern era has only just begun. Once people are asked to dream, they have a fire in their souls. In the confines of a mind, permission has been given to look inward and seek. The CCP has provided a grand vision; China is endeavoring to provide the tools for dream achievement.

On the road to China's dream attainment, we must track the missteps, course corrections, and successes. We must not jump ahead by applying an individualistic or materialistic American Dream lens but rather stay grounded in a values- and needs-based hierarchy that seeks first to honor the collective and is designed to support China's aspirations as a nation.

PART II

Chapter 3

The People of Qing

Our Celestial Empire possesses all things in prolific abundance.
—Emperor Qianlong

China's Century of Humiliation represents the period of the Opium Wars of the 1840s through 1949, with the founding of the PRC. This chapter in Chinese history—which saw China torn apart from internal warlords, external invasion, imperialism at the hands of Western nations and forced integration into Western trade treaties—is deeply ingrained in the minds of the public and the leaders of the country. Regardless of centuries of existence, it is this hundred-year period that defines at the deepest level what China intends to rectify in the future.

The Chinese Dream is about the all-important concept of "saving face." Before this period of humiliation, for many centuries, China was the center of Asia with all neighboring countries acting mostly in deference to China's superiority. There is a long history of neighboring states paying tribute to China's emperors. They were vassal states, and the heads of these states, on visiting the reigning emperor, would perform a kowtow.

For centuries China had been the dominant regional power. Its soft and hard power, which derived from its appealing culture and economic and superior political acumen, had drawn smaller neighboring states into China's orbit. China used these powers to spread civilizational proclivities and extract from neighbors the subservience China believed it was entitled to. In the minds of the Chinese elites, their superiority was not in question; they were the "middle kingdom." The world was their circular periphery.

But, as Xi articulated, China's managed tributary system fell victim to a rising international system that revolved around the idea of equal and sovereign nations. This emerging Westphalian system crashed on the Chinese shores through a British envoy, Lord Macartney in 1793, as he sought to open trade and diplomatic relations. Howard French, in *Everything Under the Heavens*, wrote, "He [Macartney] represented a country of 8 million subjects that was rapidly developing a trading system to span the globe and had recently become convinced of its status as the most powerful nation on earth. Qing China, a country of 350 million people, or more than the entire population of Europe, however, 'was the largest, wealthiest, and most populous contiguous political entity anywhere in the world.'"[1] This encounter set the stage for breaking the Chinese mindset of their ruling *tian xia* (all under Heaven). While not quite the traditional Asian tribute of the time but still a token custom today when visiting an associate in China, Macartney arrived bearing crates of gifts the English were sure would impress on the Chinese their advanced technological superiority.[2]

The English gifts represented the latest in science and technology, including modern weaponry that harnessed gunpowder discovered by the Chinese but with greatly improved effectiveness. The emperor Qianlong was not impressed and declined to establish new trade and diplomacy based on Western terms, sending Macartney back with a letter to King George III. Per French, Qianlong in part said that "barbarian" trade had been allowed in Canton. Qianlong's letter noted, "Our Celestial Empire possesses all things in prolific abundance and lacks no product within its own borders."[3] However, Qianlong expressed since China was such a generous and kind nation, it had recognized the barbarians' desire for its tea, silk, and porcelain and had allowed European nations to establish merchants in Canton in order to purchase these items. The confidence expressed by the emperor in China's own self-reliance—a belief in its people and culture to always provide what it needed—would never be abandoned by subsequent leaders. This stance has occasionally forced it to reach out to other nations to gain what was expedient for its survival, but it always turned back to itself.

This self-reliance mindset is replete in the goals and strategies of XJT. A dominant area of concern for self-sufficiency is food security. We will see how under Mao a breakdown in agriculture required China to reach out for nutritional assistance. This dark time under the CCP's rule haunts the elite. They recognize that should today's rulers fail to feed the people, it would be damning for the party. The party links food to economics but also politics. XJT says, "Our foothold and starting point are that under no circumstances should we buy or even beg food from others. Our bowl must hold the food produced on our own."[4] While this is a current aspirational statement of self-reliance, in reality food independence is not yet achieved, as witnessed by China's food imports growing from approximately $6 million in 2005 to $300 million in 2015.[5]

Xi's food fear is a callback to the words Americans heard at their dinner tables in the 1960s: "the Chinese are starving." Food as an analogy to the great wealth-building progress achieved by China since 1978 is a litmus test for the CCP's performance legitimacy and recurs throughout the seventy-year history of the PRC. *The New York Times* reported a recent example from 2020 as Xi Jinping extolled a Clean Plate Campaign. China had suffered crop loss due to extreme weather, pork markets were devastated by swine flu, and the pandemic had affected food supply chains. As the nation had grown rich, overeating and overordering had revived an old Chinese cultural custom that leaving food would show to friends, relatives and important guests their largess.[6] The state was estimating annual food waste of up to nineteen million tons, which could feed up to fifty million people.

Under Qianlong, British import/export trade did increase, but soon China's exports culminated in an unfavorable trade imbalance intolerable to England. British silver was flowing east to quench the desire for Chinese tea. Prior to the first Opium War, it is estimated that the average Londoner was spending 5 percent of the household budget for the exotic elixir. As England searched for products that could be sold in China, it looked south to India and the opium trade. The Qing emperor, unable to stop the trafficking, had the British opium embargoed as it entered the port in Canton, today known as Guangdong. The British and Chinese fought from 1839 to 1842. As the British were about to take the old Chinese capital, Nanjing, the emperor signed a peace treaty. The result was to pull China into the world of treaties and most-favored-nation trade clauses. While America was not involved in the first war, it had been trading with China as early as 1784. America soon faced the same fate as Britain: that of too little Chinese demand to match desires for Chinese products. America had become a party to these trade treaties, signing its first with China, the Treaty of Wangxia, in 1844. When the West determined China was not enforcing the agreements, a second Opium War ensued, lasting from 1857 to 1859. This war resulted in the complete destruction of Yuanmingyuan (Garden of Perfect Brightness). Today it has been rebuilt and is known as the Summer Palace.

Chinese grievance is long-lived, and today the original site of Yuanmingyuan has become one of over four hundred national sites used as a base for patriotic education.[7] In order to ensure the populace does not forget this humiliating destruction of an important cultural and historic site, children, students, and officials are required to visit, and new CCP members take their oath to party and country there. *The Economist* described one of Xi's first trips post leadership installation. He chose to visit *The Road to Revival* exhibit in Beijing. Aptly named the show's historical arc begins with the Opium Wars and concludes with nuclear weapons.[8] Xi's first speech about the Chinese Dream was delivered on this occasion, and the symbolism of the venue was clear—the party's vision was an ascendant China. By putting a media spotlight on this period of history, he reinforced the deft management of the CCP and how it leads to a rejuvenated, superpower status.

Contrasting China's experience, when comparing Western inventions to Japan's, a very different outcome resulted, and it further weakened the celestial idea of ruling all under Heaven. When American commodore Matthew C. Perry landed on the shores of Japan, demonstrating as Macartney had to China superior military technology, Japan chose a different track. The Japanese modernized, and the period beginning in 1868 became known as the Meiji Restoration. By 1895 Japan had defeated China in the first Sino-Japanese war.

An important Chinese figure emerged from the fall of China: Liang Qichao. He fled first to Japan and then Hawaii to contemplate and write about China as a modern nation and the need for China to open and change. China's history had been based on a series of ruling dynasties. In 1644 the Manchus conquered China and ruled as the Qing dynasty. To foster the idea of a sovereign nation, in 1901 Liang wrote "Introduction to Chinese History," stating, "What I feel most shameful of is that our country does not have a name. The name of the Han or people of Tong are only names of Dynasties, and the name 'China' that foreign countries use is not a name that we call ourselves."[9] His goal was to inspire the people to stand up to foreign threats and to develop. Per Liang, China's demise,

and later repeated by Mao, was to accuse the Qing dynasty of
decadence. The Qing had not kept the country safe from outside influences, nor superior, under its Mandate of Heaven.
With the fall of the last dynasty, the Qing, a search was on for
a new system of governance. A new thinking based on international governance systems tried to emerge, leading to the
establishment of an unsuccessful Republic of China.[10]

The Republic of China lasted from the fall of the last
dynasty, the Qing in 1911, until the establishment of the PRC
in 1949 under Mao. This was a period of upheaval, civil war,
and more humiliation at the hands of foreigners. As it found
no viable solution to rule the country, the country fractured,
and warlords emerged throughout the countryside. The
era saw the rise of Sun Yat-sen, who founded in 1912 the
Kuomintang, or KMT, a.k.a. Nationalists, which was soon led
by Chiang Kai-shek. Parallel to this chapter of China's history, World War I began in 1914. China's fractured country
coalesced around two opposing parties, the Nationalists and
the communist party, which was established on July 1, 1921,
with Mao Zedong as its leader. The internal war for Chinese
hearts and minds seesawed with significant cost in blood and
treasure. The Soviets had initially supported both camps,
believing they could mold either winner, while the Americans
had supported the Nationalists throughout and after World
War II.

Both Chinese camps fought the Japanese invasion beginning in 1937, but with the end of World War II, inevitably one
party needed to be victorious to unite the country and provide an ideological vision for the future. The fate was decided
in 1949, as the Nationalists held the historically important
capital of Beijing, and the People's Liberation Army entered
the gates, removing Nationalist leader Chiang's portrait from
the gate to Tiananmen Square. Chiang's portrait was replaced
by the victorious leader of the communist party, Mao Zedong.

Mao arrived at the historic Summer Palace a few months later in Chiang's custom Detroit-built, bullet-proof Dodge.[11] In early 1949, Mao Zedong, Zhou Enlai, Deng Xiaoping, and other fathers of the revolution took control of the country, and China's most recent dominant political figure, Chiang, stepped down.

One uniting thread that ran through both the Nationalists' and communist's camps had been the humiliation the Chinese people had suffered at the hands of outsiders. Throughout Chiang's rule, French said that he never forgot the humiliations of the distant and recent past: "Chiang Kai-shek wrote the characters for *Xuechi,* or 'avenge humiliation,' in the top right corner of each day's diary entry."[12]

For cultural continuity, all Chinese leaders, including Chiang, felt duty bound to reunite the nation based on the Yellow Emperor's reign. The Yellow Emperor is attributed as the first, beginning in 2696 BCE, and all Chinese are considered his descendants. His empire included Korea and Taiwan. Henry Kissinger explained China's thirteen dynastic cycles: "After each collapse, the Chinese state reconstituted itself as if by some immutable law of nature. At each stage, a new uniting figure emerged, following essentially the precedent of the Yellow Emperor, to subdue his rivals and reunify China (and sometimes enlarge its bounds)."[13] Ironically, it was to Taiwan that Chiang Kai-shek fled Mao's communists in 1949, never to return. The Nationalist party continues to be active there today.

American Theodore (Teddy) White, reporting for *Life* magazine from China in 1944, witnessed World War II and foresaw the coming civil war between the Nationalists, under Chiang Kai-shek, and the communists, under Mao Zedong, and identified what both camps wanted postwar: to make their country whole again. White described the de facto ruling government, the Nationalists, as "not only a unifying and historical force but also a product of the general impact of Western culture."[14]

White witnessed in the cities under Chiang trappings and benefits of a more modern society: transportation, factories, schools, and the accompanying middle-class citizens who ran them, mainly concentrated in Shanghai and Hong Kong. This class of Chinese wanted a unified country and were willing to utilize Western techniques to do so but were cautious of fully embracing such foreign concepts to overturn centuries of governance that relied on an historical emperor and subject hierarchy.[15] This reluctance that White identified was the degradation the Chinese felt at the hands of Westerners in their own land. White said, "I have seen my Chinese friends quiver with shame as they recalled foreign brutality toward the Chinese in China 15 or 20 years ago. This emotion is a healthy and normal reaction to an intolerable record of shame and humiliation."[16]

During White's journalistic tour, he was unable to assess if the victor would be the Nationalists or the communists. He speculated that if it were the communists, China would "be organized as Russia was, not by the rich, the well born and the educated, but by the peasantry and the working class."[17] With the last dynasty swept away, and the Nationalists and Chiang retreated to Taiwan, the peasantry chose Mao, and with the peasantry led by Mao, a new communist system was set to emerge as administer of state and soul.

CHAPTER 4

The People of Mao

Blank paper is ideal for writing.
—Mao Zedong

In the dividing and reuniting cycle of China's history, it was now to reunite under Mao and the PRC. Kissinger wrote, "Communist China launched itself into a new world: in structure, a new dynasty; in substance, a new ideology for the first time in Chinese history."[1] Idealistically, it was the proletariat that would rule this new world by force-marching through socialism to the final collective utopia of communism.

Three major periods under the reign of Mao are considered key to the destruction of old China and the development of the new brand of China with socialism and central planning at the heart of economic policy. While Chinese intellectuals are exceptional students of history, this more difficult recent history, administered under Mao, is seldom and thoroughly taught to citizens and rarely spoken of in verbal folklore. Yet the ramifications of Mao's building new China were earth-shattering to the personal, family and community experiences. Mao's leadership choices still seep into today's social fabric, affecting trust, life choices, and value systems and arousing among the people meaning-of-life questions. It is from these Chinese experiences we see the roots of issues we deal with today concerning skepticism in the veracity of data, intellectual property theft, brand quality issues, and impediments to innovation. These three major periods—the Chinese Civil War, the Great Leap Forward, and the Cultural

Revolution—have received limited inquiry because of China's closed nature during their timeframes, and only now is the wider world gleaning a better sense of what may have truly occurred.

Recently, a great number of classified documents, police reports, and nonredacted leadership speeches have become available. To provide a more complete window into this hidden history, several authors have used these resources. One, Frank Dikotter, a professor at the University of Hong Kong, published a trilogy of these momentous multiyear events. Dikotter provided insight into the personalities and styles of Chinese leaders, physical and mental atrocities the people had to bear, and the widespread destruction of life and property.

Dikotter showed how one man, Mao Zedong, led the people in victorious wars against their foes, then turned them on one another, culminating in the greatest cult of personality the world has yet known. Leaning on Dikotter's work, let's grasp the significance of Mao's reign.

After centuries of imperial rule, China's last dynasty, the Qing, fell in 1911. Its emperor, unable to unite the country or protect it from foreign interference and aggression, fell quickly to an attack from internal rebels. Thus began the great competition to fill the void of government and achieve continental unity. A series of leaders tried to emerge, most notably Sun Yat-sen, referred to as the father of the Chinese republic because of his efforts to establish a democratic structure. Sun Yat-sen founded the KMT (Nationalist Party) in Guangzhou in 1923. Japanese-trained military officer Chiang Kai-shek succeeded Sun, who died in 1925.

Another faction, Chinese communists, also supported by the Soviet Union, was simultaneously seeking a seat at China's table of governance. The most historic among this group included Mao Zedong, Zhou Enlai, and Deng Xiaoping. Zhou and Deng were leading an underground communist movement in 1927 when the first spark of the Chinese Civil War was lit, as Chiang tried to eliminate the left-right emerging division in his de facto ruling party. Chiang's attack was known as the Shanghai Massacre. Thus began the internal war for the hearts and minds of the Chinese people.

Chiang was recognized externally as China's leader, but Mao was assembling a rural, peasant band of followers. As both men's armies cut swaths across the country, north to south, east to west, they left death and destruction, and they were vicious in the execution of their respective visions. This left (i.e., Communist) or right (i.e., Nationalist) labeling followed generations of Chinese and continued to be used by Mao as a shorthand to seal one's fate until one's death.

The all-out civil war was brought to a simmer as both sides turned their weapons on the invading Japanese, fighting them from 1931 through the end of World War II in 1945. By the end of World War II, the Chinese people had suffered great atrocities at the hands of the Japanese and their fellow countrymen. In 1949 Mao was victorious; the Communists had won, and Chiang escaped to Taiwan. From 1927 through 1949, estimates count 6.5 million Chinese deaths. Dikotter, in *The Tragedy of Liberation,* explained the two competing camps. Under the Nationalists, people suffered physical and fiscal abuse. The police used brutal means to root out Communist sympathizers, and oppressive inflation and taxes ensured they lived a sustenance lifestyle. Under the Communists, people were subjected to a sophisticated propaganda machine overseen by Zhou Enlai, designed to convince that under the Communist vision, their lives would be better. The people, subjected to more than a decade of war, wanted most of all an end to the violence, even if it meant accepting the totally new concept of communism.[2]

However much the people, hungry and weary, may have craved peace, even under communism, none would yet be found. A signature Mao attribute was loyalty. Coupled with Mao's well-documented paranoia and conspiracy theory mindset, inevitably the people now had to prove their allegiance to him and the Communist party.

Mao developed many tactics throughout his reign to ensure the people bent to his will and aligned with the party's leadership. Over time, the effectiveness of various methods was drawn on not only throughout his reign but also by all following leaders, albeit with increasingly sophisticated tactics.

In the cities the Nationalists had held, they instituted a household registration system. The newly declared CPC took over the system but provided a new twist: this new version of household registration gave individuals a class label, including their family background, occupation, and individual status. The first round of classification was based on the distinctions understood by the peasants, as the Communists had used these labels in their civil war.

- "Good classes": Revolutionary soldiers, revolutionary martyrs, industrial workers, poor and lower-middle-class peasants
- "Middle classes": Petty bourgeoisie, middle-class peasants, intellectuals, and professionals
- "Bad classes": Landlords, rich peasants, capitalists[3]

But soon the classification moved to a typical propaganda technique of "othering." "Good" and "bad," or "There's us, the best, then there's all the rest."[4] The good were Red communists; the bad were Black, comprised of the middle and bad classes. This labeling allowed the party to control the fate of the household, with the labeling to be passed down through generations. Acceptance and reverence to the party were quickly adopted.

To ensure the Black class bent to the will of Mao and the party, Mao instituted a tactic he returned to many times in the coming decades—a reeducation campaign. Dikotter found that the holdover of professionals from the Nationalist government was needed temporarily as Mao established his own administration, but they could not be trusted. "All of them were sent to schools to learn the new orthodoxy. Everywhere, in government offices, factories, workshops, schools and universities, people were being 'reeducated', pouring over official pamphlets, magazines, newspapers and textbooks and learning the new doctrine. 'Everyone is learning the right answers, the right ideas and the right slogans.' It was called 'brainwashing' (xinao)."[5]

Beginning in 2014 and continuing to date, Xi has returned to the idea of reeducation campaigns. The most controversial example is in the western Xinjiang Province. The Uighurs, a Turkic-speaking, Muslim ethnic group numbering approximately eleven million, have seen their population subjected to the greatest technological and physical surveillance system devised. Orwellian in nature, the goal seems to be to pledge loyalty to the party and renounce Islam and its unique customs and beliefs.

Mao's party developed other behavior-altering and ideology-breaking tactics that endured for decades: "struggle sessions" that resulted in loss of face through forced written and public confessions and incarceration. The outcomes of these elicited "sins" were added to the person's permanent record and remained there during their lifetime. These tactics too, as we will see, have been revived by Xi and play an important role in his war on graft and in China's development of its social credit system (chapter 11).

Throughout Mao's rule, the various internal cleansing and controlling campaigns leveraged the face-losing power of labels, sometimes substituting as "rightest," "capitalist roader," or "bourgeoisie" for Black, and the confessions of "mistakes" reappeared, even within Mao's own leadership circle during purges, such as when Deng was alienated during the Cultural Revolution partially based on a confession he had given during the Chinese Civil War.

But simply labeling and reeducating people were not enough to adhere the people to the party. The population was in flux. PRC officials banished undesirables from the cities. Mao decreed that foreign market access be halted as well as foreign capital and the use of English language. The press was brought to heel.

Mao had promised the peasants land reform and that they would no longer live under the thumb of rapacious landlords, as he incited the people to turn against their local repressors. Dikotter explained the bond that was cemented between the people and party—blood; the assets and land of the "bad" classes was taken in violence and given to the poor.[6] Dikotter also noted, "Mao wanted the traditional village leaders overthrown so that nothing would stand between the people and the party"[7] Dikotter described the result: "The moral values and social bonds of reciprocity that had long regulated village life were to be destroyed by pitting a majority against a minority."[8]

The destruction of centuries of Chinese social and economic intercourse are an underlying theme throughout this book. China's culturally specific construct of unraveling morals and customs leaves fingerprints on every issue the CCP faces today as it seeks to build its much desired harmonious society.

Not all peasants were so easily brought on board with the new thinking. As the government tried to seize harvests, revolts occurred. As businesses failed, so did the coffers of the state. As unemployment skyrocketed and chaos reigned, the country entered a cycle of widespread poverty. Mao thought he saw an opportunity in this tragedy and positioned it as a state of affairs because of prior commercialization of the economy. The party developed the tactic of deflection early on. It had been victim to the Century of Humiliation. Now, while communism in governmental administration was failing, the perfect distraction emerged to channel the anger.

On the first anniversary of the founding of the PRC, October 1, 1950, General MacArthur, American commander of the Korean War, pushed past the 38th parallel into North Korea. Mao's army joined the fight. In order not to be officially drawn into the war, Mao positioned his soldiers as volunteers. North Korea's victory in this war bolstered Mao's prestige and standing among his people. The great chairman had stood down the imperialist Americans.

Emboldened, Mao was not content simply with the dictatorship of his own people. He had a vision of leading China to a utopian socialist society and thought this achievement would provide him with the credibility to become known as the world's socialist sage. Mao wanted to best the Soviet Union by beating it in surpassing Great Britain first, then America, to become a global power. He believed his advantage lay in the productive forces, his vast population. By harnessing labor, he would quickly transform China's agriculture and industry. Mao would best the West. Dikotter said, "Mao's vision of a China which was 'poor and blank' resonated with idealists who believed in the party's capacity to catapult the country ahead of its rivals. 'When you are poor you are inclined to be revolutionary. Blank paper is ideal for writing.'"[9]

From 1958 to 1962, the Great Leap Forward campaign was undertaken. This was Mao's strategy to harness the populous and achieve a leapfrog of both the USSR and the US. Mao's Great Leap Forward resulted in the Great Famine, with an estimated forty-five million dead. The people suffered starvation, coercion, terror, systematic violence, abandonment, cannibalism, poisoning, and quota killings.

To circumvent and keep his top leadership inline, Mao began the Great Leap Forward campaign by pushing management down to provincial leaders. Production output quotas were devised centrally, then pushed to the provinces, where they were expected to provide projections, then pushed down further for county-level inputs. As each descending officer was eager to please the godlike figure of Mao, they began to overestimate the crop yields they could provide.[10]

Mao's lack of scientific understanding and the natural effects of nature on agriculture soon collided and led to a food chain collapse. Mao's folly was not immediately apparent, as fear of the leader led to deception by the underlings. Mao's local officials constructed Potemkin-like fields of grain and rice wherever his local inspections took him.

This fear of speaking truth to power under a single ruler became deeply embedded throughout officialdom. The people's subservient compliance to a supreme leader continues to come to the fore, often causing China to face unintended consequences. A recent example was in 2020 as Xi sought to control both information and data resulting from the coronavirus outbreak in the city of Wuhan. As local officials attempted to hide the severity of the illness from superiors and citizens, China and its grand brand ambassador, Xi, took a major soft power hit, and internal and external trust was further eroded.

Mao, erroneously believing he had solved agricultural issues, turned his attention to steel. Steel production had become a worldwide litmus test that defined the progress and power of nations.

In 1957 the steel target was 5.35 million tons. By September 1958, Mao's edict was for production of twelve million tons. To feed the steel furnaces, the people confiscated scrap iron from homes, farm tools, household utensils, and destroyed buildings to feed the furnace fires. A migration of men to cities to work in steel mills began, leaving inexperienced women behind to tend the fields.[11]

The mirage of a successful collectivist utopia was spinning out of control. Again, chasing Mao's edicts, quality control was thrown out the window. Useless, inferior product became the norm. Cutting corners to show volume creeped into product production across the board, including food, with sand added to flour. "Corruption seeped into the fabric of life, tainting everything from soy sauce to hydraulic dams,"[12] said Dikotter. As society disintegrated, no one was left untouched. Dikotter drew the analogy of Primo Levi's Auschwitz memoir: "survivors are rarely heroes: when somebody places himself above others in a world dominated by the law of survival, his sense of morality changes."[13] Trust in local party officials and fellow humans was disintegrating. The adulteration of products as an acceptable and deceitful form of output began its legacy here and continues to plague the veracity of Chinese production, which is questioned both within and outside China's borders. In the most recent decades, harmful products produced in China in categories from pharmaceuticals to pet food and baby formula have hurt any credibility and goodwill the CCP tried to establish through laws and regulations.

While the destruction of life and property mounted, Mao kept an eye on his nemesis, the USSR's leader, Khrushchev. In 1957, on the fortieth anniversary of Russia's Bolshevik revolution, Khrushchev announced his intentions to catch up with the United States in farm products, declaring a trade war.[14]

Dikotter noted that Mao, not to be outdone, "was goaded into its own trade war, *dumping goods* (emphasis added) as if they were all surplus to internal demand in the age of plenty brought about by the Great Leap Forward. . . . [A]ll sorts of goods were sold below cost to demonstrate that the country was ahead of the Soviet Union in the race for true communism."[15] The capitalist concept of cornering a market such as steel was not what Mao sought to achieve; it was simply a quantity race, a need to point to a figure that would signify his superiority.

By the end of 1960, China was bankrupt. Mao positioned its dilemma as the result of natural disasters that destroyed crops. This allowed China to utilize a trade agreement escape clause triggered by natural disaster. To save face with communist brethren, China turned to noncommunist nations for food supplies. This is when American families' dinner table admonishments to "clean your plate, because children in China are starving" began.

In 2019 another potentially human-made natural disaster occurred with the emergence of COVID-19 from the city of Wuhan, China. In the vein of Mao's edicts of unrealistic production quotas and the lengths local officials would take to hide the truth from the chain of command, a similar hiding occurred once again throughout the country. The emergence of and warning about this novel deadly virus was leaked by a Wuhan doctor, Li Wenliang. Dr. Li had notified his colleagues of an unusual disease, and local authorities quickly apprehended him. The reflex reaction of the government to hide and deny COVID-19's existence set off a chain reaction. In a similar escalating fashion to the Great Famine, each layer of officialdom sought to build its own Potemkin village, only this time the village was a digital mirage of censorship, first designed to fool its own people and rapidly evolving into a ruse for the world.

As *The New York Times* reported, "[Wuhan] City officials struck optimistic notes in their announcements. They suggested they had stopped the virus at its source. . . . There was no evidence the virus spread between humans."[16]

News of Dr. Li's discovery, his arrest for "spreading rumors," and his death left China's internet censors on their back foot and losing control of the narrative. In an investigative report from co-publishers *The New York Times* and *ProPublica*, it became clear that the power of a propaganda machine can create a mirage. Sourcing official internal Chinese documents, including from the Cyberspace Administration of China, the article noted directives to internet censors: "They ordered news sites not to issue push notifications alerting readers to his [Dr. Li's] death. They told social platforms to remove his name from trending topics pages. And they activated legions of fake online commenters to flood social sites with distracting chatter, stressing the need for discretion: 'As commenters fight to guide public opinion, they must conceal their identity, avoid crude patriotism and sarcastic praise, and be sleek and silent in achieving results.'"[17]

Xi created the Cyberspace Administration of China in 2014 to oversee internet censorship and propaganda. The department manages tens of thousands of full- and part-time employees. For the COVID-19 mission, the article found that the Cyberspace Administration of China was to follow "strict commands on the content and tone of news coverage."[18]

Reminiscent of Mao's final understanding of the gravity of his famine, Xi faced the gravity of the escalating pandemic. There was a need for outside assistance but also, as with Mao, a desire to hide facts on the ground from the outside world. *The New York Times* and *ProPublica* reported: "News outlets were told not to play up reports on donations and purchases of medical supplies from abroad. The concern . . . could cause a backlash overseas and disrupt China's procurement efforts. . . . 'Avoid giving the false impression that our fight against the epidemic relies on foreign donations,' one directive said."[19]

Propaganda's power of revisionism in a techno-authoritarian regime is best illustrated via Dr. Li, who had been vilified by the officials who had to rectify this stance when the truth of his warning became known. He was quickly reimagined as a selfless martyr, and a museum was built showcasing the great struggle and triumph of the people over the virus, in direct violation of the initial directive to not speak in "crude patriotism and sarcastic praise."[20]

While Dr. Li was exalted, the rest of the world received from opportunist Chinese manufacturers defective Chinese-made personal protective equipment and a pandemic not witnessed in a century.

Returning to Mao's Great Famine, the senior leadership that surrounded Mao had not been blind to his insatiable need for power and had long wanted a return to a more collective leadership style. During the Party Congress of 1956, as a rebuff to Mao, they had removed from the constitution a reference to "'Mao Zedong Thought' and . . . the principle of collective leadership was lauded and the cult of personality was decried."[21]

How then did Mao carry on? The people were too physically and mentally exhausted. Leaders of riots were executed, and dissenting officials were purged. There was no alternative to the party. Dikotter found that Mao's cult still bound him to the people: "A common conviction in imperial times was that the emperor was benevolent, but his servants could be corrupt. . . . [A] distant entity called 'the government' and a semi-god called 'Mao' were on the side of good. If only he knew, everything would be different."[22]

The definition of trust is the firm belief in the reliability, ability, or strength of someone or something. "Who are our friends? Who are our enemies? This is the main question of the revolution—Mao Zedong," the opening quote to Frank Dikotter's *The Cultural Revolution, A People's History 1962–1976.* Mao sought his answer by launching the Cultural Revolution, leaving a fracture in the fabric of society that today manifests as a trust deficit throughout the citizenry. It is a deficit that Xi seeks to remedy by establishing the rule of law, reformation of Confucian values, and overt carrots and sticks that utilize a still-forming, behavior-altering social credit system.

Mao's trust question—friend or enemy?—emanated from the twin fears he witnessed externally and internally. Externally, he perceived those who were set to destroy the grand vision of socialism. He had witnessed Khrushchev denounce his predecessor, Stalin, for creating a cult of personality and committing crimes against his own people and Khrushchev's ultimate betrayal by proposing a peaceful coexistence with the West.

Mao believed he had led China in a revolution to end capitalism and had achieved socialism, but to reach the goal, communism, another revolution was needed. Dikotter clarified that with the Cultural Revolution, Mao had two goals in mind: as he approached the end of his life, he needed to settle personal scores. He needed to banish anyone who might negate his legacy as Khrushchev had Stalin's and ensure his vision of socialism would live on. Mao had been shaken by the 1964 Soviet coup of Khrushchev by Leonid Brezhnev. Mao returned to the old tactic of othering by separating the people with opaque labels such as "capitalist roaders" and "revisionists."[23]

Mao's use of vagueness in labeling perceived subversives was a communication strategy that has been perfected by the party. The lack of precision in defining adversaries' errors provides wide latitude to expand the scope of offenders. Mao's desire exceeded those simple troublemakers who harbored a merchant-class mentality and had not yet fully embraced the communist ideology, and he needed to keep his senior inner circle in line.

Mao, unable to count on his senior officials, began a new revolution and turned to the young and to college students, imploring them to ignore authorities—to bombard the headquarters. Because Mao had given permission to ignore the rules, an unexpected outcome emerged—the people turned on one another. It is estimated that up to two million people died during the revolution, but what suffered more deeply and lastingly was the assault on their centuries-old culture.

Mao had always turned to Stalin as a role model. Stalin held that to fully embrace socialism, the past ideas and culture had to be destroyed, including culprits such as religion, intellectuals and any free press. Stalin would define high culture and that culture would be for the masses.[24] Mao would follow Stalin's thinking and actions.

Mao recognized what Stalin had warned; a return to capitalist thinking had arisen among the masses. Dikotter said, "As the catastrophe [Great Famine had] unfolded, . . . the very survival of an ordinary person came to depend on the ability to lie, charm, hide, steal, cheat, pilfer, forage, smuggle, trick, manipulate or otherwise outwit the state."[25] From the lowest villager and local official, upward through the ranks, learned opacity in recordkeeping and physical goods had been the survival skill of the Great Famine, and those skills had been further honed by the beginning of the Cultural Revolution.

China's Communist Party history is replete with campaigns to change and mold the thinking of its people. Mao's answer to capitalist backsliding among the populous spawned a new socialist education campaign with the motto, "Never Forget Class Struggle."[26] Mao needed to ensure that young people would carry the mantle of his vision and maintain loyalty to his legacy for generations to come. Mao used two sides of a propaganda coin: first, a young, relatable role model was developed to engender a dictatorial-style filial piety; and second, a story device deeply seeded a historic narrative of what Mao and his revolution had done to save the country.

The 1963 Learn from Lei Feng campaign was launched. The construction of this fictitious soldier was fit for purpose. Lei was a young People's Liberation Army soldier who had died by a falling telephone pole as he worked tirelessly to serve the people. After his death, his "diary" was discovered, filled with his undying loyalty to the socialist cause and deep affection of Mao's wisdom.

Lei Feng was given the full propaganda push. From roaming village-to-village storytellers to movies, songs, plays, and exhibitions showcasing his empty uniform under glass, he stood for the great rebranding campaign of Mao. Dikotter explained the appeal: "Lei Feng was the poor man's Mao, a simplified Mao for the masses. Most of all, he was the young man's Mao, 'a rejuvenated Mao, speaking the language of enthusiastic adolescents."[27]

Lei Feng survives today as a propaganda poster boy to foster party loyalty and sanctioned behavior. His likeness, alongside Mao's, appears frequently in media throughout the country.

Mao designated March 5 as Lei Feng Day. In celebration in 2019, CNN reported that KFC opened its first Lei Feng–themed restaurant in Lei's hometown of Changsha. He Min, general manager for Hunan Province, said his staff would view Lei Feng as a role model of learning and within his province another 250 of these themed restaurants were planned by KFC.[28] KFC Yum China was spun off from US Yum Brands in 2016.

Today Xi also shoulders grave concerns of the capitalist leanings and moral bankruptcy he believes lie in the hearts of the masses. In 2019 the party released "An Outline for the Implementation of the Moral Construction of Citizens in the New Era." The document's genesis, as reported by *The Washington Post*, is: "'Strengthening civic morality construction [which] is a long-term, urgent, arduous and complicated task' . . . [due to] 'money worship, hedonism, and extreme individualism' as capitalism has flourished."[29]

To embody the desired socialist, patriotic virtues, a new, perfect hero was introduced to the masses in the campaign Learn from Huang Wenxiu. Huang, a real person who died tragically, was meant to exemplify what author Brian Anse Patrick called "The Ninth Commandment of Propaganda: Personalize and Dehumanize as Appropriate": "Personalization and dehumanization . . . [can] disambiguate—because in practice they help artificially polarize real or imagined differences between people and the policies they represent so as to achieve that simplistic cartoon worldview that is a hallmark of an effective propaganda. Positive use of personalization [provides] characteristics seen as virtuous, praiseworthy, or admirable. It invests people . . . with widely recognized better traits of humankind."[30] Patrick explained why Huang's elevation to hero status worked: Simple stories contrived to represent people are much easier for the public to comprehend without thoughtful work. To attach a face either of a villain or hero is much more readily knowable.[31]

The face of Huang Wenxiu was a model grassroots party worker. She died at age thirty when her car was swept away in a flash flood near a poor, remote village where she had worked tirelessly on poverty relief. Her backstory encompassed many of the attributes the party wished the masses to emulate.

What had Xi's campaign meant to impart? *The Washington Post* quoted Xi: "Learn from Huang Wenxiu. . . . Be brave enough to shoulder responsibilities and willing to show dedications, so as to make new and greater contributions in the Long March of the new era."[32]

David Bandurski, codirector of the China Media Project, remarked, "Heroes have a special place in the Communist Party's mythmaking around its construction of legitimacy. . . .

The point is to have figures that point people toward the need to sacrifice oneself to the interest and priorities of the party. The life well lived is the life of devotion to the party and the nation."[33]

While Mao's Lei Fung was to promote a positive role model, his second propaganda track of the socialist education campaign was designed to keep the students connected to the roots of the revolution under the motto "Never Forget Class Struggle." Senior workers and peasants were organized to roam and tell stories of their days before Mao's reign in which the Nationalists had caused great suffering from the elements, lack of food, and harsh deaths, but Mao had saved them, and they were eternally grateful.

Possibly the greatest contribution to the rehabilitation of Mao's image came in the form of the "little red book," as it came to be known. The book was part of a strategy conceived by Lin Biao, the head of the Ministry of Defense. In support of Mao, Lin wanted an easy way for the masses to study Marxism-Leninism and the book was a direct and simple method for teaching Mao Zedong Thought and memorize short sayings.[34] By 1965 millions of copies of the little red book, officially called *Quotations of Chairman Mao*, were neatly packaged in red plastic, cut, and crafted to fit perfectly in the pocket of the Red Guard uniform worn by the cultural revolutionaries.

In 2001, Apple's founder, Steve Jobs, launched the iPod using the slogan, "1,000 songs in your pocket." This technology led to the ubiquitous world of apps. Today, Xi's little red book has made its way back into the pocket in a modern-day form. In January 2019, the Chinese propaganda department released the "Little Red app" and by the end of the month it had become the most downloaded free app on Chinese iPhones. The app, called Xuexi Qiangguo, loosely translates to "Studying Xi Great Nation" and provides a plethora of Xi's thoughts, news, videos, and orders. Downloads and daily use among party members, civil servants, and state-owned enterprise employees is mandatory. So is taking daily quizzes, where points are earned for prize redemption.

Because of the app's massive distribution and required interaction, Chinese business owners spotted a promotional opportunity and began offering discounts to users. It would not be a long shot to assume that Mao would have disapproved, but under the Xi regime, an incongruent mix of ideology and effective capitalist marketing can coincide. As the edict of app usage was pushed down to local governments, some were offering free entry to tourist attractions for enough points. In a nod to the ratcheting up of production quotas of the Great Famine, *South China Morning Post* quoted an anonymous official: "I think each layer of government has added more detail to the requirements to appease the people above. Those in our city said we had to bring in users from outside the Communist Party as well."[35]

With Lin Biao's little red book in wide circulation and Mao's propaganda machine humming in the background, Mao needed a physical component of class struggle to further his ambitions. Mao, always an anti-intellectual and unsupportive of the legacy education system, turned to the students to arouse and incite them to turn on their teachers, institutions, and one another. Just as Stalin had directed, Mao enlisted the young to destroy the old culture.

In summer 1966, true chaos was unleashed. The students were to drive out demons and monsters. As the Red Guards committed violent acts on their teachers, including humiliation, torture, and murder, they also turned on fellow students who were deemed inferior.

By this time Deng Xiaoping had been forced to make a public self-criticism and was pushed aside. Lin Biao rose to the number-two leadership position and was viewed as

Mao's successor. Clique factions of Red Guards had assimilated, and by mid-August a million students had assembled at Tiananmen Square. Lin Biao had stripped the military of all visible rank. All were wearing, as were the Red Guards, green uniforms with no insignia and a cap with a single red star. Dikotter explained what Mao wanted, a "people's war," and Lin stepped forward to address one million eager students with Stalin's original advice, goading them "to destroy 'all the old ideas, old culture, old customs and old habits of the exploiting classes.'"[36] These became known as the "four olds."

In the call to destroy all trappings of the bourgeois class, everything was a target. Anyone in the service of this class was ruined, from barbers to book peddlers. Dikotter gave examples of the people's offences: "High heels, fancy haircuts, short skirts, jeans, bad books, all of these had to be eliminated at once, the Red Guards proclaimed."[37]

Quickly, the entire country was out of control as rural youth were brought to the cities, taught the revolutionary ways, and returned to the countryside armed with their little red book. Schools were closed, library contents burned, and monuments, cemeteries, and religious buildings desecrated, while homes were confiscated and hundreds of thousands were evicted. In Shanghai, the ancient Temple of Confucius was razed, and in Qufu, the hometown of Confucius, the compound and cemetery were attacked.

The carnage of destruction was broad and fast, and the people quickly fell into line. Dikotter gave examples of the offending but now obsolete old culture, including long-hair in braids and makeup and the people quickly turned to simple blue or grey monochrome clothing and black cloth shoes.[38] Their visual conformity ensured no one stood out. Today, when viewing images of the Politburo (the Chinese Party's cabinet), you would have to search for a head of hair that is not uniformly black, as the men dye their hair. A notable exception was Vice Premier Lui He, who was the representative for China in trade negotiations with the US and removed from his top leadership position when Xi claimed his third term in 2022.

In Mao's world, everything became suspect as feudal or extravagant. Entire industries and services were found to be providing the wrong products; businesses failed, and unemployment skyrocketed. It was merchants' and marketers' nightmares. Product branding and packaging style was evaluated, and if products in anyway referenced pre-Communist rule, such as emperors or dynasties, they were destroyed.[39]

You can envision the seeds of the modern-day boycott planted at this time. Today the insult to the proletariat has been replaced by the official line of hurting the people's feelings if somehow the product runs counter to the narrative the party desires. In this collectivist society, the need to fit in, to survive, can quickly be called on by the ever-evolving propaganda machine to ensure that China's economic clout can be used internally or externally to support the objectives of the nation.

At the beginning of 1967, Mao, determined to purge the party, broadened his enemy targets and opened the revolution for everyone to participate. Both the CCP and the legal system became targets; it was a true civil war. Rule of law was nonexistent. By the end of 1967 the people had grown weary of the destruction. This revolution needed an endpoint.

While the CCP's reputation was damaged, Mao's was still intact. Lin Biao used Mao's cult of personality to repair and reunite the party, people, and military. But the question arose of what to do with all the young people who had destroyed the academic institutions and were sitting around studying Mao Zedong Thought. Over the next decade, millions of students were sent to the countryside to be reeducated by the peasants. The cities were emptied; the students became the new labor force for the country's factories and mines. Up to twenty million students were sent away between 1962 and 1978. They became known as the sent-down youth.

The banishment set in motion an undercurrent of depression and disillusionment regarding personal purpose and family values. The utopian vision of a socialist paradise was lost to many. Youngsters were separated from their parents; married couples were sent to different regions.

Most importantly, Dikotter noted that caught up in this urban purge "were some of the country's most eminent scientists, physicians, engineers and philosophers, far away from their laboratories and offices, forced to do hard physical labor, shoveling mud, baking bricks, collecting twigs or hauling manure."[40] They had created their own brain drain. Henry Kissinger said, "Anyone identified as an 'expert' was suspect, professional competence being a dangerously bourgeois concept."[41] In Mao's eyes it was better to be Red than an expert.

All those who were banished also lost something more concrete than their pride and purpose: they lost their urban *hukou* status. *Hukou* status is either urban or rural. This distinction determines what benefits from the state you receive, with great preference given to the urban *hukou*. The sent-down youth were trapped in a rural neverland. The Cultural Revolution officially died in September 1976 with the death of Mao, and it was estimated that as many as two hundred million people were experiencing malnutrition.[42]

Mao did accomplish one very important objective with his Cultural Revolution: his official legacy lives on. In 1969 the constitution was amended to include Marxism-Leninism Mao Zedong Thought as the official ideology.[43] Today, as a reminder, Mao's portrait remains above the Gate of Heavenly Peace, where it was placed at his declaration of victory and liberation in 1949.

Dikotter's trilogy of the three important eras that shaped

China under Mao's reign are invaluable to help us understand the hardships and changes that China's people faced to
become the world's largest communist nation. While scholars
such as Dikotter have mined documents only recently available, uncensored, English language, firsthand accounts have
been more elusive.

Two such accounts, one captured during the Cultural
Revolution by a renowned journalist and the other more
recently through a documentary, shine a light on just how
much we may still not understand about the Chinese people
and recent history.

When Richard Nixon traveled to China in 1972, jour-
nalist Teddy White went along to report for *Life* magazine.
White's previous in-depth reporting pre-1949 had provided
Americans with detailed insights within both the Mao and
Chiang camps. White's published account from Nixon's visit
was both elegant and prescient, as he described the landscape,
the people's mindset, and the implications for the world and
America resulting from the Mao-led transformation of China.

White began by drawing a parallel between his visit to
Yenan in 1944 as they awaited the arrival of an American
major general to meet with Mao and his 1972 visit as he
awaited Nixon's arrival at Peking (Beijing) airport to meet
Mao. Both meetings revolved around the state of our relations, and as White reminded of the many setbacks in talks
that had occurred between these two historic meetings, he
observed what had been the result to date: "the dialogue had
frozen to hate and paranoia that has separated us since. We
could not understand each other."[44]

White remembered that Yenan had been a romantic symbol of a utopia for the Chinese people and of what Mao's
party had intended. "Yenan was an idea, and the idea was
simple: that people are plastic, human putty, raw material of
incredible and explosive and creative power if only properly

energized, inspirited, led. In Yenan and for years thereafter, the Communist leadership molded the minds of illiterate peasants, calling them to dignity, writing sharp new ideas on minds erased of thought by centuries of oppression and servility. On these blank minds they wrote the idea of the collective, the common will, the nobility of work, sacrifice and death for the common cause."[45]

White tried to reconcile his experiences of the past with his encounters in the present. In the cities of Peking and Shanghai, he observed a quiet, orderly sameness replacing the clamorous peddlers and beggars. He saw propaganda posters of Karl Marx, Lenin, and peasant soldiers armed with rudimentary weapons, ever ready for battle. Kissinger observed English language posters on route from the airport proclaiming: "Down with American Imperial Capitalism and its Running Dogs." With English language anti-American propaganda literature strategically placed in the American entourage's hotel rooms, Kissinger, ever the wise diplomat, found a way to express his rejection of the affront. He simply had all the materials gathered and returned, with the retort that they must have been left by a previous occupant. Kissinger's quiet message had been understood. The next day, on the route to meetings, all anti-American posters had been whitewashed, and he recalled: "Zhou mentioned as if in passing that we should observe China's actions, not its 'empty cannons of rhetoric.'"[46]

Electricity had arrived in China by 1958, and in a village home White found a radio and an electric light bulb that illuminated an image of Mao where once would have been the family's ancestral shrine. White seemed taken aback at the ubiquitous presence of Mao. The people uttered Mao's greatness and wisdom with each passing encounter. Mao's cult of personality was unavoidable. White visited the storied Peking University, noting it had been reopened for only a year and a

half, and now with only a third of the previous student enroll-
ment, Mao worship was just as prevalent among the elites as
the peasants. As White tried to engage with the professors, he
described them as seemingly lobotomized. He was shocked
that the three thousand years of Chinese history had been
swept away and now history courses began with the Opium
Wars and ended with the founding of the Communist party.
This past erasure was the beginning of the CCP's revisionism,
or rewriting the past to serve its purpose.

White tried to engage two Chinese journalists on events
of the day. He was stonewalled, but on the topic of Taiwan,
he got a bite: "Now comes a flash of anger in his dark eyes,
no smiles left. Taiwan is occupied by American imperialism, America must leave at once, there can be no discussion."[47] White explained the negotiations that were occurring
between our nations. "There is no doubt that President Nixon
yielded on the matter of Taiwan to the men who now govern
China—not all the way, not even half-way, and by a yielding
hedged in language from which any skillful diplomat, if necessary, can wiggle away [Nixon's compromise: one country,
two systems]. The Chinese, on their side, yielded not an inch
or phrase."[48]

At the closing banquet of the Nixon-Mao summit it is
of interest that White and Kissinger separately reported a
unique parting salutation. White had a relationship with
Zhou Enlai dating to the days of Yenan. As the two enjoyed a
private toast and said their goodbyes, Zhou referred to White
as an "old friend."

Kissinger noted that in this same trip, both Mao and
Zhou referred to him as a friend. Kissinger was wise to the
ploy, remarking that it was a holdover from imperial times
to manage the non-Chinese "barbarians." The Chinese belief
was that to be honored as their friend meant you had been
admitted into their exclusive club, and violating this inclusion

made it more difficult to confront or disagree with them, making negotiations painful.

In the 1980s, the US government commissioned the Rand Corporation to do an analysis of the US-PRC official negotiations for normalization of relations. The concepts of "friend" and "old friend" were studied. Rand's findings were that "the essential quality of Chinese pressure tactics is to make the foreign negotiator, with whom they have gone to some lengths to develop a personal, or 'friendly,' association, feel that his positive relationship with China is in jeopardy, that he has not done enough to warrant being considered an 'old friend,' and that he must do more for the relationship to justify Chinese support and good will. It is this tension of the relationship game that gives dealings with the Chinese much of their distinctive quality."[49]

While White tried to comprehend the changes he experienced in new China in 1972, some Chinese born after 1978 try to comprehend what came before them. Just as White was unable to engage in forthright conversation about the events that had transpired in his absence, those same Chinese today do not wish to retell their experiences during that time in a critical way.

In 2014, a documentary came out called *China's 3Dreams* by Nick Torrens, an Australian filmmaker. Torrens followed two families over the course of seven years as they tried to understand their past and what is to come. To illustrate the narrative of experience and desires of many young Chinese, key dialogue from the film's transcript is quoted below[50], and as Torrens shows, there is "a fractured line that runs just beneath the surface of contemporary life."[51]

The main family's protagonist, Lei, is a woman in her thirties. Her quest, stated in the opening, was: "People say that the gap between our past and our future is getting bigger. In the past hundred years China suffered through so many traumatic events but today the younger generation knows almost nothing about this and the older generations are silent."

Lei explains that her parents had participated in the Cultural Revolution with fervor and that after the revolution they had divorced and neglected her. Lei said, "China's problem is that there is no complete or reliable record of our history. So much has been hidden or deliberately covered up. We don't know the facts even for what is happening now. That is the biggest problem in China. . . . In the 1970s Chinese people had three dreams: a watch, a radio and a bicycle (often referred to as 'the three rounds'). Since then, many dreams came into China to make China wealthy through government-controlled Capitalism. This intensified a second dream. The dream of a better life."

Enlisting a cousin, Lei goes in search of their family's past. They interview relatives and their relatives' friends, working their way back, decade by decade, to reach their ninety-year-old grandfather. Along the way Lei discovers the experiences of relatives who were banished as counterrevolutionaries to labor camps for decades and Red Guards responsible for deaths. Youthful mayhem came at the expense of educational authority figures and a current resolve among them to let the past lie and not question it too deeply.

Lei's story concludes, "The third dream is the great but almost impossible dream. It's the dream of meaningful existence. China's social problems are huge and difficult to solve but I believe this will change. When people have satisfied their material needs, they may start to pursue a meaningful existence."

Mao's death in 1976 signaled the end of the Cultural Revolution. The CCP deemed the populous sufficiently ideologically Red. The country needed to be rebuilt and a new path forward sanctioned. The CCP by 1978 rehabilitated and elevated Deng Xiaoping, who restored the value of the educated expert. Deng opened the door to Western thinking and management theory to complete Zhou Enlai's four modernizations—agriculture, industry, defense, and science and technology.

CHAPTER 5

The People of Deng

To be rich is glorious.
—Deng Xiaoping

China's humiliation began with the Opium Wars of the 1840s, but the ideology of nationalism had its roots after World War I. A sense of Chinese patriotism also emerged in 1919, ignited by the Treaty of Versailles. As Western leaders assembled to assign the boundaries and colonies of nations postwar, a portion of Shandong Province on China's mainland was ceded to Japan as a reward for Japan's war participation with the West. China's educated youth recognized this external assault on the sovereignty of their country as another humiliation, and they directed their anger at the foreign perpetrators and their own government's weakness in protecting China.

The students of Peking and Yenching universities rose up on May 4, 1919, and the ensuing demonstrations awoke the people's will to end the foreign subservience they had long endured. Deng Xiaoping, the most disruptive Chinese leader after Mao and architect of China's reform and opening, was fourteen years old in 1919 and a witness to the May 4 demonstrations.

In Ezra Vogel's biography, *Deng Xiaoping and the Transformation of China,* he described how life-changing this event was for Deng: "The birth of Deng Xiaoping's personal awareness of the broader world coincided precisely with the birth of national awareness among educated youth. From this moment on, Deng's personal identity was inseparable from the national effort to rid China of the humiliation it had suffered at the hands of other countries and to restore it to a position of greatness, to make it rich and strong."[1] While Mao and Chiang burned with a desire to avenge China's humiliations, it was Deng's policies and politics that made China rich and strong, and today it is Xi Jinping who carries the mantle to ensure China's return to a position of greatness.

Deng dedicated his life in service to Mao and the communist cause. In 1978 when he finally achieved the pinnacle of power within the CCP, he set out to reform internal social and economic policies. He opened the country to outside financial and technological investment and educational assistance. Vogel wrote of three turning points in 1978 that led to a new spark that set the prairie fire for China's economic revolution. Under Mao, China had been a closed country. Japan also had been a closed country, but in the 1870s, the government launched the Meiji Restoration to induce modernity. Japan sent a diverse group of government officials abroad to learn ways to industrialize the country. Deng followed this model of going out and seeking knowledge. Vogel reported Deng's findings: "'Recently our comrades had a look abroad. The more we see, the more we realize how backward we are.'"[2] The returning Chinese leaders retreated from Mao's dogma in criticizing Eastern European countries who were reevaluating the strict Marxist-Leninist definition of socialism.

Vogel found that the most important trip abroad was to Western Europe, where the team, led by Gu Mu, was overwhelmed by the sophistication of the modernization they witnessed. Gu reported they expected the capitalist to be backward and decadent but admitted how wrong they had been.[3] China's fact-finding delegation was shocked to find European companies willing to offer loans and technology. The team also had a crash course in capitalism. Yes, there was openness on the part of Western companies, but these companies were operating below capacity, and in China, the Europeans anticipated a new, vast market into which they could sell goods and modern technology. Per Vogel, as the Chinese leaders were apprehensive about entering the global economic system, they asked themselves, "How could China expand foreign trade and the role of foreigners without losing control?"[4]

In Guangdong Province, across from the British-administered Hong Kong, a crisis of mainlander defections was occurring in 1978, with tens of thousands of young people escaping annually. Deng's solution was to establish China's first area of opening in Guandong, calling the region the Shenzhen special economic zone (SEZ). It became a place where raw materials could be imported, manufactured, and exported back through Hong Kong to avoid tariffs and restrictions. Today Shenzhen is a part of the mighty economic engine driving the larger region and is known as the Pearl River Delta Economic Zone. The region is often referred to as the "world's factory" with more than two hundred thousand factories in operation.

At the end of 1978, the Communist Party officially acknowledged Deng's policies of reform and opening. This also marked the beginning of Deng's reign. Officially, Hua Guofeng had been the leader since Mao's death. This was a tricky handover of power. Vogel described, "Deng met with the members of the Politburo Standing Committee and again reassured his colleagues, who were aware of his differences with Mao, that he would not become China's Khrushchev: Chairman Mao had made extraordinary contributions to the party and the party should not launch an attack on Mao like Khrushchev's attack on Stalin. He also reassured them that the country would remain united under the banner of Mao Zedong Thought."[5] Deng's assurance that he would not denigrate his predecessor set a precedent. To maintain the dynasty of the CCP, previous leaders should be positioned as nearly infallible. The successor was to remold or obscure past transgressions and seek to rectify mistakes through forward policy and politics.

Most modern texts describe Mao as the original CEO of China and Deng much more as a COO. Kissinger gives us a more culturally nuanced description. "Mao had governed as a traditional emperor of a majestic and awe-inspiring kind. He embodied the myth of the imperial ruler supplying the link between heaven and earth. . . . Deng governed in the spirit of another Chinese tradition: basing omnipotence on the ubiquitous, but also the invisibility of the ruler. . . . He ruled not like an emperor but as the principal mandarin."[6]

Deng inherited a country facing many daunting challenges, from the fiscal state of the economy to a crisis of ideology and the need for a road map. Vogel showed how through great management skills and by acting as a positive disruptor, Deng began China's long march to world power. In typical Chinese leadership fashion, Deng did not want his political elite class to dwell on the mistakes of the past or shift blame. He advised they were all to blame, including himself. The mission was to identify the linchpins of failure and correct the system going forward. Deng believed that pushing the rigid political and economic system down to the household level had overreached and created a type of paralysis that stymied initiative and progress. Deng's lifelong belief in the CCP did not allow him to walk away from the ultimate goals of socialism but to seek ways to bend it in service of immediate needs. Deng knew to create change, the country needed new ideas and knowledge. To achieve this, he sent young people oversees for training and education and to bring back the best of science and technology. Deng saw his role as harnessing the new thinking to create new processes and systems.[7]

Deng's foundational changes put China on the path to a

state-capitalism model, and his deft bridging of Mao's legacy to protect the CCP carries on today. It is now implicit that leaders should not denigrate their predecessors nor fully admit mistakes. Xi carries on that inherent rule today. Xi divides the CCP's history into two distinct yet connected phases of development: pre-1978 under Mao and post-1978 and the reform and opening period initiated by Deng. Xi admits the two time frames had different guiding ideologies, politics, and policy, but both were equally important to the development of Chinese socialism, and neither should be harshly judged. Xi said, "We should adhere to the principles of seeking truth from facts and distinguishing the trunk from the branches."[8]

If Mao represents Xi's analogy of the trunk and Deng the branches, the simplest way to describe their differences may be that Mao operated under ideological principles and Deng followed practical principles. Late in Mao's reign, Deng suffered Mao's repeated criticisms as Deng tried to restore stability and unity to the country. Vogel demonstrated the difference in the two leaders' thinking on ideological dogma and practical execution: "Mao had also protested that Deng's use of the 'white cat, black cat theory' ('it doesn't matter if the cat is black or white as long as it catches the mouse') did not make any distinction between imperialism and Marxism-Leninism; it reflected bourgeois thinking."[9]

Deng's pragmatism in reaching for a more modern, well-off society can be seen in a statement he made on a trip to the Sichuan region in 1978: "Deng mocked those who said that if a farmer has three ducks he is socialist, but if he has five ducks he is a capitalist. They should liberate their thinking from this rigid dogma. Deng argued; socialism is not poverty."[10]

Ten years later, in 1988, Xi became CCP secretary of Ningde, Fujian Province. In his book *Up and Out of Poverty*, he reissued a speech on poverty. Xi implored the people to take responsibility for themselves, saying the people should not wait for government aid or be at peace with poverty but change their thinking. Channeling his best Deng, he stated that the "weak hatchling bird can be the first to take flight and the poorest can be the first to become rich."[11]

While Deng had exercised considerable political capital to change the direction of the economic system, there were extraterritorial agreements that had to be maintained and certain philosophical concepts that were internally accepted and nonnegotiable. The Westphalian concept of sovereignty (a system adopted in the 1600s from Germany still relevant today that provides that each state has exclusive rights to govern its own territory without outside interference) was embraced by China and fit nicely within its desire to reject any outside meddling in its internal affairs or intentions to restore the territory of the Yellow Emperor's kingdom. China's dream to rejuvenate the nation and save face from the Century of Humiliation includes reclamation of territories lost through various wars and treaties. In this effort China has played a long game. Today, with China's increasing clout, there is an assertion of power to demonstrate its intolerance of outsiders' recognition of renegade (i.e., Hong Kong, Taiwan, Macao, Tibet) territories. One power tactic is economic coercion—targeting people, nations, and companies who do not fully accept or pander to China's claims on territories.

The extraterritorial agreements fall under the concept of one country (China) and two systems (territories operating under special governing rules), and their history traces to America, Britain, and Portugal regarding Taiwan, Hong Kong, and Macao, respectively. We need a cursory understanding of this unique situation, for as we will see, Chinese politics and sensitivity to these issues are quickly translating into financial and public relations consequences for US businesses.

The idea of one country, two systems is linked to the normalization of relations between the US and China. President

Richard Nixon and Secretary of State Henry Kissinger worked on a containment strategy for the USSR. In the summer of 1973, Nixon signed the Treaty for the Prevention of Nuclear War with Soviet president Brezhnev. Simultaneously, Kissinger had been negotiating with Mao and his number two in command, Zhou Enlai, on the normalization of relations between the two countries. Up to this point, the US had supported Taiwan as an independent country, appointing ambassadors and selling them military weapons. Nixon's negotiations with China were a closely held secret in Washington, as normalization of relations was not broadly supported in Congress.

In November 1973, Kissinger traveled to China to meet with Zhou and another direct report, an official translator to Mao, Nancy Tang. Zhou reported back that the Washington delegation thought they could move normalization forward through Congress if there was a carveout for Taiwan that allowed the US to maintain close relations with Taiwan. "Nancy Tang chimed in at that point, telling Mao that it sounded like a 'two-China policy.'"[12] Mao turned against Zhou and to Deng to lead negotiations with Kissinger. Deng supported Mao's view that the US was using China to achieve détente with the Soviet Union but believed a bigger picture was emerging. China and Soviet relations were at a low point, and for defensive security reasons, Mao and Zhou wanted US backing. However, Deng saw the opportunity with the US as a springboard to help China modernize."[13]

The island known today as Taiwan has passed through many hands. After the Sino-Japanese War ending in 1895, it was handed over to the Japanese. After World War II, with Japan's loss, it was taken over by Chiang and the Nationalists as they fled the Chinese Civil War in 1949. Mao had recovered a great deal of territory, reclaiming most of what had been lost during the Qing dynasty but not Taiwan, Hong Kong, or Macao. He used nationalism to galvanize the country to demand that these lost territories that resulted from the Century of Humiliation should be rightfully returned to the motherland. This legacy of rightful reuniting followed all China's leaders to the present.

Vogel described how Deng put a stake in the ground on these thorny issues: "In January 1979, immediately after becoming preeminent leader, Deng announced a policy that proclaimed Chinese sovereignty and ultimately control over Taiwan and Hong Kong, yet also granted a high degree of local independence. . . . [I]n 1982 under Deng, it was elaborated on and systematized as the 'one country, two systems' policy. As part of this policy, Hong Kong and Taiwan would be allowed to keep their very different social systems in place for half a century or even longer."[14] Deng threaded the needle brilliantly. He held firm to the territorial integrity of greater China but left open an opportunity to utilize these territories operating under a capitalist system to access both finance and technology.

On New Year's Day 1979, the US and China announced official diplomatic relations, but the US Congress, seeing the potential loss of a democratic, independent nation in Taiwan, muddied the waters by passing the Taiwan Relations Act. Thus began a history of Taiwan as a wedge between the US and Chinese governments.

Hong Kong was ceded to Great Britain after the Opium War of 1842 via a treaty that stipulated its return in 1997. Deng set his sights on wresting control of Hong Kong from England by 1997. After many years of negotiations, the Sino-British Joint Declaration on the Question of Hong Kong was signed in December 1984, with Hong Kong becoming a special administrative zone of China. Deng's plan was to allow Hong Kong to function under a capitalist system and be governed by Hong Kongers and British officials. Deng said, "*It would be called 'Hong Kong, China'* [emphasis added] . . . 'In our

Chinese constitution, there is a provision that we can establish special administrative regions with rules separate from the rest of the country.'"[15]

Deng saw both Taiwan and Hong Kong as assets to integrate China into the broader world and support its Four Modernizations campaign (agriculture, industry, defense, and science and technology). Both territories offered great potential for capital, technology, and modern management thinking. Deng's view of history covered a long arc, and he was pragmatic about reunification, saying that if it did not happen soon, no matter the wait, it would eventually happen.

In 2017, speaking on the twentieth anniversary of Hong Kong's return, Xi explained that one country, two systems had been agreed on to serve two goals: ensure national territorial unity and leverage Hong Kong as a growth engine for the mainland through its financial, shipping, and trading system.[16]

Deng's formal establishment of the one country, two systems model of governance for Hong Kong and Taiwan also included Macao. A small Portuguese island colony with a lease that was to expire in 1999, Macao had been an afterthought for the CCP as it added little economic value.

In 2014 Xi celebrated the fifteenth anniversary of Macao's return in a speech where he reiterated the continuance of the one country, two systems principle of governance. But if Macao had been a simple afterthought to Hong Kong for so long, and there were no conditions stipulated by Portugal on its return, why continue with two systems? It clearly benefited China to do so. Xi said, "[S]eize every opportunity . . . [to] promote the diverse and sustainable economic development of Macao based on its positioning as a global tourism and leisure hub [meaning gambling, which is illegal on the mainland] and a service platform for economic and trade cooperation between China and Portuguese-speaking countries [meaning Brazil]."[17]

What Xi meant by "economic and trade cooperation" became apparent in 2019 as China's trade war with the US muddled along. China found a unique leverage point in the negotiations—soybeans. Midwest American farmers had been key supporters of Trump's election in 2016. In 2017, American soybean farmers were responsible for $12.3 billion or 63 percent of the US's agricultural exports to China.[18]

As China sought to retaliate against the Trump Administration's US tariffs, this very concentrated market commodity became the target. The world's largest growers and exporters of soybeans are the US and Brazil. Combined, during their respective growing season of 2016–2017, they accounted for 83 percent of world exports. Both countries' top export destination was China, which was taking 61 percent of US total soybean production and 77 percent of Brazil's.[19]

With China's purchases shifting to Brazil, what had been $19.1 billion of US farm exports in 2017 dropped to $9.1 billion by 2018.[20] Brazil, seeking to capitalize on capturing further market share from the US, began burning large swaths of the Amazon rainforest to create more arable land. The smoke plumes were visible from space, and concerns were raised worldwide about the effects to the environment.

By the 2020–2021 selling season, US soybean sales were on track to recover a bit better than half of pretariff sales of 2016–2017.[21] American farmers' losses were being made whole through US taxpayer farm subsidies, but many farmers expressed concern about whether their relationship with Chinese customers could be recovered.

The deft Deng had turned what began as a negative for China—having to agree to governance of territories under different economic systems regarding Hong Kong and Macao—into a positive. The two systems compromise had provided China the ability to access and utilize capitalist systems to benefit the development of socialism.

With Taiwan, we face a more difficult challenge. Both China and America have vested interests in the future of Taiwan. There is no lease that will expire and return Taiwan, and Taiwan is caught between the pull of its motherland and its appreciation of independence. Taiwan has faced down potential military invasion from China, been subject to its charm offensive, and benefited from economic integration with the mainland. In 2015, Xi and then Taiwanese leader Ma Ying-jeou agreed to meet in a *neutral territory* (emphasis added as the ethnic makeup of the city/state Singapore is 75 percent Han Chinese). In Xi's speech he mined the depths of their shared cultural heritage, but he laid down markers that China would not be deterred in its goal of reuniting. "Reasonable arrangements can be made through pragmatic consultation between the two sides if they do not create 'two Chinas' or 'one China, one Taiwan.' The biggest threat to the peaceful development of cross-straits relations now comes from the forces and activities for 'Taiwan independence.'"[22]

American presidents and Congress have long viewed Taiwan as a power buffer to China as well as a source of economic activity. In the dawn of President Trump's ascendancy, Taiwan quickly became a flashpoint. In December 2016 Trump accepted a congratulatory call from Taiwan's president, Tsai Ing-wen. This broke a protocol of direct communications between the anointed leaders since 1979. The Chinese positioned this incident as an American president unaware of realpolitik; the Americans eventually positioned it as a nod to their base and getting tough on China. In February 2017 Trump and Xi met at Trump's estate in Florida, where Trump confirmed he would honor the one China policy.

Taiwan's tenuous position straddling two global powers competing in the arena of technology has become glaringly clear to American enterprise. Taiwan is home to some of the most important semiconductor foundries, and one, Taiwan

Semiconductor Manufacturing Corporation (TSMC) produces the most advanced chips in the world.[23] The innovation of chips, their manufacture, and their subsequent incorporation into the exponentially expanding, internet-connected devices industry follows a complex, intertwined global supply chain. TSMC, with 51.5 percent[24] of the foundry market, has supplied chips to both US and Chinese companies.

An FP *Insider Report* looked at Taiwan's critical semiconductor industry as it has tried to "remain insulated from geopolitics—particularly amid pressures contributing to US and China decoupling."[25] From the report's key findings: "Semiconductors represent the linchpin for US and China's mutually dependent technological ambitions (referencing our respective race for ownership of the 4th Industrial Revolution). . . . Taiwan is set to become the center of US-China tensions."[26]

As companies reevaluate their supply chain vulnerabilities, it is presently unknowable just what fate will befall Taiwan, but the island's identification as a linchpin in our nations' relationship does not seem like hyperbole.

Semiconductors, or chips, make up less than 10 percent of total trade, but of all goods exported, either directly or indirectly, 65 percent are dependent on them.[27] Behemoth US firms such as Apple, Google, and Amazon have relied on Taiwanese chips for up to 90 percent of their inputs. As the US and Chinese governments ratcheted up the rhetoric of nefarious uses of chips for military and spying purposes, the supply chain breakdown during the pandemic brought the dependency home to the everyday American in an inability to purchase many chip-dependent products.

As complacency and risk reliance came into stark relief, the US government weighed into industrial policy, passing the Creating Helpful Incentives to Produce Semiconductors and Science Act of 2022 (CHIPS Act) to support US competitiveness, innovation, and national security. The act provided billions of dollars for investment in research and development and domestic manufacturing. Taiwan Semiconductor Manufacturing Corporation committed to building an American manufacturing facility, and Apple and other US companies quickly signed on as clients.

Xi's comments that there would not be one China, one Taiwan came into stark relief when the convoluted semantics regarding country status found their way into American marketing execution. The Chinese New Year, or Spring Festival, is the most important holiday in China and lasts fifteen days. The date is not fixed but begins with the first new moon rising within the parameters of January 21 to February 20. In 2018 Chinese New Year was February 16. While the fifteen days are the official festival time, the country recognizes a forty-day traveling period known as *chunyun*, falling in 2018 from February 1 through March 12. This time is not only considered a Spring Festival but also a spring migration. Historically, it has been celebrated with a family reunion and generates a mass movement of people. In 2018 the Ministry of Transport predicted three billion trips would be made using public transportation. Six and a half million trips were expected to be outside China. The numbers are staggering and clearly include back and forth and multiple types of transport used by a single person, but the message is clear: most Chinese citizens go somewhere during this very important period.

On the eve of this great migration, you could speculate that the Chinese government used timing to make a point about one China being the guiding principle of one country, two systems. Jeremy Goldkorn, editor and chief of supchina.com, a US digital media company, said, "The People's Republic has always exerted tight control over maps and names of geographical features within its borders. . . . The Party's absolute insistence on rectifying maps and place names is now spreading beyond its borders, starting with the softest of targets: foreign companies that do business in China or sell to Chinese consumers."[28]

In mid-January 2018, one of the softest of targets, Marriott, a Maryland-based hotel and resort giant, ran afoul of the territory delineations expected by China. In September 2016 Chinese regulators cleared Marriott's takeover of Starwood Hotels and Resorts. This acquisition gave Marriott thirty hotel brands, including Starwood, Sheraton, Ritz-Carlton, Renaissance, and Westin Hotels and Resorts, resulting in it holding the world's largest market share of hotel rooms at 6.7 percent.

Upon the regulatory clearance, Craig Smith, Marriott's president and managing director for Asia-Pacific, stated in an interview with the *Nikkei Asian Review*, "China is our largest source market in the Asia-Pacific and our second-largest source market globally. . . . I am very sure in a few years it actually would be number one. . . . [a] major reason to accelerate expansion into China is to build a domestic footprint so that when Chinese tourists travel abroad, they have loyalty to the same brand."[29]

On January 9, 2018, Marriott sent an email survey to its loyalty club members that caught the attention of Chinese authorities. The offense found with the survey was the listing of countries that included Tibet (an autonomous region of China), Taiwan, Hong Kong, and Macao. Government and public outcry was harsh and quick. The governmental response was to force a shutdown of Marriott's website and app for a week in China. Lu Kang, spokesman for China's foreign ministry, explained their position: "We welcome foreign enterprises to do business in China. Meanwhile, they should respect China's sovereignty and territorial integrity, abide by Chinese law, and respect the Chinese people's feelings, which are the foundation for any corporation to do business in any country."[30] As *South China Morning Post* covered Chinese public reaction, this is a representative statement:

"'Political stance is the most important part of the brand awareness when foreign companies do businesses here,' said Zhu Guangyu, a 44-year-old consumer from Shanghai. 'I will never buy those brands or use their services.'"[31]

Arne Sorenson, Marriott's chief executive, quickly issued an apologetic statement, saying the company in no way intended any subversion to China's sovereignty or territorial integrity.[32]

Marriott quickly had to prove that it did not support anyone subverting China's claims to territories by firing one of its employees. As the Marriott survey misstep was trending in Chinese media, a group known as Friends of Tibet on X (formerly known as Twitter) congratulated Marriott for listing the countries separately. At fourteen-dollars-per-hour, forty-nine-year-old Omaha, Nebraska, resident Roy Jones was working the night shift for Marriott Rewards Twitter account. Jones was a customer care manager who spent his nights battling bots spamming the Marriott Rewards X site to earn points for a National Football League (NFL) promotion while seeking to mollify various customer complaints on all things Marriott. Jones, scrolling through the X feed, had liked the Friends of Tibet post, thinking nothing of it. By January 11, Marriott representatives were contacted again for another apology for the "like", and China expected Marriott to hold the people responsible accountable.[33]

Marriott announced that within ninety days it would roll out a plan to ensure these mistakes never happened again, including seeking collaboration with Chinese governmental departments for advice and direction and better train its employees.[34] But Marriott's first order of rectification was to fire Jones. In a Jones interview after the firing, he said, "I was completely unaware of what was going on. . . . We were never trained in the social graces when it came to dealing with China."[35]

Some Americans were questioning the values espoused by Marriott. Ben Schlapping, writing for the website *One Mile at a Time*, a loyalty points site, asked if Marriott lived by the values it explicitly stated on its website: "Take care of associates and they will take care of the customers."[36]

This issue of country listings quickly spilled over into other foreign companies operating in China, mainly airlines, resulting in more apologies, online rectifications, and modifications to country and city listings, with many Chinese netizens calling for boycotts. It is unclear what short- and long-term financial and brand damage may have occurred. What undoubtably did occur across many international companies was a thorough audit of any mentions of Tibet, Taiwan, Hong Kong, and Macau.

Deng was able to harvest great economic and technological assets by utilizing the capitalistic systems of the three territories (Hong Kong, Macau, Taiwan), but the long arc of patience he exhibited in reuniting all as one China may be ending. Under Xi, American businesses are paying the price for transgressions and lack of awareness to the sensitivity of maps and monikers.

Let's return to Deng and his early years of reform and opening. This signature policy was intended to support the four modernizations by separating the acquisition of knowledge and investment from the ideological foundation that supports true capitalism. However, what emerged was Chinese state capitalism and with it a world of contradictions. The cornucopia of access to Western wares and thinking quickly led to CCP concern: Would it be a barbarian invasion leading to spiritual pollution and cultural contamination? Australian sinologist (i.e., one who studies China) Geremie Barme observed the societal changes from Western exposure in 1983. The CCP's status as arbiter of economic ideology was being questioned by the masses. The party's policies had opened the door to a mixed economy and allowed merchants to pursue (in limited industries) entrepreneurship. As the populous enthusiastically embraced the slogan they heard in the media—let one group prosper first—many merchants were in a race to join the Wangs next door (China's version of the Joneses next door). The party felt a loss of control and attributed this new capitalist mentality to Western influence. It was the beginning of one of the party's many contradictions to come as it attempted to craft a hybrid economy—individual motivation driven by capitalism but controlled by party socialist economic ideology.[37]

Under Deng's reign, the greatest ideological challenge to the system culminated on June 4, 1989, known as the Tiananmen Square massacre. In 1987 Hu Yaobang was dismissed as China's general secretary for being too liberal. He died in April 1989, and thousands of students assembled in Tiananmen Square demanding that he be properly honored. Andrew Nathan, writing for *Foreign Affairs*, found the students were calling attention to what they saw as failures of Deng's reform: inflation, corruption and lack of political liberalization.[38]

The students of Beijing hold a long legacy of fomenting change in the political system of China. Mao turned to students in the midsixties to ignite his Cultural Revolution. But for these Hu-supporting students, it was not to turn back the clock to Mao's day but the most important student uprising on May 4, 1919, that inspired them. The May 4 movement had sprung from students' desire to see Chinese leaders of the republic stand up to the world and challenge the outcome of the Versailles Treaty, which gave Chinese territory to Japan for its support during the war. The students in 1919 exhibited a nationalistic reaction and wanted China to shake itself from imperialism: the shackles of feudalism, isolation, and authoritarianism. They wanted "Mr. Science" and "Mr. Democracy."

In the 1989 protest, the students saw an opportunity to utilize the ideas of the May 4 movement by creating the Democracy
Movement. Kirk Denton compared the two movements and
how the 1989 group co-opted the language and desires of the
original group. "Placards held by marching students proclaimed
support for the May Fourth demands of democracy, science,
human rights, freedom and the rule of law . . . Appealing to
May Fourth and embracing its values gave the movement the
substance that only historical precedence and tradition can in a
culture so intensely conscious of the force of the past."[39]

American media had a presence in China, and cable-news
channel CNN broadcast the Tiananmen protest live as it unfolded.
The American audience saw tens of thousands of protesters and
rudimentary facsimiles of the Statue of Liberty being pulled along
with the masses. While broadcasting live, a Chinese government
official entered CNN's headquarters and demanded it pull the
plug. In the darkness, the military moved in, and protesters were
killed. The exact number was never disclosed, and an icy wind
swept through our two countries' relations.

America thought it had witnessed a glimmer of hope, a
crack in communism with the Democracy Movement, but
Denton brought a realism to the witness. In the US's hubris,
we thought we were witnessing a turn to democracy and a
capitalist's economic model. But our insight was shallow as
Denton explained that the masses were really rejecting parts
of their own culture and using Western ideas as the weapon
to eradicate traditional cultural aspects that were holding
them back. What the US did not understand was "that once
the disease is cured the medicine is no longer needed."[40] The
masses were not becoming like us but simply cherry-picking
ideas to further their cause, and they would remain true to
themselves, believing that ultimately their unique identity
would always be tied to Eastern thinking.

President George H. W. Bush's response to the Tiananmen

Square massacre was to quickly impose sanctions on China, but just as quickly, realpolitik won out. Per *The Washington Post*, the US ambassador in Beijing, James Lilley, sent a cable to Washington expressing that he "did not want to interrupt US business in China, particularly the sale of commercial aircraft and satellite launch services. Maintaining business ties does not mean that America is 'rewarding the murderers of Tiananmen by selling Boeing aircraft for hard cash.'"[41]

American businesses did continue to assess their economic opportunities, with a focus on the need for China to have most favored nation status. The benefits of this status in trade with the US had been used as a carrot with China, allowing it to export to the US under most favored nation low tariffs. This status had to be renewed annually by Congress. The renewal tussle in Congress pushed American corporations to lobby for permanent status and provide China entry into the World Trade Organization (WTO).

This next step in commerce's globalization and China's entry into the WTO fell to President Bill Clinton. As US corporations and the Chinese government pushed for entry, the question became what status China would be admitted under. The Chinese wanted to be deemed a developing nation. This status would hold them to lesser standards than a developed nation, meaning it could keep limiting access to China's market (i.e., barriers to entry) and would not have to adhere to international labor standards, creating a labor cost advantage.[42]

In March 2000 President Clinton gave a speech outlining his reason for supporting China's entry into the WTO. He acknowledged the policy's critics, citing concerns over Taiwan security, human and labor rights, and the economic power it would bestow. Clinton's answer was:

The question is not whether we approve or disapprove of China's practices. The question is what's the smartest thing to do to improve these practices. . . . [I]t will be nothing compared to the changes that this agreement will spark from the inside out in China. By joining the WTO, China is not simply agreeing to import more of our products. It is agreeing to import one of democracy's most cherished values, economic freedom. The more China liberalizes its economy, the more fully it will liberate the potential of its people—their initiative, their imagination, their remarkable spirit of enterprise. And when individuals have the power, not just to dream, but to realize their dreams they will demand a greater say. . . . In fits and starts, for the first time, China may become a society where people get ahead based on what they know rather than who they know.[43]

Clinton was referencing the Chinese cultural trait of conducting business through its *guanxi* system, based on who you know vs what you know. We'll look deeply at *guanxi* in chapter 9.

Clinton continued: "There's something even more revolutionary at work here. . . . The Chinese government no longer will be everyone's employer, landlord, shopkeeper and nanny all rolled into one. [Known as the 'iron rice bowl,' cradle-to-grave governmental stewardship of the citizens' needs.] It will have fewer instruments, therefore, with which to control people's lives. And that may lead to very profound change."[44] One of Clinton's most memorable lines was uttered in this speech as he spoke about the growth of the internet in China (at the time two million users—in 2018 about eight hundred million). He acknowledged that Chinese authorities were already trying to censor and control the internet but said, "Good luck! That's sort of like trying to nail Jell-O to the wall."[45] In 2001 China was admitted to the WTO with the desired status as a developing nation.

In less than twenty years, America's conventional wisdom that economic growth pulled along values of freedom and human rights was destroyed. Chinese private enterprise did blossom, providing hundreds of millions of jobs and unprecedented and sustained gross domestic product growth, but state-owned enterprises and CCP-led industrial policy holds the key to China's greater designs on value-chain ascension, namely in its plan known as Made in China 2025. We'll look closely at Made in China 2025 in chapter 7. Regarding the internet, it did not bring the freedoms to China expected but rather has become a tool of oppression through surveillance and is a powerful weapon in propaganda dissemination. The CCP was able to harness the internet to achieve Patrick's first commandment of propaganda: control the flow of information. The most important tenet of propaganda is control, and no other nation has been as successful as the PRC.[46]

June 4, 2019, marked the thirtieth anniversary of the Tiananmen Square massacre. Andrew J. Nathan, writing in *Foreign Affairs*, accessed newly released documents memorializing CCP senior leadership speeches in the incident's aftermath. They provided clarity about what CCP leaders were thinking and insight into where they were intending to drive the nation. China's leaders, under Deng, conducted a postmortem, drawing three conclusions: the CCP was under siege from internal and external enemies; ideological adherence and social stability superseded economic reform; and internal division would cause the party to fail. Nathan wrote, "In analyzing why a 'disturbance' had occurred in the first place, and why it evolved into a riot, the speakers revealed a profound paranoia about domestic and foreign enemies. . . . [T]he party resorted to ever more sophisticated and intrusive forms of control to combat the forces of liberalization."[47]

To flip Denton's previous metaphor of the protesting Tiananmen students in taking the Western cure for traditional aspects of their society holding China back, the party took the "medicine" of Western economic strategy, only to embark on an immunization plan against the accompanying ideology.

As Deng sought a long-term solution to guard against a wholesale turn by the Chinese youth away from their socialist path and guiding principles of Marxism-Leninism, he turned to a Mao tactic, a reeducation campaign. Deng's campaign was to reject the West and turn to the unique, irreplaceable Chinese culture to generate patriotism. The execution of reform and opening initiatives had allowed foreign humiliation to recede as a driver of the CCP's savior status, but the foreign sanctions being levied because of the June 4 massacre allowed the party to repackage the grievances of old. The party was quick to link patriotic education to nationalism, and it was rather quickly adopted by the masses, who viewed the US sanctions not as targeting China's leaders but the whole of the Chinese people and their nation—the collective.

While the immunization against Western ideology and values began in earnest after June 1989, its progress and comprehensive road map for success became clear in a leaked party directive from 2013, Xi's first year in office, known as Document No. 9, issued by the Central Committee of the CPC's General Office. (It is not recommended to attempt to download this document, as a nasty computer virus may occur.)

The document's proclamations became known as China's seven political perils, and officials were called to strengthen against outside infiltration and renew their work in the ideological sphere. In brief the perils took aim at the West's foundational philosophy for governance. No Western constitutional democracy. No universal values. No civil society. No neoliberalism. No Western ideas of journalism: speech was not free but controlled by the party. No historical nihilism: any rewriting of history belonged to the party. No questioning the party's definition of socialism with Chinese characteristics.

In the thirty years after Tiananmen, the CCP has deftly proven how well it can "nail Jell-O to the wall"—shielding itself from Western infiltration and mandating party-centric ideological adherence. Case in point, the thirtieth anniversary of the Tiananmen massacre passed without mention in the press or from the people. Louisa Lim, author of *The People's Republic of Amnesia*, said, "A single act of public remembrance might expose the frailty of the state's carefully constructed edifice of accepted history," which has evolved from strict censorship and the people's willful forgetting.[48] Patrick's historical propaganda view was "the purpose of history is to control the present and the future. History does not take place in the past but in the present."[49]

George Orwell's classic novel *1984* is often referenced in trying to understand China's single-party, controlling governmental apparatus. The novel, set in a futuristic, dystopian world where the protagonist's work is to make history serve her masters, draws on an oft-quoted insight of his: "Who controls the past, controls the future: who controls the present, controls the past. . . . The mutability of the past is the central tenet of Ingsoc (Orwell's fictional party). Past events, it is argued, have no objective existence, but survive only in written records and in human memories. The past is whatever the records and the memories agree upon. And since the Party is in full control of all records, and in equally full control of the minds of its members, it follows that the past is whatever the Party chooses to make it."[50]

Andrew J. Nathan's summary findings of "The New Tiananmen Papers" provided a broader view of the chasm between the CCP and the people and hinted at the supporting source of the people's silent acquiescence. "Yet centralized leadership has not resolved the abiding contradiction between reform and control that generated the Tiananmen crisis 30 years ago. The more China pursues wealth and power through domestic modernization and engagement with the global economy, the more students, intellectuals, and the rising middle class become unwilling to adhere to a 1950s-style ideological conformity, and the more conservative party elites react to social change by calling for more discipline in the party and conformity in society. . . . China now has a large, prosperous middle class that is quiescent out of realistic caution but yearns for more freedom."[51]

Deng Xiaoping's legacy is long and complicated. For China, it was transformative and disruptive, and the consequences reverberate today. Deng did not start reform and opening; Hu Guofeng did, but it was Deng's management of the concept that brought China into the modern world.

Deng's continued support of Zhou's four modernizations saw China race toward the embrace of technology and education supporting Mr. Science, but he shunned Mr. Democracy. He did not completely abandon the party's ideological goal to achieve socialism, only bent it by adding Chinese characteristics.

His compromises opened the doors to material wealth but cleaved a populous wealth gap and furthered the hated officials' graft, which troubles the whole of society today. Deng's draconian one-child policy left China with demographic imbalances in age and gender. Introducing entrepreneurship and market forces freed the proletariat from state-controlled labor distribution but also broke the safety net of lifetime employment and state benefits (i.e., the iron rice bowl). The rush to get rich first left the environment poor and an internal values system in tatters. Deng's policies and their consequences are explored in Part III, "Contradictions."

Deng was born in 1904 under China's last official dynasty. He traveled a long and torturous road to leadership. Throughout his political journey, he demonstrated patience and strategy. He used what we consider Western management skills in creating consolidation and cohesion: power dissemination based on meritocracy and expertise. He incorporated market demand mechanisms in pricing and production, turning away from state-planned supply and controlled pricing.

Deng acknowledged the flaws in communist ideology and its incongruence with human nature, thereby loosening the binds that had kept people from striving to satisfy their personal needs and desires.

As Kissinger remarked, Deng had not considered himself an emperor, or "son of heaven," but rather a mandarin, or a son of the people of China. Deng recognized to claim emperor status was a betrayal to the cause of socialism and rejected the building of a cult of personality. For his internment, he forwent Mao's grandiosity of embalmment and permanent display, choosing rather to donate his organs for research and cremation.

CHAPTER 6

The People of Xi

Chinese people should hold their rice bowls firmly in their own hands, with grains mainly produced by themselves.[1]
—Xi Jinping

Today it is not in the government's interest for the masses to simply satisfy their individual needs and desires through material acquisitions—they are expected to raise all domestic boats and spend their way out of a potential middle-income trap by sustaining a consumer-led economy. Xi's people, to enhance China's self-sufficiency, are to be the support for a dual-circulation strategy, an economic engine firing between production and consumption emanating from the Chinese themselves.

It is in the building, maintenance, and sustainability of the goal to create a consumption-led economy with a floor for common prosperity and a pressing need to eliminate a destabilizing wealth gap polarization that Xi sought to address in his first decade of leadership.

While Mao's tenure force-marched his people through a failed collectivism experiment, Deng's intentions through reform and opening held to the socialist ideology of egalitarianism for the masses, with eventual equal improvement for all. However, the methods to achieve Deng's theory unleashed an opportunity for those with connections and ambitions to accumulate profound wealth and those without to fall into a place of want and disillusionment.

Mao's and Deng's people experienced the extremes of poverty and wealth and diametrically opposed ideologies in economic systems through orthodox communism/socialism and capitalism experiments. Those people alive under Mao and Deng and those born after their reigns now find themselves caught up in the currents of massive change emanating from Xi's leadership.

An internal Chinese name has been adopted to segregate Chinese born before and after the reform and opening period. The pre, or silent generation, endured the turmoil of Mao's years and saw their iron rice bowls broken. This tacit promise of cradle-to-grave government dependency disappeared as state-owned enterprises (SOEs) no longer offered guaranteed lifetime employment and old-age benefits. Today, those who did not excel through the reform and opening transition look back on their hardships and are known as the bitter generation.

Postreform consumers who are a part of the burgeoning middle-class and who experienced doting parents, improved education, and worldly travel have become known as the sweet generations for their lack of difficulties and their exposure to the finer things that modernity has to offer.

The gulf between the generations "eating bitter" and those "eating sweet" is wide, and their respective experiences and reference points are very different. James Palmer described people born in the 1980s in 2013 writing for Aeon. co. Palmer's discussions with two young, well-educated men show just how much had changed from their parents to their generations in experience and outlook. These sons of parents who had survived Mao's many erratic and poverty-inducing years had left this bitter generation desiring money and security for themselves and their children. As the parents sacrificed to achieve these needs for their children, especially through the children's education, the children who succeeded developed higher-level needs and values. The children who had not known struggle struggled to understand what they considered their parents' amoral behavior in the chase for the security brought by money. In the eyes of the parents, the children were becoming materialistic and divorced from the family values of their culture. They perceived the children's reluctance to marry and not have children as an affront to their many sacrifices.[2]

But those born in the '80s and '90s and those following broadly labeled as millennials and Gen X have had unique challenges in navigating massive, disruptive changes emanating from the state. While their parents and grandparents had to focus on the survival stages of Maslow's hierarchy, it is this postreform generation that has been called on to meet the challenges of the more personal, individualistic values and mores of the hierarchy matriculation.

The generations after 1978 had to carry the burden of globalization and all the contradictions it brought to their traditional values system and paradoxes to the governance system. Deng's going out and bringing the best back meant that thousands went abroad to study. Hundreds of millions of Chinese now speak English. Deng's opening brought the reintroduction of and exposure to advertising, foreign media, entertainment, awareness of other forms of government, and finally the internet.

As Xi ushered in a new vision for China, reliant on self-sufficiency and pride of country, one way to gauge the changes to the people is through the consumer, where much of Xi's strategy for dual circulation lies.

The heavy lifting to support dual circulation can be found in the reticent, yet prolific middle class. McKinsey & Company projected the *urban* Chinese affluent and middle class would reach about 304 million by 2022, comprising 40 percent of global luxury consumption and driving 65 percent of global luxury consumption growth from 2018 to 2025. Just as in America, a "1 percent" phenomenon has occurred, with wealth, coastal regions, and billionaires grabbing the bulk of consumption press and possessions as witnessed by 969 Chinese billionaires (vs 691 American) by 2023.[3] But like in America, things that can sustain a society such as consumer staples, durables, and services are quickly being gobbled up by the masses. In 2015 the Demand Institute gave the divide between the US's and China's individual annual consumption. For China it predicted by 2025 an average of $4,400 vs the 2015 US consumption of $32,000.[4] As this annual Chinese consumption amount seems very low, remember that consumer prices in America are 68 percent higher than China. (China's currency is the Chinese yuan, abbreviated as CNY or symbolized as ¥, and the Renminbi, meaning the "people's money," abbreviated as RMB, are often used interchangeably, but RMB is the name of the currency, and the yuan is the unit of currency.)

In 1937, Carl Crow wrote *400 Million Customers* in reference to China's then population:

> Any time an export manager wants to enjoy a pleasant day-dream of the future, in which fame and prosperity will unite to banish daily cares, all he has to do is to take a pencil and a pad of paper and start figuring out what sales he could make if he could only find an advertising agent clever enough to induce a reasonable proportion of China's 400 million customers to buy his goods. Merchants wore out quill-pens on the same pleasant speculations long before graphite pencils, calculating machines and advertising agents began to play an important part in the affairs of the business world. So long as people of one country make goods to sell to others, so long as ships cross the ocean and international trade

exists, the golden illusion of the sales which may
be made to China's industrious millions will always be an intriguing one. No matter what you
may be selling, your business in China should be
enormous, if the Chinese, who should buy your
goods would only do so.[5]

Given McKinsey's projections of the growth in the middle class and disposable income, it is difficult to resist a quick
back-of-the-envelope calculation to realize the trillions of
yuan that are in play—which explains why China has long
been a dream maker for enterprises worldwide.

But under Xi, are the outside world's rose-colored glasses
fading? Two sources help us understand the mindset of the
Chinese consumer at the beginning of the Xi era in 2012. After
a decade of a nationalistic sanctioned dream, coupled with
deteriorating Western relations and a pandemic, the Chinese
consumer was on a very different trajectory.

In 2014, recognizing the importance of an emerging sanctioned national dream and the role it could play in branding
and marketing, the Millward Brown agency conducted a survey in China on the subject and compared it with Americans
and their dream. Author Helen Wang published *The Chinese
Dream The Rise of the World's Largest Middle Class and What it
Means to You* in 2010. Combining these quantitative and quali-
tative sources, trends and insights emerge to paint a picture of
these two distinct groups—those born prereform and opening and those born post—and how they contributed to the
shift to a consumer-led economy.

Millward Brown set the generational divide for its analysis of the Chinese Dream compared to the American Dream.
"More than in most places, brand actions in China need to
consider generational differences. Young people are more
individualistic and older people are still inclined to rely on

government. That's because today's grandparents were born before the founding of the People's Republic of China in 1949. Their children experienced the Cultural Revolution. But their grandchildren have known only the burgeoning economic power that has developed over the past 30 years."[6]

Helen Wang summarized these postreform consumers: "Most were born after the Cultural Revolution (1966–1976) and grew up in an increasingly prosperous and fast-changing China. . . . They are also living with extreme anxiety due to the rapid changes in China."[7]

Much like Maslow's base needs, Millward Brown found the needs of Chinese and Americans were similar, with both cultures desiring health, happiness, and good lives for their families. Wang interviewed He Jie, a businessman from Wuhan, who told her, "'In today's China, people just got beyond their physiological needs, such as food and clothing. . . . Now they need to feel secure in their family, health, and property.' . . . 'For average people, our biggest dream is feeling secure.'"[8]

For the Chinese there is an interdependency between their personal attainment of a dream and the country's achievement of the dream, but for Americans, achieving the national dream depends on the individual achieving their own dream.

Wang explained the traditional Chinese cultural trait that has always put the collective society in a superior position to the individual. This intertwining of people and country—one unit—explains the natural defense and affront to the people when outsiders question China's actions, such as when the US implemented sanctions after the Tiananmen Square massacre. Wang found that the Chinese people associated their future with the future of the country.[9] Wang explained the tradition of collective unit down to the household level in their surname convention. In China the family name is listed first, and the person's individual name comes second, demonstrating the superior position of the family and the individual's subservience. In the US, the individual's first name is superior in position and helps distinguish them from the family clan. In China this individualism can connote selfishness.[10]

As the Chinese middle class moves up the economic ladder, additional needs and higher-level values begin to emerge. In 2014 Millward Brown, citing the Futures Company, found life satisfaction to be 58 percent for Chinese vs 48 percent for Americans. However, the Futures Company survey found that Chinese satisfaction would increase if they had more stuff. "Chinese realize that their lives have room for improvement, with an overwhelming 79 percent agreeing that they'd be happier with more possessions. . . . 14 percent of Americans say they need more stuff. . . . The Futures Company concludes that once people worldwide satisfy their basic material needs, adding more possessions doesn't usually increase happiness. Chinese aren't there yet."[11]

Wang explained the middle class's need to demonstrate publicly their desire for more material possessions, tying it to the unique Chinese value of saving face. From a marketer's perspective it leads to strategies and tactics that employ inadequacy marketing, leveraging product attributes improvement to a person's appearance, performance, or group inclusion. Using inadequacy messaging speaks to affiliation, admiration, and status, Asia's top-tier hierarchy needs. Wang provided a cultural insight: "Since the Chinese put great value on group expectations, they tend to measure their worth from what society expects of them rather than what they want for themselves. . . . They feel like they have to 'keep up with the Joneses.'"[12] She further explained purchase choices as dependent on the consumer's audience: "One force driving the consumption boom is that the Chinese are very status conscious. As their financial situation improves, they like to purchase items that increase their status. . . . They want to own homes, buy cars, and travel for vacations. However, for products and services that their friends and neighbors cannot see, they can be very price conscious."[13]

Millward Brown's survey found Chinese spending priorities aligned closely with Helen Wang's observations (figure 2).

Figure 2: 2014 Spending Priorities

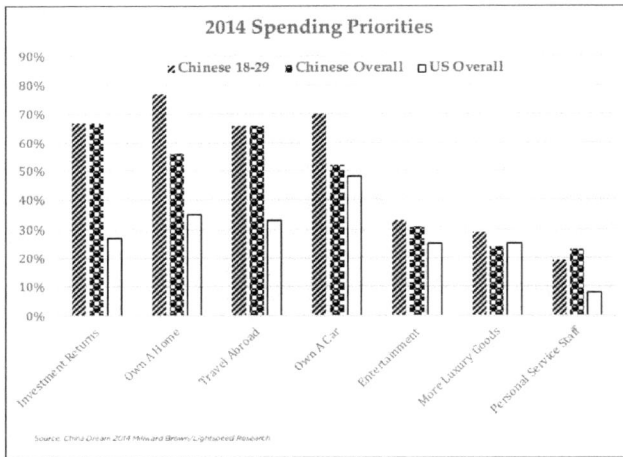

Xi has worked to usher in policies that effect Chinese consumers and Chinese and US industries as he attempts to engineer the state-capitalist model away from infrastructure and manufacturing and toward domestic consumption. McKinsey's data shows why: the value of services in China represented 52 percent of 2018 GDP growth. Its gross trade in services in 2017 was $5.1 trillion vs $17.2 trillion in global goods trade, but services were growing 60 percent faster than global goods trade. China has a lot of headroom to boost this growth, as its labor productivity in the service sector is only 20–50 percent of Organization for Economic Co-operation and Development countries.

As China's personal pocketbooks expanded and its exposure to the outside world increased, the yuan was leaving the shore. Within Millward Brown's identified priorities, we see how the government tried to control the flow of outbound funds and how they use their consumers' spending to reward or punish other countries' behavior through economic coercion. But first it is instructive to look at the consumer's evolution as documented by Crow in the 1930s:

> Without wishing to revive a controversy . . . I may say that the persistence of the hated opium traffic in China was due to the fact that opium was, at that time, the only commodity the British and American traders could sell to the Chinese in sufficient quantity to meet a substantial part of their payment for cargoes of silk and tea. Thousands of the old silver dollars (British and American) . . . have been worn smooth in domestic trade, but have never left China's shores, because the Chinese found nothing in the West worth exchanging them for. From the dawn of history everything produced by China had been superior to anything produced by the barbarians. The Chinese assumed that this was a condition of affairs which would last forever and paid but scant attention to the goods the foreign trader had to sell. The first serious blow their inordinate pride suffered came when they discovered that the barbarians could really produce good merchandise.[14]

Crow described how the first Industrial Revolution emanating from Great Britain had changed the dynamics in production and pricing, with eager Chinese willing to purchase

Western goods, and the ensuing competition that arose both from other countries and eventually by replication on the Chinese mainland. Now, as the developed world moves out of the third Industrial Revolution and into the fourth (the revolutions are covered in detail in chapter 7) with much of the output locked up in services and revolutionary inventions, China intends to be an important source of the needs of their own people. Xi's dual-circulation strategy once again seeks to keep the consumer's expenditures cycling within the country with a goal of silver worn smooth from domestic trade, only in a more technological, traceable way with an emerging government-controlled digital currency.

By breaking down each of the Millward Brown survey priority categories, we see how the government influences and controls its subjects' behavior. (For the pocketbook priority of owning a car, see the case study "Ford's Folly").

On the pocketbook priority of investment returns, the complexity of China's financial system is beyond the scope of this book. Yet there are important trends emerging within its consumer base and Chinese government actions regarding the US that should be touched on.

Hardworking, coupled with prolific savings, has been a hallmark of the Chinese consumer. Being frugal and debt free, long a revered Confucian value, and the notion of saving to provide a sense of security, have underwritten much of the prereform group. As all move to the consumption-led economy, the fundamentals of credit and investment are increasingly recognized as foundational for this metamorphosis.

McKinsey Group International provided an overview of the state of finance in China. China's unprecedented growth accelerated when it began to integrate its economy with the rest of the world. However, international capitalist systems remained relatively closed to Chinese commingling. According to McKinsey Group International, "A huge majority of Chinese firms' revenue still comes from the home economy. Operational and regulatory complexities in China's financial markets remain a barrier to international players."[15] As China reached the bounds that investment-led growth could provide, capital productivity and corporate returns were not absorbing the slack. Chinese debt in 2007 was 140 percent of GDP, and by 2018 it had reached 250 percent. McKinsey Group International found that "57 percent of national debt is corporate debt, of which 70 percent is in SOEs [state-owned enterprises] that have only 30 to 50 percent the return on assets of private companies."[16] This internal reliance on the population's savings to support state-owned enterprises fueled debt, and underperformance in the areas of capital returns, productivity, and innovation is not lost on the government.

Reliance on the consumer as a source of funding is becoming more challenging, as the consumer-debt-to-GDP ratio has also substantially increased, from 8 percent in 2000 to 56 percent of GDP in 2019.[17] This figure is shy of year-end 2018 for American consumers' debt, standing at 66 percent to US GDP. In February 2019, two US Federal Reserve economists said, "the rapid increase in household debt in China in recent years, driven primarily by growth in mortgages, has raised issues from a financial stability perspective."[18]

South China Morning Post reported that in 2018, household debt accounted for about 50 percent of all new loans, eclipsing corporate borrowing to become the driver in loan growth. A vicious cycle has been created. According to McKinsey Group International, Chinese consumers experience a dearth of investment options due to the lack of connectedness with non-Chinese financial instruments. This has forced the average household to concentrate their savings in home ownership, finding that Chinese assets are skewed to real estate at a 62 percent rate compared to only 28 percent for US households. This phenomenon has greatly driven an unsustainable rise in property prices.[19]

This lack of Chinese consumers' international financial connectedness is due to Chinese constructed barriers to entry, resulting in unique advantages for China. Its banking system is now the largest in the world, at $40 trillion, but foreign ownership in its financial system stood at 2 percent in 2019. The Agricultural Bank of China operates over twenty thousand branches. This has given the country the opportunity to build entrenched, in-market giants. Its overall banking system leads the world, and Swiss Re Institute, a Zurich-based reinsurance company, predicts China will be the largest insurance market by the mid-2030s. Swiss Re forecasts insurance premiums moving from a value in 2018 of $575 billion to $2.36 trillion in 2032 vs a 2018 US insurance market value of $1.47 trillion. It also predicts that the insurance premium growth rate over the next decade will accelerate at two times the global average, with aging demographics driving growth in the areas of retirement annuities, old age health care, and life insurance. For MNCs to reach these customers will require beating state-owned China Life, with 1.7 million sales agents on the ground.

Offering revolving consumer credit has long been closed on the mainland for American companies. Chinese government-backed credit card company China UnionPay has become the dominate player, controlling 90 percent of the Chinese market. American companies Visa and Mastercard have been trying to enter the Chinese market for two decades, including winning a WTO case against China to break the monopoly. To express the frustration with China's barriers during Trump's China trade talks, in 2019 *South China Morning Post* quoted the US's trade representative Robert Lighthizer as saying it was "a 'conspicuous ongoing example' of its failure to honor its WTO obligations. As has become clear, China's industrial policy objective is to protect its national champion,

China UnionPay, from competition in China so that it can use the revenues from a captive domestic market to fund its own global expansion."[20]

UnionPay's global expansion has been massive and strategic. By the end of 2017, fifteen billion credit, debit, and other payment cards were in worldwide circulation, with UnionPay's penetration at 44 percent and Visa and Mastercard standing at 21 and 16 percent, respectively. It is UnionPay's going out strategy that positions it for long-term market domination. By 2019 UnionPay was available to accept payments in 174 countries and had begun issuing cards in fifty countries serving one hundred million customers.[21] *China Daily*, quoting the chairman of China UnionPay in 2018, said,

> For UnionPay, the countries and regions involved in the Belt and Road Initiative (Xi's signature program designed to link China with Africa, Asia, the Middle East and Europe via land and sea) are a priority. They are not only closely tied with China in many aspects, but also are in need of infrastructure relating to transfer payments and digital payments. Apart from promoting both greater acceptance and larger issuance of UnionPay cards in these countries, the bank card organization has also been pushing ahead with the globalization of China's financial technology standards and helping those countries in need of transit networks for payments, such as Laos and Thailand, to build the networks locally.[22]

Prior to the Belt and Road Initiative, UnionPay's international business had been focused on availability in Chinese outbound travel destination countries to serve them and recapture transaction fees.

For Chinese and emerging markets, it's not just plastic but mobile payments that drive the flow of money. Alibaba's Alipay and Tencent's WeChat Pay wallets, which allow UnionPay credit card linking, have built ecosystems that provide all financial needs, from the ability to conduct transactional payments to the purchase of financial instruments and insurance policies. Ipsos, a market research firm, reported that in 2018, 890 million people used mobile payments, with Alipay and WeChat Pay claiming one billion and nine hundred million authorized users, respectively.

The state of the revolving credit market in China was best summed up by Wang Pengbo of Analysys, a Chinese consultancy: "Visa and Mastercard won't be able to change the payment culture that Chinese consumers have formed in the past decade. They have missed the golden era."[23] UnionPay is a classic example of a China state-owned business protected from competition and allowed to grow to juggernaut status.

What China does seem to need is fresh injections of capital and financial management expertise. Historically, Western financial service firms were not allowed in China to control a majority interest in asset management, equity, and bond trading or insurance firms. In 2018, with the denial of entry for financial firms on the table of US-China trade negotiations, China agreed to 51 percent US majority–owned joint ventures in these industries. By mid-2019, China agreed to 100 percent ownership and that it would go into effect by 2020 for foreign firms, a rapid about-face due to trade negotiations from the previously promised change of whole ownership by 2021.

While Chinese customers cannot buy US stocks, even though Chinese corporations are listed on US exchanges, changes in rules are making it easier for US customers to own Chinese stocks in China. Morgan Stanley Capital International is an exchange-traded fund that tracks emerging markets. In 2019 the benchmark reconfigured its holdings to better represent Chinese stocks in ratio to its emerging market dominance. In 2018, as China's stock and bond markets were seen as investment options for Americans, we went on a spending spree, investing $75 billion in their shares, and the Wall Street titans were predicting much more would follow.[24]

What does China get by opening its financial markets? To keep funds flowing to Chinese financial instruments, it needs financial credibility and performance. According to McKinsey Global Institute, China's system is inefficient in allocating its capital. Corporate debt favors SOEs, yet only produces around 20 percent of industrial output. McKinsey identifies the quadrupling of domestic debt in the last decade as leaving the economy vulnerable and that foreign experience in risk management resource allocation could improve better returns on investment. [25] *The Economist* concurred that Chinese "officials also crave more competition in the financial system for China's own good. As growth slows, they want to improve productivity, which requires better allocation of capital."[26]

By allowing more access to China's financial system, China hopes to also blunt US criticism. As Wall Street elites' support of China has waned in the last few years, a chorus of hawks has become vocal. Florida senator Marco Rubio warned that Americans investing in Chinese companies faced risks due to national security dangers and human rights violations. Former Trump advisor Steve Bannon called for blockage of Chinese initial public offerings on American exchanges, advising to "unwind all the pension funds and insurance companies in the US that provide capital to the Chinese Communist Party."[27]

In 2018, thirty-four China-based companies raised $92 billion in capital on US stock exchanges. *South China Morning Post* reported, "As the total market capitalization of US-listed Chinese companies has ballooned to US $1.2 trillion, worry has grown that US investors are assuming risks they know little about."[28]

China's quick change of heart regarding deeper US ownership and involvement in its financial system will accomplish several things. First, it will leverage Wall Street firms that desperately want to enter the Chinese market to put pressure on lawmakers in Washington. Second, Western financial institutions will raise the standards of China's capital markets.[29] Last, it may provide more trust and returns to the small Chinese investor who has not experienced any long-term investment growth.

The Wall Street titans did not disappoint. In December 2020, Goldman Sachs was the first to report it had reached agreement with the Chinese government to buy out its Chinese joint-venture partner and take 100 percent ownership of Goldman Sachs Gao Hua Securities Co., renaming it Goldman Sachs (China) Securities Co. JPMorgan Chase and Morgan Stanley were quickly on their heels.[30]

On Millward Brown's pocketbook priority of owning a home, there is a direct link between Chinese investing and owning a home. A general understanding of how the consumer must allocate their household budgets and how things are changing helps us understand where priorities lie and what funds may remain for discretionary spending. Directional answers are found in quantitative research done by the Hong Kong Trade Development Council. Looking at middle-class consumers, Hong Kong Trade Development Council conducted two rounds of inquiry, first in 2013 and again in 2017. In reviewing the findings, some results seem intuitive based on general behavior with a consumer's income growth.

The Hong Kong Trade Development Council provides a useful and market-relevant stepladder phrasing of consumer behavior familiar to our traditional American marketing product line extension strategy of "good, better, best." "It is said of mainland consumers that, as they get wealthier, there is a shift in their consumption patterns—starting at 'from (having) nothing to something,' moving to 'from something to more,' and then to 'from more to better.'"[31]

Hong Kong Trade Development Council points out that the percentage of people in their survey owned more than one property, with most having paid off at least one of the properties.[32] Since investment options are limited, Chinese have used homeownership as an investment vehicle, with the acquisition of second homes for any excess savings. Hong Kong Trade Development Council called out this rise in home mortgages to draw attention to the fact that the acceptance of and use of debt has increased.

While Hong Kong Trade Development Council looked at home ownership in China, there is a spillover effect in the US housing market. The National Association of Realtors tracks international sales of residential homes. For the period 2010–18, cumulative sales of people from mainland China, Hong Kong, and Taiwan buying US property exceeded $180 billion. The association estimated 7 percent of sales were for housing Chinese students studying in the US. The remainder was shared among Chinese immigrants (approximately 2.4 million)[33] and secondary homes as a store of offshore wealth.[34]

CNBC reported in July 2019 that the trend in US real estate sales to Chinese nationals had collapsed, posting a 56 percent decline in sales from the previous year. The contributing factors were Chinese government control of outflowing funds and rhetoric associated with the two nations' conflict.

Not only had US sales to Chinese nationals collapsed, but also by 2020 there was a destabilizing undercurrent in the Chinese housing market. As a top priority for wealth accumulation had become the need to own a home, home prices had suffered years of annual increases. With this boon of desire came massive overbuilding, supported by Chinese financial companies underwriting unrealistic investments. As the government recognized excessive borrowing in the industry, it wanted to tamp down spiraling costs and debt risk.

Evergrande, China's second-largest property developer, was the first domino to fall. Per CNN, the government "ordered a debt restructuring intended to prevent a disorderly collapse from wreaking havoc on the economy and sparking social unrest."[35] Evergrande's debt by end of 2022 had reached $340 billion, about 2 percent of China's GDP. Local governments control the sale of land and rely heavily on real estate and its related industries, which employ tens of millions and comprise roughly 30 percent of China's GDP.

As other private property developers saw their funding dry up and consumers—many of whom suffered losses on large down payments or complete purchases of unfinished apartments—closed their pocketbooks, the government moved to support state-owned enterprises. Midway through 2023 state-owned enterprise property developers grew by 40 percent year over year, achieving a 58 percent market share of the top one hundred developers.

The Wall Street Journal reported the long-term challenge faced by the government. With the housing market underpinning Chinese investors' nest eggs, the financial systems in both countries recognized the potential long-term issues to be faced from falling wealth, damaged confidence in the market, and a declining demographic base to soak up excess housing inventory.[36]

On Millward Brown's pocketbook priority of traveling abroad, before Trump's trade war and the pandemic, we could think of the Chinese traveler from sea to shining sea, as they were visiting unexpected and far-flung areas of America. They were also descending on and sometimes overwhelming new and old hotspots of international travel in search of unique, status-building selfies. Craving the great outdoors to escape their compact, environmentally challenged megacities, they topped off wilderness excursions with a swing through an important American or European city for a highbrow shopping extravaganza.

McKinsey Global Institute noted the magnitude of Chinese travel. In 2018, the Chinese made 150 million trips inclusive of domestic travel. Half the trips were in the greater China area, including Hong Kong, Macau, and Taiwan. Twenty-nine percent were within the larger Asia area, leaving approximately 20 percent for the rest of the world. Chinese accounted for 9 percent of all international trips, spending $265 billion in 2017, contributing 22 percent of worldwide spend.[37]

Resonance and China Luxury Advisors published a white paper called "The Future of Chinese International Travel." It cited Nielson, who projected outbound travel to reach four hundred million by 2030. Trip.com (a dominant Chinese travel agency) reported that in 2018 there were 120 million passport holders and forecasted that passport holders would reach 240 million by 2020.[38] As these forecasts were prepandemic, the current growth trajectory is unknown. It is estimated that 20 percent of Chinese passports expired during the pandemic and outbound trips were stopped, resulting by early 2023 in system backups in issuance of passports and visas.

The US Travel Association gave a breakdown of Chinese traveling to America. In 2017, 3.2 million visits were made, with the traveler's average age of thirty-five and the US counting $35.3 billion in revenue. However, ending 2019, the last year of prepandemic US-bound travel, data show Chinese visits had declined to 2.8 million. Also notable was the lack of a postpandemic rebound in direct flights between the countries, with April 2023 still indicating that mutual flights were down 94 percent from prepandemic levels.

Travel was an industry where we banked a trade surplus

with China, with only $5.5 billion going to China from our travel there, netting the US $29.8 billion. One note of caution: the travel category tracked by the US government includes education from Chinese nationals studying in US universities. The gross revenue breaks out as $18.8 billion associated with true travel, $2.5 billion to US airlines, $1 billion miscellaneous, and $13.9 billion on education. The US Travel Association provided a breakdown of Chinese tourists' discretionary spending while visiting the US in 2017 (figure 3).

Figure 3: Chinese Tourists' Discretionary Spending in the US, 2017

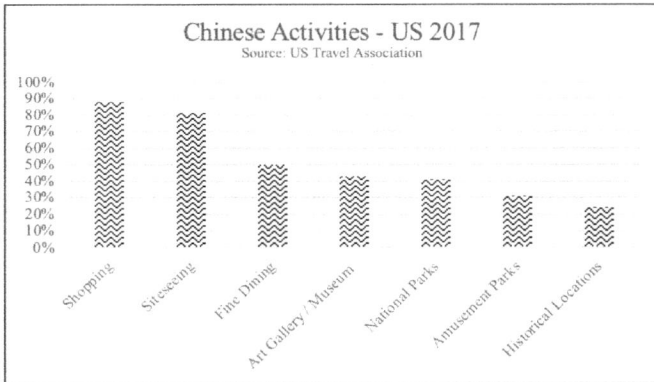

As the average age of the Chinese traveler decreased, their willingness to break away from the traditional tour group junket increased. They are quickly becoming the free independent traveler. Small groups of friends or families are increasingly reliant on their phones to guide them, providing GPS, translation, site and restaurant reviews, and mobile wallets for payment. For self-driving trips, the US was the preferred destination. In 2015 Hertz estimated it provided ninety thousand rides per month for Chinese tourists and businesspeople.

With substantial money and desired foot traffic for places such as museums and national parks on the line, America's recipient industries invested much capital to court these consumers. Hotels have tried to cater to the Chinese visitor with Chinese language TV channels and traditional Chinese meals. A clue that a hotel may be preferred by Chinese, especially in Las Vegas, is the absence of the number four in floor or room numbers. Much like Americans' aversion to the number thirteen, four's pronunciation sounds like their word for death and is considered unlucky.

Because China is becoming a mobile payment, cashless society, many American companies installed the ability to accept WeChat Pay, Alipay, and UnionPay for transactions. The hiring of Mandarin-speaking staff proliferated, especially in high-end retail shopping. Resonance and China Luxury Advisors research found "that Chinese-speaking salespeople are an important motivator of return visits, with several (interviewees) noting that they feel self-conscious being helped by non-Chinese speakers."[39]

Not only did establishments invest in the infrastructure and human power to serve these customers, but also a great deal of marketing in language was produced. Resonance and China Luxury Advisors ranked Chinese destination decision factors as safety, quality of natural environment/scenery, iconic landmarks, and the country's political climate.

The US National Parks noted the benefit tourists could bring and created smart video campaigns, including using a Chinese travel influencer to provide safety tips and itineraries. Utah, Wyoming, Montana, and Idaho jointly produced a self-drive guide around Yellowstone National Park, a favorite of the Chinese.

With the rest of the world clamoring for Chinese travelers, the Chinese government took note. By harnessing the power of the yuan, they are leveraging it to achieve two purposes.

First, at home, to build pride in Chinese culture and bolster homegrown consumption, they embarked on building domestic tourism. China set a goal to develop a national park service. By the end of 2010, they had over twenty-five hundred nature reserves, two hundred national scenic areas, and 650 national forest parks, but none of them qualified as a national park by international standards. These areas had become victims of commercialization and were undermanaged and funded. China's Development and Reform Commission partnered with the US think tank Paulson Institute to study successful tourism models, especially the US's, to pattern a 2020 plan.

In 2015, when Beijing was awarded the 2022 Winter Olympics, the party realized the internal interest that would be sparked in winter sports. The party developed a plan to have 650 skating rinks and eight hundred ski resorts built by 2022.

To supplement the renewed and increasingly sophisticated interest in China's own culture, the party set on a sweeping construction of museums. *The Economist* reported China had twenty-five museums when the communists took control of the country. With Mao's Cultural Revolution, the idea of revering the ancient was further decimated. Museums had not traditionally been accessible to common folks, with important imperial relics viewed only by the elite. As China integrated with leading nations, it realized it did not have trophy museums. China's museum count at the end of 2012 was 3,866.

Second, China has turned its outbound tourists' yuan into a unique and unsettling leverage point. Succinctly explained by *The Economist*, "China even uses the term 'tourism diplomacy.' The Communist Party's mouthpiece, the *People's Daily*, says this has become an 'important and indispensable' tool of China's foreign policy. And, just as Chinese tourism can win friends, so its curtailment can be used to show displeasure. Some analysts call this tactic 'weaponizing' outbound tourism. In countries where Chinese visitors play an important economic role any twitch by China that may curb the flow soon spreads anxiety."[40]

In terms of winning friends, tourists' yuan can grease the wheels of the Belt and Road Initiative. *The Economist* cited in early 2019 that Chinese tourists were treated to the pyramids of Giza and the Sphinx bathed in lights of Chinese red and accompanying audio narration given in Chinese. The Chinese government was encouraging its citizens to travel to Egypt as it is an important regional hub in China's Belt and Road Initiative.[41]

In March 2019, Italy became the first of the Group of Seven countries and largest country in the European Union to sign onto the Belt and Road Initiative agreement. The deal provided $2.8 billion in projects, notably three ports, to enable faster access of Chinese goods into the EU. By May 2019 China had granted new flights from China to Rome, widening the funnel for Chinese businesspeople and tourists into Italy and the home of the Belt and Road Initiative inspiration, the Silk Road of Marco Polo. However, in 2023, before an automatic five-year renewal of the agreement, Italy announced it would not continue. Italian luxury businesses should have taken note of the severing, as the CCP's rhetoric was harsh, and the ramifications of retaliation were not yet clear.

It is the punitive use of tourism diplomacy that is most troubling to those industries with sunk costs and future earnings tied to this important, emerging customer. Resonance and China Luxury Advisors reported that the government designates which countries tour packages can travel to and promote and that it grants this approval at will, effectively turning it into part of its tourism diplomacy strategy.[42]

While various countries have felt the ire of this sharp

diplomacy, it is the US, and those associated with it, who are becoming the main targets. As tensions rose between China and the US, the Associated Press reported on June 4, 2019, that China had issued a travel alert on America. Issued by the foreign ministry and the US Chinese embassy, visitors were warned of being interrogated and other forms of US law enforcement harassment. Separately, China's Ministry of Culture and Tourism warned that shootings, robberies, and theft are frequent in the US.

While Resonance and China Luxury Advisors had found a country's political climate was low on the travel destination decision tree, it pointed to an important cultural insight. The Chinese were increasingly willing to venture out independently, but they were not confident in going to destinations that were viewed as politically incorrect: "many Chinese are loath to explore unsanctioned destinations, risking their social standing among their peers."[43] In other words, a selfie in the wrong place is a face-losing proposition.

By mid-2019, 2018 travel data was in, and 2019 trends were becoming apparent. The US National Travel and Tourism Office counted 2.9 million Chinese travelers for 2018, a three hundred thousand decrease from 2017. US tourism experts were bracing for the 2019 decrease to be more dramatic. They feared a similar fate, a 50 percent drop in Chinese tourism, as was experienced by South Korea in 2017 after the US had deployed a Terminal High Altitude Area Defense system there as deterrence to North Korea. China feared US weapons so close to its borders and in turn weaponized its South Korea–bound Chinese travelers. With the Chinese government angrily threatening South Korea, Chinese citizens stayed away.

Economists pointed out the power of propaganda at the disposal of the CCP to deter US travel. *The New York Times* quoted Michael O. Moore, a George Washington University economics professor: "That is potentially an enormous advantage in conflict if you can control the message, without question . . . There's an increasingly patriotic spin to everything and the US is portrayed in a negative light, and that can play a role in people's decisions."[44]

Postpandemic 2023 saw the Chinese consumer maintaining a wanderlust for travel, concentrating their trips in the Asian Pacific region, while the US and Europe continued to wonder if the tourism yuan would return to their shores.

The US counts revenue from foreign students studying in the US under the travel category. By 2019 the offshoot from the travel category of education, which had in 2017 provided American universities with $13.9 billion, was under extreme pressure. The scrutiny of Chinese students and university-based researchers had become a focal point of US politics and national security concerns.

By the numbers, since 1978 the US has educated approximately two million, full-tuition-paying Chinese nationals. These students were heavily concentrated in the science, technology, engineering, and math disciplines. In 2017, six hundred thousand Chinese students went abroad to study, with the US receiving approximately one third. In the 2000s, only about 20 percent returned to China after graduation. However, once China's focus turned to innovation, the CCP realized that its legacy education system, which relies on test-focused, memorization techniques, did not necessarily foster creative thinking. Therefore, China placed great emphasis on luring these students back, and by 2017, 80 percent were returning.

Education is highly regarded in China, and a US degree has traditionally been seen as very prestigious. The US stance toward continuing to accept these students is causing great concern among the Chinese elite and among some US colleges who reap significant tuition fees. So far, the value of the

US degree seems to have escaped the ire of the CCP, with a count of 298,000 Chinese students enrolled for the 2021–22 school year.[45]

Millward Brown's pocketbook priority of entertainment is a broad category that encompasses everything from e-sports to place-based experiential forms, all of which are squarely under the thumb of the CCP. PwC's Global Entertainment and Media Industry Outlook 2022–2026 estimated that by 2026 China's in-market gross (including advertising) will be just shy of $530 billion.[46]

The value of entertainment as a vehicle of soft power, propaganda, and cultural identity represents one of the highest barriers to entry the US faces. One form of entertainment, film, had been an important revenue stream for Hollywood from China, but as Americans taught the Chinese technical skills of modern cinema and China continued to bend US filmmakers to its will, US revenue, story authenticity, and soft power eroded.

It is within cinema where we find an informative look at the career arc of a Chinese princeling whose wealth and ties to the CCP show just how much control over the outbound flow of yuan China yields. Most importantly the CCP's ability to use censorship, whether overt or self-induced, to bend this industry to its edict that all art is to serve the party is rampant through propaganda, patriotism, and nationalism in the service of the Chinese narrative. Hollywood has paid a great price to reap billions of dollars over the past decade, but Hollywood's party seems near an end. Read more in the case study "Hollywood Hijacked: The Politics of Art."

On Millward Brown's pocketbook priority of buying more luxury, This is a category that is and will continue to experience a great deal of disruption from Xi's goal of internal dual circulation, coupled with more than a decade of heavy indoctrination into Xi's proclaimed version of patriotism and nationalism. It is helpful to look at the morphing behavior of the people's mindset as consumers from early in Xi's installation as paramount leader to the present to see subtle and monumental changes in consumer behavior due to patriotism, nationalism, and the economic effect of the pandemic.

Returning to Helen Wang's 2010 findings that consumers spend on luxury consumption that is publicly visible but choose to economize on items consumed privately, this provides an indicator for understanding consumption across all products. Laddering customers up through product line extensions and a product's perceived status is the holy grail of profit margin and brand equity. In 2013 McKinsey identified a new challenge as the middle class split between mass and upper middle and emerging inland-tier Chinese cities became important. The premium status of products and the aspirational value they contribute begins to rely more on emotional rather than functional benefits. McKinsey's research found that Chinese consumers had been too new to so many product options, and coupled with pragmatic and conservative spending habits, the key selling point had been product functionality. But within a couple of years of exposure to what emotional benefits could be achieved from higher perceived value, the emotional advertising appeal was moving to the top of the buyer's consideration.[47]

As the world entered the pandemic, the split between mass and upper middle class identified by McKinsey revealed cracks in the materialistic frenzy giving rise to CCP concern. As millions of Chinese have excelled, just as in the US, a large group is seeing the upper-middle-class ladder being pulled beyond reach.

There is a bifurcation occurring among the younger urban class. As the realities of moderating growth and competition became a headwind, individual needs were rising to the fore. In the major metropolises of tier one and tier two cities, housing costs were becoming untenable, and job opportunities that matched educational attainment were dwindling.

American author Zak Dychtwald lived among the young Chinese trying to make their parents proud and better their own lives. He described a woman named Bella who graduated from college in the largest group to date in 2014.The competition for a job that matched her credentials was difficult. She had received good grades and attended a good university, but good wasn't enough. She couldn't differentiate herself from the millions of other graduates.[48]

It is in this emerging disillusionment with the ability to get rich and differentiate oneself that new profiles of the future consumer are emerging. Doug Sanders, writing for *The Globe and Mail*, described China's millennials as unique, assertive, and potentially destabilizing. Sanders described their backstory by observing China's annual migration during the Spring Festival as hundreds of millions returned from the coastal areas to their hometowns. Sanders assessed the psyche of these millennials as unique Chinese experiences that contribute to unique expectations and anxiety. Many of these children, he estimated as many as one hundred million, were left in the rural countryside with family members as their parents went to the cities to make money. The parents returned annually to visit, but most likely their only child became alienated and rebellious. Other children, whose parents remained in the countryside but focused all their resources to get the only child the best education, ended up with a child who carried guilt if they did not find a well-paying job.[49]

There seem to be two broadly emerging groups within this mass middle class: those whose consumption has become a psychological crutch and civic duty—think of them as the apprehensive strivers—and those who have adopted a defeatist mentality, calling themselves the *sang* (loosely translated: dejected, frustrated) culture. You could think of the *sang* as like the free and unfettered that emerged during the Cultural Revolution.

The apprehensive striver was illustrated through a *Sixth Tone* report in 2018 told by Li Xueshi, a professor at the Chinese University of Hong Kong in Shenzhen. She attended a conference on China's environmental problems regarding how extreme consumption was destroying the environment. Li recognized the contradiction in her and her friends' lifestyles as they spent their days studying and teaching about Marx's theory of commodity fetishism only to regroup with friends to compare notes on their recent purchases of society's must-have consumer goods such as iPhones. She described their plight: "The act of buying things offers us a break—a precious relief from our lonely lives, our crippling debts, and a world verging on ecological collapse—even as each purchase brings us one step closer to the brink of financial and environmental ruin. Consumption has become a psychological crutch." [50]

Li equated the ability to purchase goods by choice as an expression of freedom since previously what could be bought or was allowed for purchase was tightly controlled. But as Xi moves the country toward self-reliance and dual circulation, the people are expected to make and then consume their own goods, feeling the pressure to do so coming from the media, CCP, and peers. Li exposed what this empty consumerism did to them—temporary joy—and admitted the shallowness of the emotions, saying, "And even if they were motivated to stop shopping: What next? Finding meaning in life is hard when we're discouraged from most beliefs ending in '-ism'—except, of course, consumerism."[51]

Li's disillusionment with and the futility of a consumerist mentality seeping into young shoppers' minds hints at the much larger structural problem the CCP faces in its desired shift to a self-sufficient consumer-led economy. With youth's anchors unmoored from centuries of China's value systems,

environmental carnage in plain sight, and doubts about ful-
filling employment to match the educational sacrifices made
to acquire it, fleeting luxury brand badges are beginning to
tarnish.

The *sang,* also known as the "lie flat," group represents
those who have willfully stopped trying to seek affiliation
through acquisition. Lie flat "literally means loss or depriva-
tion, [and] now describes a mentality of idleness, depression,
apathy and lack of self-motivation."[52]

But the malaise and questioning have been seeping in
for several years, as Helen Wang wrote in 2010. Interviewing
Veronica Chen, a young, middle-class urbanite, Chen told
Wang: "There is nothing for people to hang on to. Family
relationships have changed dramatically, I don't have religion, my soul feels empty. My central question is: why are we
living—what's the meaning of life?"[53]

As the CCP continued to push toward a consumer-led
economy and the financial titans of banking and investment
were maneuvering for market share, an opportunistic Chinese
behemoth emerged to keep the consumer in the game by serving the underbanked Chinese person with revolving credit.

Chinese billionaire and founder of Alibaba, Jack Ma,
following the mantra of dual circulation through consumer
spending, created an offshoot, Ant, from his financial company, Alipay, designed to offer the young and small businesses quick access to online loans. Ma implored, "You're
young, just spend," and by mid-2020, five hundred million
people were using Ma's microlending apps. A Nielsen report
found that 86.6 percent of eighteen-to-twenty-nine-year-olds
were using credit services. The idea of buy now, pay later was
anathema to previous generations who had suffered through
generations of little money.

Ma's methods of packaging the debt and selling it off
to banks, akin to the US housing mortgage debacle of 2008,

ran afoul of the CCP. This risky strategy coupled with Ma's outspoken criticism of the government banking regulations resulted in his highly anticipated Ant initial public offering being stopped by the government and Ma disappearing from the public for many months, with the Ant Group acquiescing to a rectification of its misdeed and agreeing to be reorganized and regulated like a bank.

By early 2021, as the youth-spending credit spree slowed down, many in debt began to question what they were trying to achieve with their material bounty. The *Los Angeles Times* reported one interviewee, Shen Xiaoli, age twenty-five, finding herself heavily in debt and amid the pandemic chose her own rectification solution by binge watching anticapitalistic videos: "Through baptism in the spirit of communism, I controlled my desire to spend."[54] Another young woman, Eva Wang, was more introspective about the challenges a consumption-led economy faces: "After I stopped shopping, I found a lot of my consumption was to fill up a kind of emptiness in my heart, not because I needed those things."[55]

During the pandemic and without the availability of international travel, where Chinese nationals could purchase duty-free European luxury items (25–45 percent less expensive than on the Chinese mainland), they discovered homegrown, culturally relevant luxury fashion, and domestic fitness and wellness companies also emerged to create tenacious competition to traditionally US/European strongholds.

McKinsey's 2023 China Consumer Report illustrated the changes to the consumer's mindset. "There was once a time when consumers paid a premium for foreign brands; those days are over. . . . And with the introduction of trendy innovative local brands, many foreign brands that once enjoyed a leading position in the mass or mainstream segment are feeling the pressure, and have seen steep declines in sales. . . . [N] ational pride is not the only driving factor. Today, domestic companies are reacting faster to trends, are closer to the consumer, and are making bolder investment."[56]

While domestic brands were capitalizing on an inward shift in consumer behavior, a larger trend was surfacing. The graduating class of 2023 minted 11.5 million college students in search of meaningful employment. As youth unemployment (in China calculated as age sixteen to twenty-four) was hovering around 20 percent, the CCP stopped publishing unemployment figures. The sentiment of the *sang* group that emerged pre-COVID became a growing cohort of restless, disillusioned youth referring to themselves as the lie flat group. With confidence dwindling, those lying flat were questioning an unforgiving and unrewarding intense work culture and all the social expectations that came from upward mobility.

As the pandemic held the Chinese hostage for three years, a vast number of consumers locked their pocketbooks. The old Confucian value of frugality and debt-free living was back in vogue. By the end of 2022, McKinsey's survey found that "58 percent of urban households indicated their desire to 'put money away for a rainy day,'—the highest since 2014."[57] The magnitude of this shift in discretionary spending to savings was evidenced by year end 2022, showing Chinese bank deposits had grown 80 percent year over year, with a record contribution of $2.6 trillion.[58]

By mid-2023 Xi's administration was grappling with potential destabilization that could arise from educated but unemployed youth. A bit reminiscent of the educated but idle youth of Mao's Cultural Revolution who were sent to the countryside to learn from the peasants, province-level administrators began to circulate campaigns, policies, and propaganda seeking solutions to clear burgeoning tier one cities of the idle with visions of serving their country by returning to the interior hinterlands.

The people of Xi face a myriad of contradictions, aspirations, and societal pressures. They carry grievances with one another, the CCP, and the outside world resulting from their educational indoctrination into the Century of Humiliation storyline. They have been raised under socialism with Chinese characteristics and participated in consumerism yet realize they are empty. Their hearts cry out for more. It may be another -ism that is needed to salve the wounds—spiritualism.

To quell the masses, Xi will reach back to remold and co-op traditional values and philosophy, create newly sanctioned social values, and lean on the teachings of Mao and Marxism. He will also assume the role that the supreme leader has had in solving society's contradictions. XJT outlines the six contradictions that must be solved and shepherds their evolving solutions. It is within these contradictions that we will see the country faces wicked problems—complex problems without straightforward solutions. And Xi's proposed solutions will not only affect their people but also send currents around the world.

PART III

CHAPTER 7

E²: Ecology and Economy

Two mountains, three phases
—Xi Jinping

XJT Contradiction 1—Ecological: There is only one earth for human beings.
"Thus, sharp contradiction is formed between the huge population and limited resources. . . . Solving the contradiction between man and environment and paying special attention to ecological progress are not only related to economy but also in association with the society and politics."[1]

Author Thomas Friedman noted of the Chinese Dream that if it meant consumption patterns based on the American Dream, another planet would be needed. Xi tacitly concurred by referencing a report by the Club of Rome titled *2052: A Global Forecast for the Next Forty Years.* The report's bottom line: current worldwide lifestyles need the resource support of 1.4 Earths. Early in his first term, Xi cited China's own data to support the enormity of the challenge. While referencing China's contribution to world GDP of 10 percent, it was his list of China's global consumption of resources that was eye-opening. Of the world's oil, coal, steel, and cement, China was using 20, 40, and 50 percent, respectively. His point was that this natural resource consumption was unsustainable for China and the rest of the world, and ultimately, even if no other country stopped it, it must stop itself, as the path was a dead end.[2]

The degradation of China's environment resulting from its breakneck modernization is legendary, and both its party and people acknowledge its glaring evidence. Regarding XJT, Xi explained that when China's 1.4 billion people reached the living standards of developed nations, it would more than double the world's developed countries' living standards, leading to the exhaustion of the planet's resources.[3]

Pew Research Center's *Global Attitudes & Trends* looked at China's population concern with pollution in 2012 and 2013. Its findings showed that within this one-year time span, the percentage of people who saw air pollution and water pollution as enormous problems rose 31 percent and 21 percent, respectively. The population's heightened awareness had resulted from Western expats on the ground making public air quality data about Beijing known. XJT, without citing Pew or outside data, appeared to acknowledge the problem. The party recognized that any issue that could cause social unrest and negative foreign press had to be addressed. The solution was to make ecological progress a strategic task, and it foreshadowed how this strategic undertaking could give rise to economic benefits: "We believe that our efforts will be rewarded."[4]

At first blush the rewards Xi referenced to be reaped may lie within the usual expectations of the CCP in self-preservation and a stable society, but it also signaled the identification of more lucrative and strategic payoffs. XJT referenced an article by Xi from 2006 entitled "Ecological Environment from the Perspective of 'Two Mountains.'" In order to describe the harmony between human and nature, the economy and society, Xi sought to summarize the historical disharmony between them and how harmony could be restored and monetized.

Xi described the two mountains. One is a gold mountain, meaning financial, and the other is a green mountain, meaning environment. He said these two mountains are contradictory but can be dialectically united. He saw the evolution of understanding how these two mountains could coexist as passing through three stages. In the first stage humans consume the resources of the environment to reap economic rewards with disregard for the environment costs. At the second stage, still utilizing the resources of the environment, they try to establish environmental protection and balance it with economic profit. At the third stage, there is an understanding that economic rewards can be reaped from ecological progress. "[E]cological advantage can be turned into economic advantage, and the two are integrated to and harmonious with each other. This stage represents a higher realm that embodies the concept of developing circular economy and building a resource-conserving and environment-friendly society."[5]

It is at this third stage, where ecological and economic advantage converge, that the CCP seeks to reap the rewards. The world consensus sits mainly in the second stage, with most of the intellectual elite understanding that a tipping point has been reached in what Earth can sustain environmentally. Solving the sustainability contradiction provides China many internal and external benefits. Internally, it fosters a more harmonious, healthy society by reducing pollution, increasing agricultural self-sufficiency, creating new industries that support higher value chain production and output, and it shows the people that they are innovators leading the world. Externally, it allows them to better shape the fourth industrial revolution, with their imprint on the standards and the inherent intellectual property rights and associated fees. There is no guarantee that China will solve this contradiction on its own—there are many impediments to success—but what is important is its recognition of the issues and the resources they are marshaling behind it in the attempt. The all-encompassing plan it outlines to resolve this contradiction will go to the heart of the conflict between China and the US.

Xi's reign has been designated as the New Era, and with it, new concepts for development were formulated. Recorded in *Xi Jinping The Governance of China, vol. II*, are remarks on the Thirteenth Five-year Plan for Economic and Social Development and its blueprint. Xi outlined state capitalism to drive industrial policy. The CCP will use environmental transitional innovation to drive value-chain ascension in achieving new economic sources and to tamp down socially destabilizing pollution.[6] It is of note the amount of real estate concerning new development Xi devoted to the environment. He referenced Frederick Engels's *Dialectics of Nature*, ancient Chinese texts *The Analects of Confucius* and Lu's *Spring and Autumn Annals*, and the American environmentalist Rachel Carson's *Silent Spring*. Xi outlined many of the humanmade environmental disasters of the twentieth century to demonstrate understanding of the challenges and a recognition of the unsustainability of the current path as a party in the eyes of its people and more generally their contribution to the planet's survival or failure.

Xi highlighted the harmony between humanity and nature that can be obtained from low-carbon technologies, stating: "We have huge potential in this regard, which could give rise to many new engines of growth."[7] Later, in his green development model, Xi listed as a key task the pursuit of environmental innovation to speed the transition to a new economic model "which is oriented toward the future and gives full play to *first-mover advantage* [emphasis added]. This is an important part of supply-side structural reform."[8]

With the American withdrawal under the Trump Administration from the Paris Agreement, designed to provide an international redress on climate change, Xi stepped in to plant a soft power flag. Soft power is tricky, akin to rocks in glass houses, and there are many environmental issues China would rather the international community not focus on, such as exotic and endangered species abuse, exportation to developing economies of dirty energy technology along the Belt and Road Initiative, a domestic food takeout culture generating tons of plastic waste, and ubiquitous face masks to shield against choking pollution during daily commutes. Nevertheless, a marker was laid, and it may be China's current undertaking—electric vehicle (EV) domination—with which they intend to point as proof of the development concept in solving the ecological contradiction.

By the end of 2023, the world recognized the leap China had made in EVs, but innovation across the board within China is not creating consistent economic momentum. Xi said, "Innovation makes a much lower contribution to economic growth in China than in developed countries. This is the Achilles' heel for such a big economy as China."[9]

Chinese leadership is determined to move China up the technology value-add chain. Xi implores workers to have vision, expertise, and the capability to invent and for the young to dare to innovate as it provides "an inexhaustible source of a country's prosperity."[10] But will top-down directives to innovate be able to overcome legacy issues in a society that has been conditioned to not question those above them and an educational system founded in memorization and test taking? Bluntly, can innovation occur through invocation?

Just as Deng realized the deficit in innovation and technology in turning a backward country around, Xi has elevated this key area as strategic in realizing the rejuvenation of the nation. He recognizes the world's winners and losers will be parsed along the lines of tech breakthroughs and insists, "We cannot afford to lag behind in this important race. We must catch up and then try to surpass others."[11] Xi, recognizing that China's previous world's workshop economy will not sustain it, said, "The extensive development model featured by economic growth mainly driven by factor inputs such as natural resources is not sustainable."[12] He called out China's population load and that its recent experience in natural resource consumption is not viable, declaring, "The old path seems to be a dead end. Where is the new road? It lies in scientific and technological innovation and in the accelerated transition from factor-driven and investment-driven growth to innovation-driven growth."[13] He broke from the decades of communism and Mao citing the labor of people as the economy's primary productive force and replaced it with "science and technology as the primary productive force."[14]

How Xi views China's current lot, his ambitions for the country, and his foreshadowing of how it will rewrite international rules and gain self-sufficiency are telling and candidly stated by pointing to its weakness in original creativity, which has left it dependent on others for core technology. China's lag in basic and future technologies have allowed others to hold the keys and write the rules of the road. China's innovators must excel to allow them to write the rules. But not just any innovation will do; strategic opportunities must be identified and to achieve this, resources must be allocated with the nation's overarching goals.[15]

This inability to innovate, to hold the valuable keys of intellectual property rights, has long been a thorn in the side of China. Three times in Vogel's Deng biography, he wrote about Deng's tours of industrial inspection for learning. First, in 1978, as Deng was formulating ideas for reform and opening, he visited Japan to learn its secrets of modernization. He visited Matsushita factory, which was legendary for its growth from a bicycle parts maker in the 1920s to a world leader in electronics. Deng thought highly of its founder, Matsushita Konosuke, and "called him the 'god of management' and urged him to teach the Chinese all the latest technologies. Matsushita explained to Deng what apparently Deng's advisers had not, that private companies like his earned their living by the technologies they had developed and so they would be reluctant to pass on the latest secrets."[16]

During Deng's famous southern tour of 1992, undertaken

to ensure the CCP did not turn away from his reform and opening policy, he visited the SEZ of Shenzhen. While admiring bamboo trees imported from Chengdu to the Xianhu Botanical Gardens, "Deng teased his local guides, saying that they should pay Sichuan province for intellectual property rights. The joke had a deep resonance for Deng: everyone knew that Deng had complained to Westerners about China having to pay large sums for intellectual property rights, and that Deng had reminded the Westerners that China had not charged other countries for borrowing Chinese inventions such as gunpowder and the printing press."[17]

In the waning days of Deng's southern tour, he was quoted as stating profoundly what his core belief was behind reform and opening: "China had been humiliated by the foreign imperialists, but that era had passed: 'Those who are backward get beaten. . . . We've been poor for thousands of years, but we won't be poor again. If we don't emphasize science, technology, and education, we will be beaten again.'"[18]

How prescient Deng's admonition was. Today the fear of what form "beaten" might take appears to be driving China's strategy for the future and its desire to not be caught in the middle-income trap, meaning its population might grow old before rich. Xi, speaking of its economic development, said, China was in a transition stage to achieve high-income country status and that international historical experience had shown that imbalances and weaknesses were bound to be encountered.[19]

There may have been a recognition of its deficit in innovation and the mercy this placed it at the hands of the developed nations, but one event kicked off a chain of policy decisions that led to a whole of government focus and a retrenchment of state-owned enterprises through the plan known as Made in China 2025.

The recession of 2008 affected economies around the world in various degrees of severity. For China, it seems to have been a wake-up call about its critical dependence on globalization. As astute students of history, and its wise use of the developed world's experiences with capitalism, it dug deep to understand what it must change, avoid, and seek to check future interruptions on its journey through the middle-income phase of development and ultimately world leadership.

Harvard-educated Chinese national Liu He was, until 2022, one of four vice premiers under Xi and in charge of economic and financial affairs. Beginning in 2018, Liu became the representative for China in US trade talks. Liu is believed to be the architect behind moving the country from a demand- to a supply-driven economy and was charged with addressing the dangerous debt level of 260 percent to GDP in 2017. This high debt level had been accumulated since the recession and resulted from massive internal fiscal stimulus designed both to keep the engine of its own economy going as well as provide a worldwide floor to the economic downturn.

The genesis of some of Liu's thinking may be derived from an analysis he undertook comparing the Great Depression of 1929 to the recession of 2008 and later disseminated through a Harvard Kennedy School paper published in 2014 titled *Overcoming the Great Recession: Lessons from China*. In the foreword, Graham Allison and Lawrence Summers, two China experts, advised, "In the wake of the financial crisis and China's rapid growth it is inevitable that China will take a much more active role in global economic governance in the future than it has in the past. It is important therefore for all of us in the West to better understand Chinese perspectives on global economic history."[20]

Liu's analysis was published in China in 2012 and looked at the differences and similarities between the two financial crises. In his findings it becomes clear that he identified many of the issues China is currently experiencing, and he laid out a broad picture of the steps China should take to mitigate future repeats of previous missteps. Key differences and similarities between the Depression and the 2008 recession are applicable to China today and are found in the areas of demographics, technological revolutions, debt ratios, income and education gaps, globalization, and Kissinger's law.

The clarity of Liu's astute analysis and the implications and opportunities for China to leverage its knowledge of the US's financial mismanagement provided a road map of avoidance for it in the future. Liu's findings of the Great Depression and 2008 recession are summarized for brevity (figure 4).

Figure 4: Differences and Similiarties Between the Great Depression and the 2008 Recession

SUMMARY: Liu's Differences/Similarites between the Great Depressions & Great Recession			
ATTRIBUTE	DEPRESSION	RECESSION	KEY TAKEAWAY
Demographics	Age 65+ 5.3%	Age 65+ 12.6%	"The welfare system and the age factor have weakened the labor force's market adaptability; people are more ready to keep what has been arund than to change."
Technology Revolutions	2nd rev: electrification	3rd rev: information tech	"A lesson for us is that when a future technology revolution arrives, we must not only understand its progressive role and grasp any opportunities that come with it, but also be fully aware of its significant consequential changes and be well-prepared for its shocks and challenges."
Preceeding Economic Boom supported by excessive laissez-faire policies	'Coolidge Prosperity'-'A chicken in every pot'	Clinton: 'National Homeownership Strategy'	"the government remained silent on the market economy's operations and allowed financial interest groups to play a decisive role in pushing the easing of regulation and financial liberalization."
Global Trade % of GDP	16.7%	51.6%	"Although there are bouts of protectionism and beggar-thy-neighbor policies, they are destined to be short-lived because they eventually hurt their own governments, businesses and consumers."
Income Gap			
US Debt to GDP	1933: 299.8%	2009: 369.7%	"In the former crisis, the Fed's policy makers generally had no awareness of aggregate demand management, while in the latter one, the Fed held a flawed comprehension of the globalized world economy and a monetary policy the U.S. should have pursued as an international reserve currency country."
'Kissinger's Law': 'A new world power will emerge every 100 years'	Europe to America	America to Asia-Pacific	"after a big crisis, what is to be redistributed is not merely wealth within a country, but the relative power of all nations The redistribution effect is irresistible, and the world economic order will continue to experience a steady and irreversible change."
ATTRIBUTION: He, Liu, "A Comparative Study of Two Global Crises." Discussion Paper, Belfer Center for Science and International Affairs, Harvard Kennedy School, June 2014			

Liu provided the Chinese government with three policy recommendations, summarized for brevity:

1. Prepare responses for the worst possible scenarios—in particular, external crises and wars started by countries in crisis to shift their burden.
2. China's economic engine must change from a reliance on export-driven market share growth and international capital inflows to a domestic consumer market, acquiring the technologies of developed countries and continuing to develop infrastructure.
3. Concentrate on important areas of future research. Avoid international conflicts and stay focused on domestic issues.[21]

Liu is a long-time close confidant and advisor to Xi. Liu's analysis and recommendations appear to have been taken to heart. Parsing the words of Xi, it becomes clear that Liu's advice is in action. In an October 2016 speech, Xi said, "We must identify strategic priorities, make key breakthroughs, seize the strategic initiative, prevent systemic risks and avoid being swept away by crisis, so as to ensure the sound progression of our great cause."[22]

How might Liu's recommendations manifest? Possibly with one of the grandest "moonshots" ever attempted: Made in China 2025. In May 2015, China's State Council announced this far-ranging initiative to comprehensively upgrade Chinese industry. Deputy director Scott Kennedy of the Center for Strategic and International Studies provided a great, high-level summary of key takeaways. Made in China 2025 draws inspiration from Germany's Industry 4.0 (fourth industrial revolution) plan.

The heart of Germany's plan is to move to intelligent manufacturing driven by information technology. Kennedy saw China's challenge of success in achieving a similar plan as more difficult due to Chinese producers' unevenness in quality and efficiency. These challenges require China to quickly address its issues as it is squeezed by new emerging markets for low-cost products and must compete with advanced industrialized economies.

Kennedy defined the principles, goals, tools, and industrial-sector focus of Made in China 2025. The plan's principles are innovation-driven manufacturing, quality over quantity, environmentally focused tech development, and workforce education. The goal is to upgrade industry, allowing China to reach the highest levels of the production value chain to obtain monopolistic share for self-reliance and leverage in core technologies and resources. For better positioning in international standards and intellectual property for business strategy, China should use state coffers to create research and development centers and strengthen intellectual property laws.

The plan focuses on ten primary sectors:

- New advanced information technology
- Automated machine tools and robotics
- Aerospace and aeronautical equipment
- Maritime equipment and high-tech shipping
- Modern rail transport equipment
- *New-energy vehicles and equipment* (emphasis added)
- Power equipment
- Agricultural equipment
- New material
- Biopharma and advanced medical products[23]

As a member of the WTO, the Chinese government may not unilaterally subsidize and dictate local industry product substitution to the exclusion of foreign goods. The Mercator Institute for China Studies (MERICS), a German private foundation that studies China's political and economic decisions, provided the most value in understanding. The Mercator Institute for China Studies has gone beyond the official Made in China 2025 documents and sourced information from various commissions and expert working groups within China. It is from these findings we glean insights into what China's targeting of key industries could mean to the international business community.

The Mercator Institute for China Studies performed an analysis of Made in China 2025 and determined that China's goal is to become a top global manufacturing superpower through technological smart manufacturing. "This industrial policy will challenge the economic primacy of the current leading economies and international corporations."[24] The report found that in the short-term this upgrading of Chinese manufacturing may be a boom for foreign companies that can provide the technology to accomplish this, but over the long term China's plans may hollow out other countries' strategic advantages and lead to further barriers of entry for foreign MNCs in Chinese market participation. The Mercator Institute for China Studies warned that Made in China 2025's vision is to disadvantage foreign competition and substitute with homegrown innovation and to ultimately position Chinese technology in international markets.[25]

The Mercator Institute for China Studies echoed the sentiment heard from companies and countries around the developed world: Chinese high-tech companies enjoy a strategic advantage from the hand of the government through artificial barriers to entry, financial backing, closed market information data, local subsidy schemes, and forced foreign data collection by the state.[26]

In 2017, cueing off the Mercator Institute for China Studies paper and previous proprietary reports, the US Chamber of Commerce published *Made in China 2025: Global Ambitions Built on Local Protections.* The chamber's overarching theme was "The US and China share a highly interdependent, yet complex relationship that is critically important to both nations and the world. Our economic and commercial ties have long been the ballast of our relationship. Paths like MIC 2025 and their implementation are putting the two economies on a path of separation rather than integration in critical commercial areas."[27]

What had been to date the integration of our economic ties and the division of innovation and labor was best illustrated by *The Economist*: "'Designed by Apple in California. Assembled in China.' For the past decade the words embossed on the back of iPhones have served as shorthand for the technological bargain between the world's two biggest economies: America supplies the brains and China the brawn."[28]

Less visible than the China-US tariff trade war but potentially more important has been the reaction by the American government to use the Committee on Foreign Investment in the United States to review Chinese acquisition of strategic American corporations. The denial of acquisition may have various reasons, but the Mercator Institute for China Studies laid out the key concerns. "To speed up China's technological catch-up and to leapfrog stages of technological development, Chinese companies are acquiring core technologies through investment abroad. China pursues an outbound industrial policy with government capital and highly opaque investor networks to facilitate high-tech acquisitions abroad. This undermines the principles of fair competition: China's state-led economic system is exploiting the openness of market economies in Europe and the United States. Chinese high-tech investments need to be interpreted as building blocks of an overarching political program. It aims to systematically acquire cutting-edge technology and generate large-scale technology transfer."[29] The strategy of foreign technological acquisition was precisely what Liu He recommended in the second of his three-point policy recommendations after the 2008 recession.

In 2017 Trump Administration appointees spoke out against China's plan, with US commerce secretary Wilbur Ross describing Made in China 2025 as "an 'attack' on 'American genius.'"[30]

Trump's then strategist Steve Bannon said, "The forced technology transfer of American innovation to China is the single biggest economic and business issue of our time. Until we sort that out, they will continue to appropriate our innovation to their own system and leave us as a colony—our Jamestown to their Great Britain, a tributary state."[31]

US trade representative Robert Lighthizer said, "The sheer scale of their coordinated effort to develop their economy, to subsidize, to create national champions, to force technology transfers, and to distort markets in China and throughout the world is a threat to the world trading system that is unprecedented."[32]

Through a combination of state-enforced restraint on China's part and increased barriers erected by the US government, China's foreign direct investment into the US fell precipitously in 2017 as demonstrated by Rhodium Group (figure 5).[33]

Figure ES-1: Annual Value of FDI Transactions between the US and China, 2000-2020

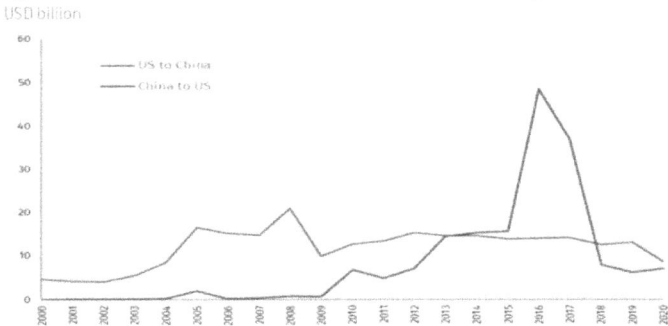

Source: Rhodium Group.

The Rhodium Group conducts deep tracking and analysis of cross-border investment, noting in May 2019 that US investment into China fell only slightly from 2017 to 2018 and by 2020 remained higher than China's reciprocal investment in the US. Despite US corporations' protestations of forced technology transfer on setting up shop in China, the market opportunities still seemed too great to not cautiously forge ahead.

Throughout the past forty years of China's opening, American companies have faced many barriers to entry, including competition from China's state-owned enterprises and forced tech transfer, so why are these issues now rising to the foreground of our geopolitical relations? The Mercator Institute for China Studies stated the catalyst best: "Global industry is at the brink of the next technological revolution."[34]

History shows that industrial revolutions are disruptive and can lead to shifts in the power and economics of countries. The Mercator Institute for China Studies described this forthcoming revolution in cyber-physical systems, where "connected machines collect massive amounts of data through smart sensors, communicate with each other and independently make decisions."[35]

For decades China has been the world's factory floor, providing the brawn. Today it is declaring its intention to be the brain. We should not consider this transition an easy feat for China but rather an enormous leapfrog attempt. The Mercator Institute for China Studies posited that an impediment to Chinese industry was the heavy concentration of their output still relying upon the methods of the second industrial revolution and many were just beginning to use the tools of the third industrial revolution.[36]

As we enter the fourth industrial revolution, let's take a cursory look at the where we have been and where we are going.

Industrial Revolution (1700s–mid-1800s)

Beginning in Great Britain in the late 1700s with a machine to spin yarn, the revolution saw the steam engine generate power. England became the workshop of the world as agrarian labor moved from the farm to the factory. Growth in mechanical manufacturing was driven by technological advances, education, and the use of capital stock for funding. The early 1800s gave us the term *Luddites* as those who did not want to embrace industrialization attacked factories to thwart mass production evolution.

In the US the mechanization of farm equipment increased efficiency and productivity. The transcontinental railroad was built from the east to west coast, greatly improving the movement of goods. Railroad construction labor represented a dark period in American history as Chinese people were recruited to build the railroad but then not allowed to obtain US citizenship. Congress passed the Chinese Exclusion Act in 1882 making Chinese immigrants permanent aliens. Shunned by communities, they cloistered in Chinatowns, which still dot some of the US's major population centers.

Second Industrial Revolution (1870–1914)

Driven mainly by US inventions, power was generated from electricity and oil. The era also ushered in telephone communication, airplanes, and Henry Ford's moving assembly line for production of automobiles.

Third Industrial Revolution (1950s–2010)

Nuclear energy was harnessed, but the significant change came from electronics and computers, enabling programmable devices to automate processes.

Fourth Industrial Revolution (2010 to present)

This era is experiencing further digitization of manufacturing driven by connectivity, analytics, data, human-machine inter-action, improved robotics, quantum computing, and artificial intelligence.

In two separate speeches, Xi described the evolution of the industrial revolutions and the benefits the first-mover countries received. Xi said, "Each and every scientific and industrial revolution has profoundly changed the outlook and pattern of world development. Some countries have seized the available opportunities, so they achieved rapid social and economic development, and increased their economic, scientific and military strength. Some have emerged as world powers."[37]

In an earlier speech, musing as to why China had been left behind, Xi said Qing Emperor Kangxi was interested in learning about Western science and technology and Western missionaries who gave him and designees lectures and books to study, but they had not applied the education for their social and economic development: "Rather, they simply talked about the knowledge."[38]

Xi's retelling of the Qing's acquisition of knowledge, without creative utilization of it, aligns with the collective, hierarchal nature of China's people and governance system. To color outside the lines is not an innate trait.

In the race to own the fourth industrial revolution, the Mercator Institute for China Studies sees impediments to China's ability to accomplish its goals rooted in the foundations of the differing economic platforms. Utilizing China's state-capitalism model, the strategy is top-down: "The leadership imposes its policy priorities and strategic vision for industrial upgrading on a manufacturing industry that has so far been largely hesitant about industrial modernization."[39] Whereas in Western capitalism, it is a bottom-up strategy, driven by enterprise initiative. Again, this begs the question: Is China's strategy to invoke innovation congruent with the masses, or is it anathema to who it really is as a collective, hierarchal society?

We can question the realistic accomplishment of the Made in China 2025 goals through observations made by the Mercator Institute for China Studies on core disadvantages inherent to China. Some of these include a herd mentality, fueled by local governments' rush to support central government edicts, resulting in provincial competition and overcapacity in certain manufacturing sectors. See an example of China's native internal combustion engine (ICE) auto manufacturers' overproduction of entry level sport-utility vehicles in case study "Ford's Folly."

The Mercator Institute for China Studies listed the impediments of a government-led, top-down, strategy.

> Industrial upgrading more than a technical task of installing modern equipment: True optimization is derived by continuous improvement reliant on management and talent—gap areas for China.
>
> An inefficient allocation of funding: The government seeks first to fund those with political connections.
>
> Absence of pure competition: Enterprises do not historically react to competitive pressure with innovation solutions. Move to focus on mass production of low-tech products.
>
> Skilled workforce for complex processes requires expertise across the fields of automation, engineering, and software: Chinese education system is unable to provide enough skilled experts to fill its talent gap.
>
> Potential political and social unrest resulting from displacement of workers from advanced automation: Service sector does not absorb enough of the additional migrant labor. The current manufacturing industry has reached limits in providing job growth.

The Mercator Institute for China Studies illuminated four key challenges[40] for high-tech developed countries:

- Western tech hollowing out by Chinese state-led foreign direct investment: China has promoted investment in foreign tech companies to acquire and transfer technology.
- Data/cyber regulations put manufactures' industrial data at risk: China's extreme control of its cyberspace limits data transfers and demands access to in-market business data.
- Increasing market access restrictions for multinational tech suppliers: China courts industries into China that can help it catch up technologically, then once lessons are learned erects barriers to entry and foreign ownership to safeguard its own market share
- Domestic standards support industrial policy goals: China desires to set international standards based on its technological specifications, often intentionally creating standards that exclude foreign specs to reduce its intellectual property royalty fees, protect its own market, and eventually export intellectual property to other countries.

The Mercator Institute for China Studies analysis concluded: "China's industrial policy will have an enormous impact on the entire national economies of many industrial countries. The largest industries that will be affected by China's industrial policy are *automotive* [emphasis added] and machinery."[41]

For a deeper understanding of how Xi intends to resolve this contradiction by doing good for China's ecology while serving the economy, see the first proof point of Made in China 2025 through the auto industry (case study "Ford's Folly").

CHAPTER 8

Creating a Moderately Prosperous Society

As delicate as frying a small fish.
—Xi Jinping

XJT Contradiction 2—Between Rich and the Poor: How to Achieve Common Prosperity

"Comrade Deng Xiaoping gave an important definition to socialism: 'the essence of socialism is to emancipate and develop the productive forces and eliminate exploitation and polarization in order to finally achieve common prosperity.'"[1]

Solving this contradiction has been the opportunity and conundrum of the Chinese people since their beginning. Communism is the path they chose as the ultimate answer to their question of the ages. XJT says, "Since human society entered the stage of class society, the contradiction between the rich and the poor has become the primary social contradiction. The revolution of China was, in the final analysis, a campaign in which the poor overturned the rich. A batch of rich people was overthrown through the new-democratic revolution, and another batch of rich people was transformed through the socialist revolution."[2]

It is this new "batch of rich people," resulting from reform and opening, that the Communist Party must address, not by revolution and tearing down but by raising up those left behind and tamping down the excesses displayed by the rich that the poor gaze upon with envy.

Deng uttered of the reform and opening policies he instituted. His famous line was "Some will get rich first." Deng's willingness to introduce economic inequalities in 1978 brings us full circle to this second contradiction the party must solve. XJT reflects on Deng's thoughts about this change in China's communist direction and what outcomes might arise. Deng was concerned about wealth creating polarization among the people. He warned that if the CCP allowed this to happen, it should consider its policies had failed. Deng knew with China's enormous population that even if half became rich first, a half-billion people would not be, and he believed this situation would lead to another civil war.[3]

XJT states that the plan was for this initial inequality to move all toward prosperity, and it was not bringing along the lagging class quickly enough to depress the rift growing among the classes.[4] Two data points shed light on how intense this contradiction between rich and poor has become. The first is a measure of how the people themselves rate the importance of the wealth gap problem as measured by Pew Research. In a survey published in 2015, Pew found that fourth from the top in concerns was the "Gap between rich and poor," with 75 percent reporting it as a problem and 33 percent agreeing that it was a "very big problem."[5] The second confirmation is found in the Gini coefficient. The Gini index is a way to measure the extent to which the distribution of income or consumption among individuals or households within an economy deviates from a perfectly equal distribution. The Center for Strategic and International Studies explains the ranking of income inequality on the Gini scale as zero equal to 100 percent equality and one indicating the maximum inequality possible. China almost doubled its inequality number from the 1980s to 2015, registering 0.055. The US in 2015 was 0.039, meaning the US population enjoyed greater economic equality.[6]

How does China plan to rectify this wealth gap contradiction? The CCP made the people a promise: "By 2021 when the Party will celebrate its 100th anniversary, we will have built a well-off society in an all-round way, doubling the 2010 GDP and per capita personal income."[7] After the Cultural Revolution, China's leaders knew they must bring prosperity to their people if they wished to remain in power and be seen as the international arbiter of socialism. XJT also recognizes that unless the party can improve the people's livelihoods, all the ideological rhetoric about the superior benefits of a socialist system will prove to be empty words.[8]

The CCP based its promise in terms of doubling GDP. But it realizes the folly of simply chasing GDP. XJT points out that the unprecedented annual Chinese GDP growth rate based on speed and mass output was not sustainable, and the new growth pattern needed to switch to efficiency or productivity growth.[9] Why must China transcend the narrow barometer of success tied to GDP annual growth? This is explained well by Yuwa Hedrick-Wong for *Forbes*: "As the largest exporter in the world, however, China's export cannot grow much faster than the global economy. To try to do so China will have to take market shares away from other exporters continuously, which will be economically challenging and politically disastrous."[10]

What does the CCP see as the key to creating an efficiency-driven country? A policy switch from human migration to urban areas and an increase in domestic consumerism. As urban areas received the bulk of investment and growth, rural areas were allowed to lag. The new plan is to better integrate urban and rural areas and allow the rural areas to excel by expanding domestic consumer demand.[11]

The PRC's planned government-controlled economy directs not only industry and infrastructure but also the movement of human labor. Its history of labor distribution was formalized under Mao Zedong in 1958 with the establishment of the current *hukou* system. The policy calls for one's *hukou* to be assigned at birth based on birth location and parents' classification within the system. An individual is either rural or urban. The *hukou* status designation is the gateway to participation in and receipt of social services. Its determination rules access to basic services such as health care, education, and old-age pensions, where the value of urban greatly outweighs rural.

From the PRC's inception through the Cultural Revolution, the control of labor movement kept rural workers in the fields to produce food for urban dwellers as the country moved through the development and execution of a heavy industry base.

The benefits of the *hukou* policy serve a core interest of the CCP—social and political stability. The management of this policy has and will continue to morph over time to meet the needs of the economy and to engineer the flow of human capital.

The pent-up, rurally tied labor force had its first real chance to improve its lot under Deng Xiaoping when he began the creation of SEZs, which allowed for foreign investment in certain industries and areas of the country. Four cities initially received this designation, the first being Shenzhen. Today it is one of China's riches cities and sits on the mainland coast across from Hong Kong. The area has become known as the Pearl River Delta.

The SEZs became a magnet for foreign and domestic manufacturing, and a great rural migration filled the factory floors. Rural labor could move, but their social services remained tied to their *hukou* registration location. *The Economist* reported the outcome of three decades of urban growth. "Migration from the countryside has helped expand the urban population by 500m—the biggest movement of humanity the planet has seen in such a short time."[12]

As labor costs have risen, China is becoming less the

world's factory floor, and the government wishes to steer the economy from manufacturing and export-driven to consumer led. Again, with social and political stability a prime priority, and consumer consumption the future economic model, the *hukou* policy will continue to be used to steer a gradual and smooth transition.

It is estimated that 275 million migrant workers live in urban areas without the benefits afforded those with urban *hukou* status. The State Council's plan called for 60 percent of the population to live in urban areas by 2020. In 2012 it was estimated that 53 percent of the 2020 goal was urban, and of those, 35 percent had urban *hukou* status that allowed for participation in all social services.[13]

To achieve the 2020 goal of 60 percent urbanization, another hundred million needed to migrate. Managing the current and continuing migration and maintaining order is a tremendous challenge. As the thriving coastal cities struggle to accept more migrants, and the government fears slums surrounding their cities, many experiments are conducted to find a way to push migrants inland to newly growing cities and, for those already ensconced in urban areas, to have a way to earn urban registration.

While the State Council's plan was to have 60 percent dwelling in urban environments, it called for having only 45 percent of that population holding urban *hukou* registration by 2020. While the achievement of the population goal appeared to be reached, it is unclear if the social safety net is in place, as urban planners have historically ignored the migrant count in the development of hospitals, schools, and other basic services to meet demand.

The *hukou* registration policy adds a special layer in thinking about its people, as it shifts their physical location to urban, but their official status is still rural. The disconnect between their physical and official statuses changes the priorities of the consumers' disposable income, forcing purchases into areas not as burdensome for those who have urban status.

One experiment for earning urban status was a point system developed in Guangzhou, tied to required compliance of family planning quotas, social security payments, and no criminal violations. The point system placed the most emphasis on higher educational achievement and employment skills as well as income tax payments.

If gaining urban status in Guangzhou was a primary driver, then a college education and paying for primary and secondary education, plus base-level survival needs, may be where most of the income goes over many years. If you are without a social safety net and without access to public services, you can expect to see a higher savings rate and lower tier products as the target for earned income over your life cycle.

The issue of *hukou* status, its known drag on consumption, and its motive for savings are well-known issues. The CCP knows *hukou* reform must be addressed if it is to meet the goal of an economy heavily supported by domestic demand. The plan refers to these rural migrants as the "three 100 million." They are segmented by the CCP as the first hundred million who are currently permanent migrant farmers living in cities. They estimate that about 70 percent of the two hundred million migrants living in cities wish to remain, and this desire increases substantially if they were born in the 1980s or 1990s. The CCP Central Committee stated that by 2020, one hundred million migrants would become urban residents. This appears to be in response to the *hukou* drag on consumption. XJT says that in order to ease the tension of the urban/rural *hukou* within the cities, the burden of financially transferring urban status to these hundred million registered residents should be borne by all—the local government, industries, and urban-*hukou*-bearing individuals.[14]

For the second hundred million migrant farmers already in the cities, the CCP wants to avoid what it perceives as emblematic of the middle-income trap—cities littered with shantytowns. XJT says, "The success of urbanization lies in whether we can transform urban shack dwellings and villages within cities and improve the living conditions and public facilities and gradually dissolve and eliminate internal urban dual structure."[15] The plan is to build homes and utilize subsidized housing.

The third hundred million addresses those in China's central and western regions. While the east coast SEZs acted as a magnet for labor and investment, the central and western regions were an afterthought. The CPC Central Committee edicts that the midwest is to be the focus of effort, with coordinated development to build major and medium size cities and small towns, with the plan to draw nearby agricultural labor at a lower transfer cost to narrow the gap between rural and urban areas of the country.[16]

Anecdotally, *South China Morning Post* ran an article in early 2019 that supported the idea of a growth engine forming in the rural inland regions. It reported that a Chinese investment and retailing firm was projecting a 50 percent increase in revenue, with half of that increase attributable to less developed cities and rural areas. The company, Five Star Holdings, operates an e-commerce and logistics operation that services over seventeen thousand rural area villages covering twenty provinces. In the interview with Frank Hu, Five Star's strategic development manager, Hu reported rural consumers were now spending 70–75 percent of their annual disposable income. Hu broke down the rural spenders' allocation as "about 30 per cent of their income on household appliances and products, including mobile phones, another 30 percent on food, 20 per cent on housing, and the remaining money on clothing and shoes."[17] While there is hard data to support inland growth in domestic spending, it is important to keep the ratio of growth in perspective. *South China Morning Post* reported that in 2018, both disposable income and the actual amount spent grew faster in the rural areas than urban areas. However, "National urban sales last year topped . . . US \$4.82 trillion, with rural spending a mere 16.8 per cent of that."[18] *South China Morning Post* spoke with Jennifer Ye, PwC's China consumer market lead, who projected 90 percent of the rise in retail sales would come from these rural areas, but she "believes it will be at least another five years before smaller cities will have a significant impact on overall consumption."[19]

Xi may have signaled the CCP's awareness of the fallacy of unending GDP growth, or he may have been hedging. As the party worked toward the goal of doubling per capita income by 2020, it stated that sacrificing the pace of the breakneck annual growth rate was no longer necessary. "In whatever undertaking, one has to look far and plan wisely to take care of both short and long-term needs. Killing the goose to get the eggs or draining the pond to catch the fish is no formula for sustainable development."[20] In the CCP's shift from export-delivered moderate prosperity to one based on a consumer-led economy, it may have realized that the goose's output could no longer be absorbed by a world economy not growing at its output pace, and a greater external threat to political stability could arise if it sought growth through taking international market share continuously.

Xi said that the slowdown in the economy was intended, and "GDP growth means everything" is no longer the measuring stick. But shifting focus away from GDP figures is not simply said and done—not for Wall Street, their own internal provincial officials, or media outlets. *South China Morning Post*'s headline in February 2019, reporting on 2018 year-end metrics, said, "China's wealth gap widens as more than half

of its provinces missed growth targets last year." The data
showed that seventeen of thirty-one provinces had failed to
meet their GDP goals and the 6.6 national rate was the slowest
in twenty-eight years. Citing the Midwest city of Chongqing,
the article said, "[o]nce the nation's fastest growing region,
was its worst performer last year. The 2018 growth rate of the
inland manufacturing powerhouse slumped to 6.0 per cent
from the previous 9.3 per cent and was 2.5 percentage points
behind the targeted 8.5 per cent set at start of the year."[21]
The article said that not only were inland provinces struggling to meet goals, but also typically strong, coastal regions
were experiencing actual-to-goal gaps as well. It cited that
the wealth gap between the richest provinces and the inland
provinces was growing. "China's northern and northeastern
provinces, once the heart of the country's state-owned industries and enterprises, now not only rank at the bottom of the
list, but are also struggling to upgrade the value chain, overcome a brain drain and statistical frauds."[22] In early 2021 as
the world assessed the GDP fallout from the pandemic, China
was the only major economy to post positive results, logging
a 2.3 percent gain, with GDP per capita reaching $10,000 for
the first time.[23]

At the end of 2020, Xi declared that the goal of eradicating poverty had been reached ahead of the all-important 2021
centennial celebration of the founding of the CCP. But victory,
when based on data, can be deceiving in its context. In a poverty alleviation study provided by the China Power Project,
the data show China has lifted millions from the depths of
extreme poverty, defined as $1.90 per day, but in truth, China
should be applying a higher benchmark of $5.50 per day, and
that would leave 237.2 million Chinese in poverty to end
2018.[24]

As questions arose that some government bureaucrats
may have hidden pockets of poverty to report meeting the

2020 goal, a government-sponsored tour of poverty work was organized for journalists. *The Economist* reported from a trip to the Sichuan Province and a visit to a Ms. Jizi's home. Ms. Jizi, from a nearby impoverished region high in the mountains, had been relocated to a newly built apartment complex named Gratitude Community and given a job as a cleaner in the complex. As the journalists visited with Ms. Jizi, she expressed in timid Mandarin that she owed her good fortune to General Secretary Xi.[25] Most striking about *The Economist*'s report was the propaganda and cult of personality observations: Ms. Jizi sat "beneath a color poster of Mr. Xi with the caption: 'Be grateful to the party. Listen to the party. Follow the party.' . . . Every flat visited by the press was decorated with the same photograph of Mr. Xi. A second poster on display in each apartment featured photographs of residents' old and new homes, and slogans like 'Relocation warms our hearts, and we are forever grateful to the party.' . . . The whole housing estate is hung with party slogans and banners."[26] The scene observed was one of eerie similarity to the one witnessed by Teddy White for *Life* as he visited and reported on the homes of common people during the Nixon visit. The shrines to ancestors were gone, replaced with Mao, who had given the people everything. Only now it was Xi who has taken center stage.

Xi, as the leader of the people and CCP, has a very complex task ahead if China is to deliver the promise of a moderately prosperous society in an all-around fashion. Solving the contradiction of the wealth gap between the rich and poor requires moving hundreds of millions of people, both physically and psychologically. The people must keep faith that the evolving ideology of state capitalism can provide a level of prosperity that allows them to live a better personal dream, that an economic transition from exporting to consumption can be smoothly managed, and they must trust that the still-developing social safety net will emerge. Xi's fondness for the expression of his job as "governing a big country is as delicate as frying a small fish" seems most appropriate.

Chapter 9

The Antigraft Campaign

Catching "Tigers and Flies"
—Xi Jinping

***XJT Contradiction 3—Between the Officials and the People:
How to Prevent the Opposition between Powers and Rights***
"The core contradictions in the Chinese society are two 'divorces,' namely, the divorce of the rich from the poor and the divorce of the officials from the people. Two 'hostile' sentiments of 'hostility to the rich' and 'hostility to the officials' have been fermented in Chinese society over the years. They are typical manifestations and the 'hostility to the officials' is more popular and severe than the 'hostility to the rich.'"[1]

The CCP strategizes, plans, and operates with the goal of ensuring that it remains in power. To accomplish this, a great deal of focus is directed toward identifying issues to maintain stability throughout society. There is a continuous feedback loop of monitoring society to gauge where potentially disruptive public sentiment lies and propaganda and actions to check and reshape those public perceptions and negative sentiments.

Pew Research monitored public sentiment in China and published in 2013 areas of Chinese populous concern. Between 2008 and 2013, rising prices was the top concern, but it had fallen 13 percent over this period. Concern about the income gap rose 11 percent, and worry about corrupt officials rose 14 percent. These three areas held the top three spots on the public concerns list out of seventeen issues tracked. When Pew again published this same tracking research in 2015, corrupt officials had risen to the top concern, with 84 percent saying it was their main issue of concern and 44 percent agreeing it was a big problem.[2]

Looking at contributing factors to the endemic corruption, Xi may have been viewed by the CCP as a good candidate to tackle this issue. Anyone doing business with China will learn about the concept of *guanxi*. American *guanxi* brokers are businesses that position themselves to create *guanxi* for an organization and describe the concept on Western terms, such as relationship building or networking. US-Pacific Rim International, Inc., a US-based Chinese market-entry consulting firm says the concept of creating *guanxi* is to develop relationships that create mutually beneficial ties and to do so requires out-of-office wining and dining. This *guanxi* relationship with both Chinese companies and government officials is valuable in overcoming obstacles in business transactions.[3] US-Pacific Rim recommends having a native-born Chinese person who understands the cultural niceties of developing *guanxi* and facilitates relationship building. It is preferable that the person has experience working in or with the government to exercise leverage.[4]

In a white paper for the University of Pennsylvania, Jin Guan looked into how the Chinese view *guanxi* beyond the Western notion of relationships and networks. Guan said Westerners see *guanxi* as "a form of social capital," but the Chinese view the *guanxi* relationship differently—it is based on "reciprocal obligations and indebtedness," with no time limit on the obligation's expiration.[5]

Guan argued Westerners focus too much on trying to generate favors through gifts and elaborate dinners and are not truly creating reciprocal value. He said "the best way to cultivate guanxi is to identify and satisfy the other party's greatest needs and desires."[6] Guan traced the roots of reciprocity back to Confucius, from the Confucian rule of propriety. This ancient understanding still informs Chinese social behavior and requires that both sides must give something of value, not necessarily material value, and if this is not reciprocated, it is improper.[7]

Both US-Pacific Rim and Guan attributed the continued prevalence of the *guanxi* system to the lack of a formal rule of law governing transactions. Guan noted throughout China's history there has been no sound, adhered-to legal system to protect the legal interests of the common person.[8] US-Pacific Rim said that in order to overcome this recourse deficit, "Chinese people needed to develop another means of ensuring trust amongst themselves in personal and business matters. . . . [T]herefore guanxi has become a means of building trust that law cannot always provide."[9]

Crow's *400 Million Customers* provided an excellent first-person account of how pervasive and long running in the modern era *guanxi* is as a prerequisite for business transactions.

> Very few foreigners, even including those who live in China, realize the very important part that friendship plays in all Chinese business transactions. A Chinese wants, first, to do business with members of his own family, next, with his friends and will not have any dealings with strangers if it is possible to avoid it. If two strangers are parties to a business deal then it is absolutely essential that there be a go-between, a mutual friend who will conduct the negotiations, . . . act as joint guarantor for both parties, making himself personally responsible that the contract will be carried out and the money paid.[10]

In 1937 Crow observed that this technically informal yet essential system of deal making led to large concentrations of industry or goods in trade in certain geographical areas and legacy family domination. "It is because of this desire to confine one's business transactions to the circle of family and friends that residents of certain provinces or of certain localities within a province tend to monopolize certain lines of business. Nearly all the silk dealers in the country are Soochow men, while the tea dealers come from Anhwei."[11]

It is easy to see how in the ensuing forty years of reform and opening this centuries-old type of trust building through *guanxi* in business transactions can no longer bear the sheer weight of transactions. Due to the massive migration to urban centers of industry, connections with fellow countrymen have been severed. It is the idea of the consistent and equitable establishment of and adherence to the rule of law that Xi proclaimed he will create to bring trust into the equation.

XJT says,

> There are two basic ways to govern a country: 'the rule of man' and 'the rule of law.' The disadvantage of the 'rule of man' is that it varies with the individual and can't avoid the phenomenon that 'the policies and rationality of an organization shift with the change of the person in charge.' The advantage of 'the rule of law' is that it relies on the strength of systems and gives play to the permanent mechanism of systems. . . . China has been ruled by men for thousands of years. . . . China has long been in the shift and transition from the rule of man to the rule of law.[12]

How endemic is China's corruption? Transparency International, a nonprofit organization, ranks countries annually via experts and businesspeople on their perceived levels of public sector corruption. The scale is zero to one hundred, with zero being highly corrupt and one hundred representing very clean. The Corruption Perceptions Index ranks 180 countries and ending in 2023 found the average to be forty-three. When Xi took office in 2012, China's score was thirty-nine. In 2023 it rose to forty-two. The US scores were seventy-three in 2012 and sixty-nine to end 2023.[13]

China does operate under a constitutional system, albeit one more fluid than America's, as is witnessed by the addition of XJT. Another difference between the two nations' constitutions is the idea that all are equal under the law or that no one is above the law. In China there is a separation of adherence and consequences to the laws of the constitution between the masses and the CCP members. XJT says the rule of law means governance by the constitution, but the CCP must practice self-governance per the constitution.[14] The party administers enforcement of its own members.

XJT is forthright in exposing the corruption and lack of adherence to the rule of law by calling out the lack of enforcement and punishment of lawbreakers. There is great prevalence of deals cut with power, money, favoritism, and bribes, and this inequitable system is recognized and despised by the common person.[15]

As Xi and China seek to rise to global preeminence, they must cure the contradiction of corruption with not only their own people but also in the eyes of other nations. Attacking official corruption is a top priority. Due to the historical legacy of official malfeasance, self-policing under a one-party system, and the disparity between the potential for personal wealth to be created via private enterprise and public service, this contradiction proves quite challenging. XJT says, "China is a country with a long-term tradition of feudal autocracy and a culture deep-rooted in the rule of man. The Chinese society is an 'acquaintance society,' . . . personal connections greatly obstruct the effective enforcement of laws. . . . The fundamental reason is that the authority of the rule of law is not really established, and people don't have enough feeling of awe and veneration toward the Constitution and law."[16]

Is Xi the man to inspire awe toward the constitution? XJT says, "The Constitution is the fundamental law of the country. To make the rule of law authoritative, the primary thing is to make the Constitution authoritative."[17] In Xi's inaugural term, he declared December 4 China's Constitution Day. Also, at the eighteenth CPC Central Committee meetings, he enacted an oath system to the constitution, saying, "Among the 142 countries with the written constitution, 97 countries stipulated that civil servants should make an oath to be loyal to the Constitution."[18]

Rooting out official corruption has been a euphemism within the CCP historically to remove rival factions and consolidate power among tightly knit circles. As Xi came to power, a war on graft began, and much speculation said this same cycle of purge and merge was underway. However, under the course of his reign, it is worth looking at both his deeds and words.

The Bloomberg report on Xi's extended family's wealth said, "Xi . . . has a reputation as a clean politician." In a WikiLeaks cable from 2009, a credible Xi acquaintance said of Xi that he "was not driven by money" and was "repulsed" by official corruption and materialism.[19]

Throughout Xi's rise to power is a history of Xi speeches and articles written about corruption and CCP officials' conduct. While prudence would suggest caution in the veracity of English translations, sometimes going back decades, as they could be subject to revisionism, the words should be judged by the actions and outcomes. A frequently attributed admonishment of Xi is if you want to make money, do not join the CCP.

In the late 1980s, Xi was party secretary of Ningde, Fujian Province. In 2016 a collection of his pronouncements and speeches from that era was published as *Up and Out of Poverty*. On official conduct, he said an official's duty was to serve the people and that they must not seek power and personal gain. Should they try to serve both masters, they would be caught.[20] Xi even invoked the American idea of the Jones effect: "We should consider whether we are trying to outdo our neighbors in terms of 'position, wealth, house, wife, and children,' or whether we are willing to roll up our sleeves and toil alongside the people."[21]

This desire to keep up with the Joneses, while the wealth disparity becomes more apparent in China, is not a new phenomenon for rank-and-file officials. During World War II, prior to the Chinese Civil War, correspondent Theodore (Teddy) White, working for *Time* and *Life* magazines, spent two years in China to provide insight into life on the ground. He reported there was no resource for real revenue and inflation was rampant. "This inflation is a serious menace . . . not because of purely economic reasons but because of its moral consequences. Corruption, official and private, monetary and moral, exists throughout the length and breadth of the land."[22] White reported on the challenges and corruption in the military in trying to feed their troops but also among officials who administratively ran the country. White compared Chinese civil servants to other countries' white-collar workers at war and found that the Chinese endured the greatest bitterness. Many were decent and honest, selling their clothes, valuables, and enduring hunger, and they maintained their moral compass. But they were "hungrily, envying the profiteers and their more practical friends."[23]

Throughout XJT, Xi returns again and again to the original contradiction and his desire to move official corruption from Pew's top spot of dissatisfaction with the public and the potential demise of the CCP inherently related to it. "The masses have complained a lot that some cadres (officials) seek personal privileges."[24] Citing a history lesson, XJT says, "What is the fundamental lesson of the falls of the Chinese feudal dynasties that lasted for 2,000 years? . . . Corruption is a social tumor. If it is left unsettled, it would eventually lead to the destruction of the Party and the nation."[25]

Today, while corruption flows throughout the daily administrative functions of bureaucracy and the judiciary, it is officials' public displays of excessive behavior that are most visible to the masses. Xi has a history of calling out glaring excesses. *Up and Out of Poverty* said, "We must address the problems of banqueting, entertaining guests, gifting, gambling, and arrears on and illegal possession of public funds."[26]

In XJT forbidden activities are spelled out in detail, including no extravagant banquet food items such as shark fin or bird's nest soup. He notes the money that could be saved with more modest fare. As the CCP is in control of the budget and since it is not required to provide line-item disclosures, if these expenditures became known to the public, "the people would boil with resentment over our behavior!"[27] Xi called out officials' travel excesses and how they took advantage of their positions to be offered high-end accommodations: "we are arranged to stay in a very good place, equal to a presidential suite, but the local leaders would still say 'sorry' to us for the simple treatment. In fact, it is even better than the presidential suites abroad, and much better than the Waldorf Astoria Hotel I stayed in before."[28] The irony should not be lost here. As of mid-2019, the Chinese government owned the Waldorf Astoria, having taken it over from the Chinese firm Angbang, as its chairman was charged with financial improprieties.

Xi's antigraft campaign began in full force in 2012 and continues to date. *South China Morning Post* reported in October 2017, "More than one million officials have been disciplined, including several prominent party and military leaders."[29]

ChinaFile.com launched an interactive tool to track the numbers of people ensnared in the campaign, showing how pervasive the corruption is and how widely the campaign reaches down to the province level and across all sectors of industry, government, and military. The Central Commission for Discipline Inspection continues to be strengthened and used to suppress corruption among high- and low-ranking officials as well as high-profile entrepreneurs. Xi's campaign of catching tigers and swatting flies shows no sign of abating.[30]

Did the campaign influence sentiment among the masses? Zak Dychtwald, living in China and getting to know the people, published *Young China* in 2018, giving a firsthand account of a conversation with a Chinese friend who related the experience his parents were having as they tried to open a restaurant. To make their way through the bureaucratic red tape, they had spent significant funds for bribes of cigarettes and liquor, mainly Maotai *baiju*—a coveted Chinese drink. Xi put the fear of the CCP watchdogs into low-level officials—flies—and it made a positive impression on people.[31]

Not only were the people noticing, businesses were, too. The luxury market was roiled. *The Guardian* reported that in anticorruption crackdowns people tended to freeze, unsure of what the new rules are.[32]

No industry felt the pain quite like the top-shelf liquor purveyors. Per the World of Chinese website, heavy drinking is a required social skill in China. Luncheons and banquets with frequent toasts, especially in honor of high-ranking officials, had been the norm, and the serving of *baijiu*, especially Maotai, was considered a power play. [33] However, as Xi's crackdown on frugality took hold and specific callouts were made against serving luxury brands of alcohol, both the English and French MNCs felt the pain. *The Economist* reported that England's Diageo, "the world's biggest maker of spirits, completed its acquisition of Shui Jing Fang, a maker of baijiu . . . had to write down the value of its purchase, after its sales had fallen 78 percent in response to the Chinese government's ban on the giving of 'gifts' to officials."[34] France's Rémy Cointreau had been posting double-digit growth, but as word spread throughout officialdom, the acceptance of ultra-expensive items such as cognac ceased. The company gave forward guidance to expect at least a 20 percent drop in profits for 2014.[35]

While the corruption campaign continues, with public shaming of officials and guardrails on official extravagance, fundamental changes supporting a fair, consistent rule of law are still not apparent, as witnessed by the 2018 US Chamber survey of US businesses and their greatest concerns regarding business practices in China. China's lack of transparency and a functional legal system that guarantees binding rules be consistently applied left US businesses with little trust that they would receive fair treatment.[36]

China seeks to move its economic engine into the world of innovation and technological specification ownership to dominate the fourth industrial revolution. China's ability to demonstrate respect for and safeguarding of intellectual property rights will begin, for the first time, to benefit its businesses and people. Simple self-dealing may force it to better establish rule-of-law systems.

However, if the end result is to move away from *guanxi* business practices, which must be brokered by a go-between due to lack of trust among China's own people and bribing officials to perform what is an official's contractual duty, China must carve a path that leads to true rule of law. By enshrining XJT in its constitution, it is perpetuating rule by man, and with self-policing in the CCP, the contradictions between people and party will not find a long-term solution. The antigraft campaign may have quelled the masses for now, but Xi may spend his tenure catching tigers and flies.

CHAPTER 10

Offspring: Nature vs Demand

Turn the population load into population resource.
—Xi Jinping

XJT Contradiction 4—How to Achieve the Long-Term Balanced Growth of Population

The major contradiction in the population growth of China has significantly changed from the control and restriction of population size to the improvement of population quality and structure. . . . Chinese leaders have to tackle the following tasks assigned by the times: how to transform the huge population into high-quality population and turn the population load into population resource; how to effectively improve the age and gender structures of the population; how to, from the perspective of the long-term development of the nation, innovate the fertility strategy, accomplish the transformation from family planning to scientific fertility, realize the balance respectively between population development and economic and social development, between aged population and young population, and between male population and female population, so as to boost the long-term balanced development of the Chinese population.[1]

The world has never witnessed human intrusion on nature's human reproductive evolution on the scale the CCP has undertaken. Population manipulation began under Mao and is on course to continue as long as the CCP reigns. Under Mao, reproduction directives were erratic, swinging between extremes. With the cessation of World War II and the Chinese Civil War, the population began to grow. Mao viewed this increasing manual labor capacity as a positive, and the party regarded growing population figures as an output advantage. Soon this growth began to strain its food supply, leading to the promotion of birth control. With Mao's Great Leap Forward campaign, famine erased millions. After famine recovery, the population again began to climb, and by the time of Deng's ascension, the total population had more than doubled pre-PRC levels.

Deng was a witness to and complicit in an estimated forty-five million deaths under Mao's reign as well as the failure of his economic policies. Deng assumed power with an estimated population of one billion. To pull the country out of poverty and create a modern society that could participate in the world, he launched a campaign, previously conceived by Zhou Enlai, dubbed the four modernizations. The four tenets were agriculture, industry, science and technology, and national defense.

To support the Four Modernizations campaign, Deng's policy of reform and opening began. To attack the poverty issue from the ground up, the decision was made to hold the population to 1.2 billion by the turn of the century.

In 1980 China's State Council issued an open letter regarding the problem of controlling population growth in the country. The letter was to the members of the Communist Party and the Communist Youth League. It stated the population goal of 1.2 billion was to be borne first by the CCP members and Chinese Communist Youth League members.

By example and with propaganda, education, and enforcement, the general population was to bear no more than one child. The objective was to increase the speed of modernization by shifting resources from sustenance living needed to serve the rapidly expanding population to investment in the four modernizations.[2]

The Economist reported that the one child policy had exceptions based on ethnicity. China recognizes fifty-six ethnic groups who comprise 8 percent of the total population. One group, the Uighurs living in Xinjiang, who were mainly comprised of Muslims, were allowed two children if they lived in cities. Regardless of ethnicity, those living in rural lands were allowed two children.[3]

Ezra Vogel explained there was strict enforcement of the one-child policy in urban areas. But in the countryside, where the government budget was too thin to care for the older adult families whose first child was a girl, families were allowed a second child in hopes for a male heir who could care for the parents in old age.[4] In the urban areas, the policy was enforced with vigor. Enforcement utilized every tactic available: the powerful propaganda machine, heavy fines, peer policing, forced sterilization, and near-birth abortions. Finally, one child became the norm of the nuclear family.

The uneven application of the policy across the rural/urban divide and by Han, non-Han minority groups gave rise to uneven fertility rates by geographic locations. As *The Economist* pointed out, the migration and fertility rates led to uneven population aging across provinces. Old-age pension payments are administered and funded by local provinces. The unevenness of the one-child policy had the consequence of leaving urban areas with demographic imbalances with too few children moving into the workforce and contributing to pension plans. As the imbalance grew over time, the dependency ratio of worker to pension beneficiary fell to near unsustainable levels in some areas.[5] *South China Morning Post* reported the reality of this looming dependency cliff: nationwide, from the 1990s to present, the ratio fell from five contributors for every one recipient to 2.8 for one today.[6]

Possibly the most destabilizing consequence of this policy was to add a gender skew that ripples through today's and future generations of Chinese. For the population to maintain its current rate, women must give birth to an average of 2.1 children. As is the case with many developing nations, the birth of a male heir is highly prized. Gender selection in nature produces on average 105 males to one hundred female births. To comply with the one-child policy, gendercide was waged on the female sex. The introduction of fetal sex determination technology led to significant abortions, and prior to that, the abandonment, neglect, and infanticide of baby girls was prevalent. *The Economist* reviewed data from the UN Population Fund and demonstrated how extreme the gender mismatch estimate was in 2020—China was sixty-six million women short due to sex selection in favor of males.[7] While there is much question of the veracity of Chinese-provided data, government officials reported on the progress made, citing that in 2004, the ratio of boys to girls born was 121 to one hundred, and by 2015 the ratio imbalance fell to 114 boys to one hundred girls.[8]

This unnatural skewing of gender has repercussions across the lifecycle of Chinese consumers' economic activity. The effects of this policy show up in three main areas: males as a financial liability, forcing parents to increase their savings rate; a decreasing and aging workforce, destabilizing the social safety net; and a cultural heritage clash, pitting modern thinking, which increasingly puts the individual's needs above the greater family unit, with the traditional filial piety system.

The Economist noted that a more destabilizing demographic issue lingers, as by 2030 the ratio of marriage-aged men to women may be 160 men for every hundred women.[9] This creates incredibly difficult odds for finding a wife and necessitates a way to create a competitive advantage. Successful advantages are currently found in education, employment, home and auto ownership, and other material goods. Hence, the parents of sons have a unique financial burden.

These items have put an up-front cost on the prospect of marriage for both a man and his parents, forcing them to save more and direct the funds to a marriage-oriented priority. *The Economist*'s data proved this point by finding as much as half the increase in these households' savings occurred between 1990 and 2007. This excess savings was earmarked to purchase their only child—most likely a son—homes, consumer and durable goods, and extravagant weddings.[10]

While the prospect of marriage puts an upfront drag on consumption spending by the son and his parents, a lifetime financial burden has emerged, and it is referred to as the 4-2-1 family unit. *The Economist* reports on a significant change in China's centuries of filial piety: "For the first time in the history of Chinese family life, the child-rather than ancestors or parents—is regarded as the center of the family."[11] The family unit is now often comprised of a couple (2), often single children themselves, raising a single child (1), while caring for their parents (4). The urbanization and migration of people has also put a financial strain on the historical norms of raising children and caring for the elderly. The typical couple often migrates to a metropolitan area, where they are physically unable to care for their parents, and their parents are not present to assist in rearing the grandchild. The breakdown in this lifecycle of care giving is testing both cultural norms and social services needed from the government.

The effects of the one-child policy created ramifications, from multitudes of "bare branches" as the single, childless men are referred to, and the graying, aging population. *The*

Wall Street Journal reported that the working-age population would peak in 2015 and then begin an accelerated decline.[12] There is much speculation that China may grow old before it grows rich, the crux of the middle-income trap. This rapid deceleration in the working population is expected to leave a labor shortage of sixty-seven million workers by 2030.[13]

In 2015, recognizing the untenable demographic anomalies, the CCP began to relax the policy and endorsed two children per couple if one of them was an only child. *South China Morning Post* reported 16.55 million births for 2015. *Bloomberg* cited 18.5 million births in 2016, but that may have reflected the pinnacle of growth under this new policy, as annual rates began to drop, with 2017 recording 17.2 million. *The Wall Street Journal* reported that by 2022 the birthrate was 9.56 million, less than the number of births at the height of the Great Famine in 1961.[14]

Several factors contributed to this lack of an on-demand baby boom. *Bloomberg* said, "A paradox has emerged in China: As the country relaxes its one-child policy, factors such as lower sperm counts and attempts to get pregnant later in life are making it harder for many to succeed."[15] As witnessed by an interview with a thirty-eight-year-old construction businessman: "Now that our economic conditions are better, we all want children, but it's hard for a lot of us. . . . All the years of smoking and drinking and business dinners take a toll. It's difficult for me and my wife to conceive naturally, and we needed help."[16] While *Bloomberg*'s interviewee may have attributed his infertility issues to lifestyle, other factors such as environment may play a role, as nationwide *Bloomberg* reported that the sperm count average had dropped 80 percent between the early 1970s and 2012.

Maybe most importantly has been the change in mindset of the people who have taken to heart Deng's original intent of the policy, that of population control and how it is linked to upward financial mobility. *The Economist* reminded us there were many years of propaganda to seed the notion that China had too many people, and this belief firmly took root. As the established smaller nuclear family had to carefully manage its resources to care for the elderly and provide a single child with the best possible advantages, multiple children did not make financial sense.[17] This more developed nation mentality of quality of life over quantity is showing up in the big urban areas such as Beijing and Shanghai, where it is estimated that women are giving birth to approximately 0.7 children. *The Wall Street Journal* reported, "In such settings, scrapping the One Child Policy will make no demographic difference whatsoever: People aren't even using their given birth-quota permits now."[18]

This cosmopolitan quality of life thinking runs counter to the quality of offspring that the CCP seems to reference in its population contradiction. In an op-ed for *The New York Times*, Leta Hong Fincher, author of *Leftover Women: The Resurgence of Gender Inequality in China,* succinctly gave insight as to what the party really wanted in this next phase of reproduction and why no baby boom materialized. The CCP wanted the majority ethnic Han women who were well educated and urban dwelling to marry and produce the next generation of more evolved children. Hong Fincher called out a eugenic approach to the production of superior Han offspring and that the minority ethnic groups, especially the Muslim Uighurs in Xinjiang, were to be coerced to not give birth.[19]

A few key phrases in XJT regarding solving the population contradiction and improved quality of offspring may have stood out to one enterprising Chinese scientist: He Jiankui. Educated in top Chinese and American universities, he conducted an experiment in 2018 to edit embryo DNA in search for a gene effect against HIV. Dr. He's outcome was twin girls, who as of this writing appear to be healthy, yet the efficacy of this experiment is unknown. *The Economist* reported that many Chinese researchers came out against Dr. He's conduct, pointing out that it should not be a surprise that this happened in China. Chinese colleagues attributed this to Chinese scientists who are overly eager to elevate their scientific breakthroughs on the world stage. But the objecting scientists said it was also a perversion that left behind higher morals in service of official directives open to interpretation on how to achieve the objective of quality vs quantity in the population.[20]

The relaxation of the one-child policy presented two unexpected business outcomes. First, the anticipated baby boom caused an uptick in the stock prices of multinational corporations (MNCs) who distributed baby milk products. This focused a light once again on what was one of the largest breaches of trust in China's consumer products market, which had come at the hands of one of its own companies— Sanlu Group, maker of baby infant formula and among China's most trusted brands. In 2008 dairy production could not match demand, so melamine, an industrial chemical used in plastic and fertilizers, was used to water down the formula. This practice continued for many months until Fonterra, the company's New Zealand partner, blew the whistle. Melamine was linked to six infant deaths and another three hundred thousand ill.

With one child now the center of the family unit, protecting this child became paramount. The door was open for US and European companies to fill the gap with what quickly became trusted products. By 2018 Euromonitor International estimated four companies held 40 percent of milk formula market share.

As the fear factor of protecting parents' most valuable asset, their child, roiled the market, multinationals found that they could charge premium prices for their products. In 2017

Caixin reported that families with two- to three-month-old children spent $286 a month on milk formula or around 40 percent of the average monthly household income. Rena Lau of Globalization Monitor attributed the premium price differential of global standards not to be based on scientific product differentiation "but on parents' willingness to pay."[21]

Second, the expected baby boom did not result in increasing sales of infant formula and other necessities such as diapers. However, a very different business opportunity did emerge. Families that needed help conceiving turned to in vitro fertilization. *Bloomberg* reported that BIS Research estimated China's in vitro fertilization market was $670 million in 2016 and projected it to reach $1.5 billion by 2022. The desire for children has given rise to medical tourism by the wealthy. The US in vitro fertilization industry may be contributing to the perpetuation of gender inequality. *Bloomberg* found in an interview with California Reproductive Center cofounder Mark Surrey that since gender could now be determined before birth, although gender selection is now illegal in China, the center was treating well-off Chinese mainlanders with the reproductive technology of their choice, regardless of the criteria the couple based their decisions on.[22]

Moral and ethical questions of price gouging, genetic modification experiments, and embryo sex-selection questions aside, the gender and aging issues that today's marketer must understand add significant wrinkles to segmenting the population. The substantial savings priorities of the son's parents artificially shifted discretionary income into a very limited bucket of consumer and durable goods. If you are targeting a young male, your product or service must speak to an ability to help him get a girl. If the target is the beleaguered parents, the message needs to assure that the purchase or investment supports a successful continuation of the family and security in old age.

In solving the population contradiction and achieving the desired outcomes of gender balance, higher intellectual aptitude, a steady replacement rate, and decreases in non-Han ethnicity, the party will have to fight on several fronts: internally a culture that continues to prefer male heirs, a rising middle class that desires more money to more offspring, and some within China's scientific community who see creating designer babies as a badge of international arrival. Externally, the developed world may decry an engineered society that reminds them of a dystopian future they reject and who then may reject China.

Chapter 11

Spiritual Wealth and Values

Accelerate the building of a value system that fully reflects the characteristics of China.
—**Xi Jinping**

XJT Contradiction 5—"At present, the major ideological contradiction in China is that the ideological and cultural construction cannot satisfy the needs of comprehensively deepening the reform and national rejuvenation, which is remarkably embodied by the weakened ideals and convictions, loss of values, degradation of moral quality, insufficient cultural creativity, disparity of ideological work, weak national soft power, etc."[1]

XJT gives credence to the miraculous creation of material wealth China has generated since the reform and opening policy. However, during this time society failed to make progress in the areas of spiritual wealth and create national core values to sustain the country's rejuvenation.[2]

How is China's materialistic bounty and spiritual void manifesting? Ian Johnson for *Foreign Affairs* observed that millions of Chinese forced to live in a secular society are devoid of answers on how to achieve a better life beyond materialism and are turning to faith and religion.[3] A pastor in Chengdu told Johnson, "We thought we were unhappy because we were poor. But now a lot of us aren't poor anymore, and yet we're still unhappy. We realize there's something missing, and that's a spiritual life."[4] Johnson saw this grappling with religion as a "conversation about how to restore solidarity and values to societies that have made economics the basis of most decisions."[5]

The most effective marketing messaging seeks to align with its target's underlying values. The Chinese value system is in a period of reconstruction by the CCP. With certain goals in mind, the party is conflating historical foundational practices with broader universal concepts to make its core values more palatable to both domestic and international audiences.

As China seeks to rebuild the Middle Kingdom to its former, pre-eighteenth-century apex and build a new socioeconomic structure of governance for its people, the at times contradictory positions it must assume, such as state capitalism, have found a fungible moniker to give latitude to its initiatives—"Chinese characteristics." This identification of and subsequent co-opting of historically unique Chinese cultural traits as an explanation for China's melding of incongruent philosophies can be traced to the pragmatic but clever Deng.

Regarding the genesis of Chinese characteristics, Xi said that Deng Xiaoping Theory raised socialism to a new scientific level by adapting and creatively developing Marxism-Leninism and Mao Zedong Thought.[6] This gave rise to socialism with Chinese characteristics and answered the question of how to shape an "economically and culturally backward China."[7]

In 1984, with the economy moving positively, Deng wanted to speed up development by adding new SEZs. Vogel noted in late October 1984 that Deng was able to pass the formal decision to reform the economic structure and termed it as "socialism with Chinese characteristics." The adoption of this vague terminology allowed the creation of policies to expand markets and reform industries. The difference between socialism and capitalism was not about a planned economy but whether there was public ownership with a final goal of common prosperity.[8]

The foothold of socialism with Chinese characteristics appeared in 1978, as Deng had ascended to power and faced a multitude of issues resulting from previous administration missteps. In an oft-quoted aphorism, Deng challenged China to "feel for stones while crossing the river." Looking outward, he was aware of the success enjoyed by his neighbors, the "four little dragons" (South Korea, Taiwan, Hong Kong, and Singapore), and knew he must open China to science, technology, and management systems. As Deng searched outwardly for solutions to meet these goals, he did not assess them based on the source's political system, even if capitalist, as he knew those founding principles would be too foreign to a nation with a long cultural history of unique governmental administration. Deng knew that simply opening markets to outside interests would not hold, so he encouraged his officials to scan the globe for ideas and slowly build unique systems that would fit the engrained mentality and incrementally change thinking through experimentation.[9] Deng's patient prodding paid off; he expanded markets with pragmatic policies and housed them under an ideologically acceptable banner. But Deng's North Star had always been raising the living standards of the people and shaking off this backward mentality. He seemed to not consider the psychic toll of the belief systems long held by the people. The whipsaw changes the populous had experienced under Mao and the destruction of relic thinking and beliefs were wiped out during the Cultural Revolution, and no sanctioned replacement had been provided by the party.

It is in building Chinese values in the new era that Xi may be leaning on Deng's precedent by aggregating what can be combined to create China's spiritual wealth. Xi draws on the sovereignty of the culture and government. Xi concedes that China's governance system needs improvement and it has a long history of looking outward for new concepts and ideas, but ultimately the values China needs to develop must reflect the characteristics of the Chinese nation.[10] Just as Deng sidestepped the ideology of Mao's leadership and its adherence to strict communist dogma, Xi must navigate Mao's legacy and the destruction of traditional culture.

XJT says, "A nation's culture is a unique feature that distinguishes that nation from others." In creating a value system and its definition of core values, they should look back and creatively develop traditional Chinese virtues that are both eternal yet provide contemporary value. [11]

Xi alluded to several important ideas driving the trajectory of the party and nation. At the top of the food chain is the idea of culture. We can find a seminal look at the importance of understanding culture and civilizations in Samuel P. Huntington's *The Clash of Civilizations and the Remaking of World Order*. If we do not understand our differences, search for our commonalities, and find a way to incorporate these into our strategies, we as marketers will never be truly successful. Why does the rhetoric around the Communist Party so often veer into the idea of the culture of the Chinese people? Per Huntington, after the Cold War, global politics began to cluster along cultural identities, and therefore people's identities and symbols of those cultures began to emerge.[12] Huntington believed that world leaders would have to understand, accept, and cooperate with other civilizations to avoid war.[13]

Huntington stated the central theme of his book and broke it into five parts. The theme was "Culture and cultural identities, which at the broadest level are civilization identities, are shaping the patterns of cohesion, disintegration, and conflict in the post-Cold War world."[14] The five parts were that modernization is not Westernization and does not produce a universal civilization; power among civilizations is shifting and the West's power declining; countries group themselves around core leader states of their own civiliza-tions; Westphalian ideas bring China into conflict with oppos-ing civilizations; and the West accepting its uniqueness and not the universality of its ideas.

Since 1978 China has embarked on the world's greatest creation of wealth. The Communist Party, before celebrating its centennial in 2021, faced massive challenges. If China is to avenge its self-dubbed Century of Humiliation and remain true to its mission, it must answer the question posed by Huntington to all civilizations: Who are we? Huntington's answer: people look to their history and ancestry to find their language, customs, and values. Further, people identify with ethnic groups, religious groups, politics, and ultimately their civilization.[15]

Civilization and culture are often used interchangeably, and in many texts about outsider interactions with Chinese dynasties, the outsiders are referred to as barbarians. Where and how do these ideas join our lexicon? Huntington explained that the French in the eighteenth century devised civil vs barbaric to differentiate a formed society that was urban, literate, and settled from more primitive groups. This black-and-white divide of civil or primitive evolved into dif-ferent definitions of what was civil, and people moved to the idea of civilizations that allowed for more nuanced attri-butes specific to groups. The nineteenth-century Germans furthered the idea of civilizations by drawing a distinction between those who could utilize technology and create inven-tions requiring higher literacy to recognize a difference and also based on culture that brought into the equation different ideas of values and moral qualities.[16]

As marketing seeks to attach to the underlying values and ideas held by a particular culture, where do we look to under-stand these attributes? Huntington found the most important objective used to delineate a specific culture was religion.[17]

Modern religions—Christianity, Islam, Hinduism—support distinct civilizations, but Buddhism does not. Buddhism was exported throughout the Asian civilization beginning in the first century, spread throughout China, and assimilated into Confucianism and Taoism[18] As we will see, the CCP is grappling with religion and Confucianism and how they play in the Chinese Dream. Confucianism is not a true religion but experienced more as a system of social and ethical philosophy. This Confucian philosophy is rich with opportunity to mold and address many issues the CCP faces as it moves into a new economic and demographic stage of their development.

The co-opting of the Confucian system by the government appears through its construction of the core socialist values campaign, which is laced throughout Xi's speeches and ever present in day-to-day encounters through propaganda.

Separated from Confucianism, the Communists have an official policy on religion. In 1982, the Central Committee put out Document No. 19, *The Basic Viewpoint and Policy on the Religious Question during Our Country's Socialist Period.* The document summed up China's experience with religion historically as well as its relation to the party, its near and long-term future in China, and the party's intentions for religion in achieving its objectives. The party's thoughts are based on Marx's views on religion, simply and broadly stated as religion not being a disease but rather a symptom of the problems in society. The CCP's position is that oppressors, to make people feel better about their poverty and the exploitation they experience, have used religion. Hence, the idea supports Marx's infamous line: religion is the opium of the masses.

Mao Zedong sought to separate the people from religion, wanting nothing to come between the party and the people. During the Cultural Revolution, many physical expressions of religion were destroyed. However, religion did not disappear, and Document No. 19 took a pragmatic approach to managing its existence.

It is worth a few minutes to look at specific excerpts from this policy. Document No. 19 posits that religion is an historic phenomenon, and with the banishment of the oppressive class by socialism, it will eventually disappear when socialism and communism are completely formed and accepted. In the meantime, the people's consciousness has not caught up, and their old habits and ways of thinking still linger.[19]

Document No. 19 states that the current policy on religion is a long-term strategy to allow it until the masses catch up psychologically with the political ideology. The policy demands that true communists and party members must maintain atheism and propagate this ultimate stance. In the area of religion, the party does not support use of coercion to achieve its means but rather to step gently so as to not divide people and cause instability. The party advocates propaganda to suppress superstition and push scientific education. Further, religion will not be tolerated in affairs of the state, schools, or to oppose the party or socialist system.[20]

There are several important points in this policy on religion. Communist party members are required to profess atheism. But even atheists sometimes lapse into a belief of something greater than themselves when facing death. Ironically, it was the leader who decried religion the loudest who acknowledged God in his waning days. Kissinger wrote of his last meetings with Mao in late 1975 that the topic of discussion was the future of Taiwan. Mao was struggling with the importance of Taiwan vs the much bigger picture of global order. Mao was concerned about Taiwan's counterrevolutionaries and that it might be worth fighting for in one hundred years. Kissinger questioned this long time frame, and Mao's reply was, "It is hard to say. Five years, ten, twenty, a hundred years. It's hard to say. And when I go to heaven to see

God, I'll tell him it's better to have Taiwan under the care of the United States now."[21] Mao went on to indicate that he believed God did not bless him as he was a "militant warlord, also a communist."

As the party attempts to educate and wipe out superstitions, this will prove a long-term task, with fifty-six ethnic groups, many of whom have generational customs and beliefs. It is difficult to avoid many antiquated and fervently practiced celebrations such as tomb-sweeping day, which stands out as particularly egregious in its excesses. It involves revering ancestors and honoring them annually by pilgrimage to their graves. Many earthly goods are purchased and placed at the grave for use in the afterlife. Items can range from burning real and fake money to food items and toy luxury automobiles.

That religious interference is to be divorced from government sounds familiarly like America's professed separation of church and state, but it goes several steps further. Under the pretext of ensuring that the Muslim majority of Uighurs in the province of Xinjiang cannot escape their assimilation into the Han majority ethnic group, reports are rampant that more than one million Uighurs are currently in detention camps, receiving reeducation and indoctrination to "correct thinking." This includes forced rejection of religious observances of dietary restrictions and dress.

To allow yet control religion, the document's policy is to train and indoctrinate incoming clergy to better control these institutions. Clergy should be taught to "fervently love their homeland and support the Party's leadership and Socialist system."[22]

The party's position seems to indicate if we can't beat them, let's co-opt them and have them become an arm of our propaganda machine. The irony is that propaganda originated from the Christian religion. The term *propaganda* emerged from the Catholic Church in the seventeenth century as missionaries were sent far and wide to propagate the faith, and a College of Propaganda was created to train the missionaries.[23]

The outcome of this long-term policy was for religion to eventually disappear. Document No. 19 says, "At that time, the vast majority of our citizens will be able to deal with the world and our fellowmen from a conscious scientific viewpoint, and no longer have any need for recourse to an illusory world of gods to seek spiritual solace."[24]

In other words, once the party has fulfilled the population's material needs and they are indoctrinated with the core socialist values, the banishment of reliance on anything other than the party and nation will be achieved.

The document recognizes specific religions but in several areas makes clear that the religion of Western civilization faces specific hurdles, stating that there is a long history of religions in China, including Buddhism, Daoism, and Islam, but Roman Catholic and Protestant religions emerged in China only after the Opium Wars.[25]

Here the party has tied Christianity to the Opium Wars and its Century of Humiliation. In its instructions for how it is to work with religious professionals, the party points out that the Chinese Catholic Church is to be separated from answering to the higher power of the Vatican. Thus, clergy education must include independence from and self-governance of churches as directed by the party. These Western religions must be guarded against to ensure no outside infiltration, as they are deemed "hostile foreign religious forces."[26]

An example of how the party intends to groom the Chinese Christian clergy in the doctrine and ensure independence from outside influence occurred in December 2017. Pope Francis was negotiating for better ties with China. However, many Catholic churches are considered underground and run by bishops appointed by the Vatican. In order to further what may be broader Vatican goals, and as a sign of concession, Ian Johnson reported for *The New York Times* that there are approximately ten to twelve million Chinese Catholics, and half worship in underground churches vs party-sanctioned churches. The party insisted that two Vatican-appointed bishops step down and that the party would appoint their replacements. Pope Francis acquiesced.[27]

Demonstrating the intensity of resistance to unsanctioned infiltration and the general public's acceptance of this policy, *The Washington Post* reported on Mercedes-Benz's dilemma. In February 2018 Mercedes-Benz posted a photo on Instagram of a Mercedes on the beach, superimposed with the call to "Look at situations from all angles, and you will become more open" with an accompanying line underneath the photo: "Start your week with a fresh perspective on life from the Dalai Lama." Public outrage immediately ensued. Mercedes-Benz quickly apologized for hurting the feelings of the Chinese people by allowing an international ad to appear on China's social media site, Weibo. Mercedes-Benz offered its own rectification by stating, "In light of this, we will immediately take measures to deepen our understanding of Chinese culture and values, including our overseas colleagues, to ensure this won't happen again.'"[28] The CCP considers the Dalai Lama, the spiritual leader of Tibet, a threat to inciting separation from China in a region they consider part of China that operates as an autonomous region. Traditionally, when the Dalai Lama dies, he is reincarnated and discovered by the high lamas. The party has made clear that they will choose the next Dalai Lama.

So if religion is to eventually fade away, and religion is a key construct of a civilization, what is to replace it? It appears that the core socialist values (CSV) currently being derived from Confucius are meant to fill the spiritual yin to the material yang. Confucius's date of birth is 551 BCE, and his thoughts centered on ethics, virtues, and government leadership. Howard French, writing for *The Wall Street Journal*, said, "Mao Zedong vilified the sage as a source of bourgeois ideas and blamed him for China's backwardness, unleashing Red Guards to attack shrines to Confucius."[29] Xi's party must now rehabilitate Confucius.

Confucius is making a semi sanctioned comeback. French said, "Finally, in the past few years, successive leaders in Beijing have celebrated him anew as an answer to a materialist void in modern Chinese life and as an alternative to supposedly corrosive Western values."[30] *The Economist* reported that Xi "evidently sees Confucianism as a powerful ideological tool, with its stress on order, hierarchy, and duty to ruler and to family. Confucianism has the advantage of being homegrown. It appeals to a yearning for ancient values among those unsettled by China's blistering pace of change."[31] The CCP is creating a value system to support its ideology with a thread to tradition but layered with one cohesive theme—self-reliance through belief in the past and future.

Confucian values help the party address issues such as an aging population that is weighing on the pension system by fostering filial piety, the need to upgrade and elongate the individual's educational endeavors addressed by leaning on the ancient maxim of continuous learning and self-improvement, and the propriety of honesty and righteousness that speak to the issues of graft and the resulting public scorn of party officials from the grassroots to the top.

But simply rehabilitating Confucius will not support the CCP's ultimate goals. Digging deeper into China's imperial time, we glean a better idea of how the CCP will serve both Chinese personal morals as well as its societal obligations. If the goals are a powerful nation, symbolized by rejuvenation and social stability coupled with continuing credibility and viability of the CCP predicated on more than just economic advancement, simply mandating a set of core values will not be enough.

An excellent thesis by Huijie Cher, *The Political Utility of Morality*, pulled apart the underpinnings of what these core values are intended to do through a "morality-politics nexus" lens. Cher provided background reminding us that throughout China's history there have been many attempts to instill virtue and morality. There have always been close ties between morals, politics, ideology, and the leaders of government administration. Cher argued that the CCP has lost stature in the area of moral ideology and has relied on economic improvement and nationalism for legitimacy. This disconnect has weakened the political power due to its lack of moral justification, and without change the party's extended rule is in question.[32]

If the party is to extend its rule, underpinned by more than economics, it must look back to imperial times to meld a culturally relevant philosophy to fulfill the historic tradition of ruler as moral arbiter who can mete out consequences for amoral activities. Imperial China's legal system was born of two competing philosophies, Confucianism and Legalism. Confucianism was to rule by virtue, using moral persuasion vs Legalism which was to rule by law, using punishment and coercion.

Aris Teon, writing for *The Greater China Journal* blog, said, "Confucius philosophy revolved around two concepts: the nobleman and the establishment of a well-ordered society."[33] The nobleman, or gentleman, was historically born into a hierarchy that bestowed this upon him, but Confucius brought the concept of equality into the equation, believing one could achieve this status through merit as opposed to simple birthright. Further, he believed that humans were inherently good and endowed with four virtues: humanity, righteousness, propriety, and wisdom. To achieve a harmonious society, these virtues were the priorities of gentlemen.

Confucianism relied on perceived inherent good and

morality, reinforced through ritualism, and this would be the driving force to control and create stability. Per Teon, these rules were bounded by individuals who knew their place in society and practiced rituals and rites to exhibit proper social behavior.[34] These relationships were codified between parents and children, siblings, community, and ruler with specific expectations for each. The people were not viewed as, nor did they believe that they were, free individuals but rather part of a complex social network and as such had duties to their society and emperor.[35] It is a collectivist society.

Confucius taught that violation of these virtues and hierarchal structure were because of a lack of education and negative influences. Rectification came through education and moral persuasion where the wrongdoer could be taught to recognize improper actions through shamming.[36] This self-correction of behavior through shame and moral persuasion can be thought of as the currency of "face." While the concept can be understood subconsciously to a Westerner as grounded in ego and judged by society, for China it has its own unique characteristics. Face has been described "as the 'guiding principle of the Chinese mind.'"[37] Chinese society continues to operate personal relationships guided by accepted social roles and hierarchies. While to the outsider these accepted interactions are nuanced, they are a delicate standard by which judgment is passed.

There are two types of face in China that can be overlapping or discrete. First, *lian* is personal and held by everyone. This value of face depends on personal behavior and its alignment to society's moral code. It links back to the social standards, societal roles, and obligations devised by Confucius. It is violation of those obligations and rituals within the hierarchy that cause loss of face. Modern-day realities are challenging some of these traditional moral obligations and garner much press coverage and generational conflict. Two occur in the long-observed and revered area of filial piety. Foremost is the emphasis on early marriage and the production of children to carry on the family name. The tradition is hindered due to gender imbalance, female career attainment, cost of child rearing, and the rejection of arranged marriages.

Second is the child's obligation to care for the parents and to acquiesce to all their wishes. The pervasiveness of the financial and emotional burdens the younger generation face in their 4-2-1 family unit is uncharacteristically represented in a popular Chinese TV show that began airing in March 2019. The show, *All Is Well*, represents a widower who places hardships on his children via excessive demands. Per *The Economist*, the father was difficult, always expecting his sons to financially cover his lavish lifestyle, leading to fighting between the brothers who wanted to avoid being considered unfilial. Further, reporting that China's state media gave the show mixed reviews presumably because this was not the image censors want portrayed in parental care.[38]

So intent is the state on fostering elder care on the family under the guise of filial piety, it enacted a law in 2013 that requires children to physically visit their parents. The law, Protection of the Rights and Interests of Elderly People, had by 2019 become the basis for some parents suing their children for emotional and financial support.

The second type of face, *mianzi*, is acquired by a person's status and position in society. This currency is not necessarily dependent on individual behavior but rather exhibited by wealth, power, and social connections. This face is lost from the abuse of these privileges. The loss of face and public shaming of party officials caught up in corruption campaigns best illustrates the *mianzi* issue. One method of shaming created must-see TV shows devoted to ousted high-ranking officials making confessions and demonstrating contrition.

The second philosophy of imperial China's ruling system

was Legalism. Teon described a system that could not be more opposite to Confucian beliefs. The legalist believed that man was inherently evil, greedy, and selfish, and without strict control and punishment the state would not be able to function.[39] While Confucius saw an equality among people, albeit within their appropriate hierarchy, the legalist saw humans as naturally unequal, but the law should apply equally to all humans regarding reward and punishment.

The Legalist school of thought contributed greatly to building the rule of state, but its excessive use of punishment led to its diminishment, and the Han Dynasty (206 BCE–220 CE) turned back to Confucianism as a ruling philosophy.

Teon gave a powerful insight regarding the ruling philosophy of China. The Legalist established a powerful state under an authoritarian monarch. The Confucians sought a harmonious state through indoctrination in propriety and moral values, led by a monarch. But neither considered a Chinese state led by any form other than a single ultimate leader.[40] The people's acceptance of one-party rule is inherent in their thinking on the administration of state and soul.

As the CCP seeks to fulfill its ruling duties as developer of moral, self-regulating citizens and provide a harmonious society that can administer rewards and punishment for amoral behavior, it cannot turn back to pure Confucianism or Legalism. It is constructing a set of core socialist values. These values will serve multiple needs and hence, as Cher posited, provide a new type of political utility. These core socialist values are intentionally vaguely defined. Collectively looking at these values, they seem incoherent, but this adds to their utility in pulling in various opinions found throughout Chinese society.[41] "[T]he flexibility of political slogans is a source of political utility—flexible slogans can be politically manipulated or interpreted in numerous ways, and appeal to various audiences for different reasons."[42]

The core socialist values are not arbitrary. Cher pointed out the party has grounded the core socialist values in history and refer to them as inherited yet upgraded from China's traditional culture.[43] Why does the party seek so strongly to tie to tradition? Cher explained that tying the core socialist values to tradition offers a feeling of continuity and stability, uniquely indigenously Chinese, and distinguishes Chinese values from Western values.[44]

The party's ability to mine Confucianism is a classic use of what Patrick deemed the second commandment of propaganda: reflect the values and beliefs of the audience. Propaganda works most effectively by piggybacking on beliefs and values that are already in people's heads and not by trying to install entirely new cognitive equipment.[45] Patrick explained that beliefs become common knowledge and acceptance through cultural conditioning. For the propagandist, the molding of preexisting beliefs is much easier than trying to wipe out ingrained experience and replace it with an entirely new set of beliefs.

For the flexibility and political utility of the core socialist values construct, let's examine a speech given by Xi on May 4, 2014, at Peking University. Xi noted the date of the speech and tied it to the spirit of the May 4 movement—to stand up for the country. He turned to his main topic, the core socialist values. As he implored the students to embrace them, he said, "Today, we should still adhere to and carry out these core values, highlighted by patriotism, *progress*, democracy and *science*."[46] Emphasis was added to progress and science, as they are not consistently referenced in the twelve core socialist values but may have been added for audience relevance.

However, in the same speech Xi explained the twelve core socialist values and tied them to their corresponding societal hierarchy. "The values of prosperity, democracy, civility and harmony are for the country; those of freedom, equality, justice and the rule of law for the society; and those of patriotism, dedication, integrity and friendship for citizens. They explain what sort of country and society we are striving for, and what kind of citizens we are cultivating."[47]

Cher pointed out that the core socialist values are a shorthand for a moral-ideological code of conduct. The definition of the individual values is intentionally vague, which serves several purposes. For the citizens it is harder to question their validity, and hence they speculate leading to self-censorship. For the party, they can be used arbitrarily to define moral behavior and mete out rewards and punishments. The party's goal is to reduce resources required to foster correct behavior through coercion and specific law enforcement and move to self-governing citizens who regulate their behavior based on unseen red lines.[48]

As the party professes to focus on legal reform and rule of law as opposed to Legalism, or rule by law, it is experimenting with a new concept aimed at self-regulation and offerings of reward and punishment. This new system is known as the social credit system (SCS).

The social credit system is best defined by Germany's Mercator Institute for China Studies: "China's Social Credit System is an ambitious, information technology-driven initiative through which the state seeks to create a central repository of data on natural and legal persons [corporations] that can be used to monitor, assess, and change their actions through incentives of punishment and reward."[49]

Rogier Creemers of the University of Leiden provided an overview of how law intertwines with social credit and the CCP's objectives. China has struggled with legal reform due to compliance and enforcement of laws. The enforcement problems cover a wide range of issues from civil judgments to intellectual property infringement, environment, and food safety.[50]

On legal background, Creemers said that China, since its communist inception, relied on the Leninist system with the judiciary's first responsibility to the party. Under Mao's reign, a sound legal system was not created. After his death the party began building a true legal system. It relied on Chinese characteristics, as it had few modern systems to access. China's legal reform has been an incremental process that has attempted to marry some of China's previous political systems to ideas borrowed from the West.[51]

Combining its historic political system and communism's scientific ideological systems, the CCP seeks to leverage the social credit system to support its goals of consistency, compliance, and ruling mandate. Creemers described it as first, the state recognizing it has an obligation to develop social morality as well as sustain legal authority. Second, due to its ideological adherence to social systems theory, through science it can engineer society.[52]

Creemers saw the outcomes for the party as cultivating people's morality and worldview, which will lead to social harmony.[53] For the people it will bring confidence and a restoration of trust in the government, enterprise, and their country. How will the party achieve the objectives? Per the Mercator Institute for China Studies, by leaning on the power of science and requiring the people to believe in "the Chinese government's portrayal of big data-driven technological monitoring as providing objective, irrefutable measures of reality."[54] By adopting this strategy, the party signaled it cannot completely remove graft, nor restore innate trust in fellow humans, so it is turning to the artificial solution of data to do so: techno-authoritarianism. There is fallacy in this thinking, as the early computer scientists' maxim was always garbage in, garbage out.

Creemers traced the genesis of social credit system to market reform to provide a solution to the untrustworthiness and amoral behavior that has resulted in many abuses, including intellectual property theft and unsafe food.[55] To address the legacy of shortcomings in economic reform and to understand where the social credit system goes, Creemers pointed to the 2014 "Planning Outline for the Construction of a Social Credit System. . . . [T]his new plan combined the economic aspects of credit, both concerning financial creditworthiness and trust in the market, with the broader initiative to enhance social harmony and discipline government."[56]

For business transactions, with a side benefit of society control, one could think of the system it is developing as FICO+. China was predominately a cash-based society. As China moved to e-commerce, lack of credit became a hindrance. Alibaba, China's dominant online commerce platform, needed to address this barrier to growth and serve as an intermediary between buyers and sellers. They developed a spinoff known as Alipay as a processor of electronic and mobile payments. Beyond fostering the movement of payments from buyer to seller, the legacy trust factor found in the *guanxi* system of a guarantor who sat between the two was still not present. To establish credit, Alibaba created Ant Financial, a credit service, and developed a FICO-type system. Utilizing Alibaba transaction history, the outcome was a proprietary credit system called Sesame Credit.

While Sesame Credit is prevalent and credible, this one system does not provide all the necessary data capture and levers of enforcement the CCP ultimately envisions for a fully formed social credit system. Currently, the massive and disparate sources of data necessary to support the system are being assembled under, and administratively led by, the People's Bank of China, which created a united credit-scoring bureau named Baihang. To further standardize data related to individuals and enterprises across the country and with various bureaucratic agencies, it is introducing what you could think of as a social security number called the unified social credit number system, which is a unique eighteen-digit number.

By developing a system to support 360-degree surveillance of enterprises' actions, the government seeks to address a pressing concern of the people beyond the mere ability to pay; it desires to address a lack of trust in the quality and efficacy of products and services. Two areas that garner heated press and populous outcry are food and medicine safety. Per the Mercator Institute for China Studies, one outcome the government promises to deliver through the social credit system is consumer rights protections and "trustworthy" information about products and companies.[57]

For society, the objectives of the social credit system, per the Mercator Institute for China Studies, is to create a culture of integrity and trust, with official Chinese media stating it will transform society by removing untrustworthy actors.[58]

Creemers noted that underpinning the development of the social credit system is administering the government through systems engineering techniques that not only take in data but also push it out to create a feedback loop to individuals and entities to foster self-governance. The system will ultimately provide fast responses to noncompliance and quickly administer appropriate consequences.[59] The aggregation of activity data from individuals and entities across legal and social mores creates an unavoidable, pervasive system, leading to a tagline used by the CCP: if trust is broken in one place, restrictions are imposed everywhere.

If the goal is to create a self-regulating society adhering to the core socialist values, supported by social credit system, it is unclear if the objective can be met without potentially creating more divisive social issues and creating an unrecoverable loss of face and fortune, at least through a transition period that allows a viable rule of law to be implemented and administered.

While province social credit system level system tests vary, the Mercator Institute for China Studies found that all carry the basic criteria of sorting, reminiscent of Mao's classification strategies, such as "blacklists of non-compliant individuals and legal entities [and 'red lists' for outstanding companies and individuals]."[60] Or, as in Shanghai, one can access a database by entering the state ID number and determine if an entity or individual has been rated as very good, good, or bad. Other systems assign points, akin to American auto insurance deductions for traffic violations, or grades similar to bond ratings of AAA to D.

The range of punishment is also diverse, with a theme of public shaming most prevalent. Loss of face methods include city-wide electronic billboards with mugshot-type images for jaywalking, apps that identify nearby debtors, and forced voice mail recordings urging the caller to encourage the recipient to abide by court orders due to legal infractions. Creemers found that beyond *lian*-type loss of face, the system can enforce *mianzi*-type loss of face: "blacklist entrants (and where it concerns a legal entity, their senior staff) faced restrictions on conspicuous consumption. They were no longer allowed to travel first class, on high-speed trains, or on civil aircraft to visit star-rated hotels or luxury restaurants, resort, nightclubs and golf courses, to go on foreign holidays, to send their children to fee-paying schools, to purchase particular kinds of high-value insurance products, to buy or renovate their homes, or purchase cars."[61] As of this writing, millions of plane and train tickets had been blocked from purchase.

Early in 2020, as the COVID-19 pandemic swept the world, a crisis with an opportunity for enterprising yet untrustworthy Chinese entrepreneurs arose. There was a dire need for personal protective equipment. Because China is the world's largest producer of personal protective equipment (17.2 percent market share in 2019)[62], orders rolled in at an unprecedented rate. Quickly, countries discovered they had paid millions for defective, fraudulently labeled equipment. Under the social credit system it should be expected that in China a few companies made the blacklist. For the rest of the world, the party received a black eye.

While such a complex system will take years to reach ubiquitous, standardized rollout, it will be the younger generations who will be most innately indoctrinated. A carrot system of compliance of note developed by the Communist Youth League Central Committee called China Youth Credit Management (CY Credit) is being rolled out targeting approximately 450 million aged eighteen to forty-five. CY Credit is based upon a numeric range (350–800) with anything greater than 640 as "excellent credit." Data inputs include personal information, volunteer work, social connections, credit history, consumption history, and track record of honoring contracts. The incentive perks include discounts, waiver of deposits, and automatic elevation to second-round interview status in job applications.

Alluding to how broadly this positive behavior system may evolve, Meng Jing of *South China Morning Post* interviewed Shi Yanying, president of CY Credit. Shi, channeling Harvard MBA-type language, said in order to foster good citizenship, "data needs to be used to realize its value. . . . Shi said she simply views social credit as the invisible assets of a person, something that if used properly can bring benefit to a young person's life."[63] Shi stated to further actualize the data, CY Credit "is looking at plans to offer more credit-based services in the areas of overseas education, flat rentals, travel, dating and even marriage."[64]

With a credit score potentially touching every part of one's life, what will help or hurt? *South China Morning Post* reported that college students can create positive marks by publishing papers, creating intellectual property, or volunteering in places such as nursing homes. Negative marks include items such as plagiarism and exam cheating.[65] In a country where the youth reference themselves as the "996" generation, meaning to work from 9:00 a.m. to 9:00 p.m., six days a week, they may find that the seventh day of Christian rest will become the socialist's volunteer day of credit repair.

On the consumer front, American MNCs operating in China are required to maintain information on Chinese nationals' interactions with their products and services in China, which by default requires them to feed data into the social credit system. What is unclear is how American companies will be able to utilize this data in segmentation and targeting strategies. While credit scoring may be typical in data dissection, the addition of behavior monitoring will require building new types of psychological profiles. This leads the marketer to ask: Does the excessive risk taking of a repeated jaywalker preclude one as a target for fast cars?

On the corporate front, in mid-2019, the European Chamber in conjunction with Sinolytics, published "The Digital Hand How China's Social Credit System Conditions Market Actors." The report's concern, urgency, and warning for foreign companies was dire: "It is no exaggeration to say that the Corporate SCS will be the most comprehensive system created by any government to impose a self-regulating marketplace, nor is it inconceivable that the Corporate SCS could mean life or death for individual companies."[66] The report provided details on rules and regulations across a swath of internal corporate disciplines subject to compliance. It noted that some of the arbitrary friction that has been prevalent in business dealings due to individual officials' power brokerage may be dissipated. But it is in the monitoring required of employee behavior and all those affiliated companies in one's supply chain where operations could become unwieldy. Should a critical component supplier fall into a category of heavily distrusted entity, the consequences will ripple throughout the supply chain. Should the marketing department send out a survey incorrectly labeling Chinese autonomous regions or a vice president be found to personally be in arrears on his home mortgage payments, the corporation will take a hit on their corporate credit score and be expected to mete out internal punishment as well.

In the artificial development of values and trust, corporations will face an onerous task. One could imagine in the future to find alongside normal corporate compliance functions a new title of corporate social credit officer, with fingers in every facet of the business, from human resources to taxation.

As the CCP grapples with the need to make up for a functioning, credible rule of law legal system, the people grapple with a loss of trust, meaning of life of questions and a disconnect to a Confucian-centered value system that for millennia had regulated the family's moral code.

With the party's implementation of a set of sanctioned yet fungible values, a techno-authoritarian carrot-and-stick system to create self-governing citizens and businesses, it remains unclear how its solutions square the contradiction of a spiritual void and produce spiritual wealth.

Chapter 12

One Mountain, Two Tigers

War is the extension of politics by other means, economy is the root cause of wars.
—Xi Jinping

XJT Contradiction 6—Sino-US: There Can Be Only One Champion in the World

XJT says,

> The second largest economy in the world is the achievement of China, but also a danger to China. . . . The "runner-up" should keep a low profile, bide his time and remain modest and prudent, but should not be content with the "second place" and give up striving for the "first place." . . . Both Sino-US contradiction and relationship are significantly related to the destinies of both countries and the future of the world. In the next ten to twenty years, the cooperation between China and the US will be deepened continuously, thus intensifying their competition and unavoidably sharpening their conflicts sometimes. China should not only compete with the US in a brave and benign manner but also have the initiative of strategic competition in hands. . . . How to control the Sino-US relationship and properly solve the Sino-US contradiction is an unprecedented task testing the wisdom of the statesmen and the strategists of both countries.[1]

Strategic competitor has been adopted by both China and the US as reference to this next stage in a globalized world, and the outcomes will heavily depend on our respective visions and strategies. On a deeper level, it may be thought of as an ideological struggle to be decided by economic competition. Ideology takes the form of the most attractive governance system, either democratic or techno-authoritarianism.

The old Chinese idiom of one mountain, two tigers is one of supremacy. As American enterprise forms the front line in the battle for the mountain, can the mountain accommodate two tigers?

The Chinese are known for their great wit, puns, and creative plays on words and use of symbolism. Throughout this journey, the symbolic actualization of concepts often referenced animals. In researching the tiger, an interesting analysis of the tiger's behavior as a parallel to business strategy was discovered, written by Ayyappa Nagubandi, about types of business leaders symbolized as animals. Nagubandi compared the entrepreneur to a tiger. Just like the tiger, they do not hunt in packs. Once they have identified the perfect strike, they practice patience, sneaking up and, once striking, hold the target's throat until it dies. The tiger and the astute entrepreneur are able to find opportunities and solutions before others.[2] As tigers are loners, they are seldom referenced with a unique name to designate their pack, but should you wander upon a pack, it would be referred to as an ambush.

China has only one formal alliance—with North Korea, called the Mutual Aid and Cooperation Friendship Treaty between the PRC and the Democratic People's Republic of Korea. Tsinghua University published a working paper to illustrate the two camps within China on their discourse of the pros and cons of formal alliances. China has had a strategy of no alliances since the early 1980s. Pro-alliance scholars argue that the US's current alliances throughout East

Asia could jeopardize China's security interests and contain China's rise, and they should therefore seek to create a formal alliance with Russia. The scholars who have traditionally guided China's foreign policy of non-alliance believe it will erode principles of self-reliance and independence. The paper concludes a belief that the going forward strategy, without significant internal or external security threats, China will continue to develop various versions of quasi-alliances and create unique entanglements to pull in partners.[3]

If a formal alliance requires mutual military defense in service of national threat, a more lucrative benefit can be derived by economic entanglement resulting from China's Belt and Road Initiative. Through this initiative China created financial obligations with mainly developing countries to provide needed infrastructure. The cumulative investment in this program since 2013 is estimated at $1 trillion. Many of the recipient countries soon found that either by subpar construction or onerous repayment terms, they are indebted to China. The agreement struck becomes a new form of economic coercion, leading to a new era of one-way imperial tributary status without any of the benefits a formal alliance would provide.

The CCP exhibits a great deal of angst about the Western world seeking to contain and circumvent its rise in achieving the pinnacle of the Asian version of Maslow's hierarchy need of status—to be number one in the world. China sees an important defense against Western infiltration of its culture and ideology through a self-sufficient economy.

China's self-reliance economic strategy, as evidenced by Made in China 2025, served as a wake-up call to the Western world's industrial complex. Western eyes opened to the potential of a world divided, one in which China aligns other nations to its center and attempts to bifurcate the world. This division manifests through dissemination of techno-authoritarian governance models, new technology specifications, intellectual property rights, and ultimately the rules of the economic road.

XJT says, "Economy is the foundation of governance. As the foundation of national security, economic security is the material premise for military, political, social and scientific and technological security. If something goes wrong with economic security there will be the dangerous plight of 'devastating the foundation.' . . . Clausewitz had a wise opinion, 'War is the extension of politics by other means.' Then what is politics? Vladimir Lenin once said, 'Politics is the concentrated expression of economics.' Therefore, although war is the extension of politics by other means, economy is the root cause of wars."[4]

China's ultimate answer to the threat and how to alleviate it was articulated by Liu in *The China Dream*, who said champion nations are the strongest, most prosperous nations that are also able to set the tone of the times and therefore yield worldly influence. Liu saw China and the US squaring off in this race to the mountaintop. Liu believed this strategic competition would benefit the world by driving progress for all.[5]

What are the benefits accruing to the champion of this great competition? Liu said, "Champion nations are those that design the world. This design includes crafting the international power layout, establishing new codes of behavior for nation-states, new international institutions, a new world order, and new international systems. . . . Champion nations cause the world to reform itself in their image."[6]

Why after forty-years of reform and opening and integration into the global system should this be the time for China to assert itself? As the world enters the fourth industrial revolution, China cannot be left behind. If it is to achieve its objectives of creating new international systems and laws and holding key valuable intellectual property, hoisting it higher in the value-add chain, the time is now.

China's political elite's conventional wisdom says that the US is on the decline. Liu's *The China Dream* provided an analogy for China's thoughts on the US's prospects and democratic system.

Liu, in citing the book *1940: the Fall of France*, provided a cautionary tale due to the failure of political unity and national goals. Liu noted that France had a good, stable economy, but it lacked political unity. As France had no visionary leaders, as war began, there was no unity among the people to fight for the country. "Prior to the war, a German writer made a vitriolic remark about this: 'France is a standard dying people. It has no goal or value. Its people have lost their tradition, honor, and spirit. We should let it run its own course, without paying it any attention.'"[7]

Liu's *The China Dream* pointed to two key US weaknesses: time horizon and political vision. In the area of patience, the differences between long-term and short-term thinking are stark. The party has witnessed US MNCs acquiesce and turnover valuable intellectual property to Chinese joint ventures to meet the demands of Wall Street's quarterly profits vs China's state-owned enterprises that, while inefficient, benefit from long-term support through state capitalism.

Liu made a case that the US political and economic systems are not geared toward visionary, generation-spanning goals and the weakness they introduce to our ability to win the strategic competition. Liu argued that China's vertical democracy fits its history of a single ruler, and the advantage lies in the ability to create and follow through on long-term plans such as Made in China 2025, allowing China to forgo addressing short-term promises due to electoral pressures. Liu characterized the West as practicing horizontal democracy, giving rise to wasted campaign time and endless variations to solutions for current pressing problems and leading to confusion, division, and instability. Liu's bottom line: "The largest consumers of a nation's strategic resources are internal struggle and external conflict."[8] If we follow Liu's logic, this points to the political system he sees as having a competitive advantage.

In this battle for the mountain, China seeks to change the rules of competitive engagement between the tigers. In this modern era of great power competition, which has witnessed hot wars, China seeks to dethrone the champion through new rules. Liu summarized what he saw as geopolitical competition from the beginning of the twentieth century until now. First, hot wars like World Wars I and II, where "you die, I live"; second, the Cold War, where "you decline, I prosper." Third, "It will be more like a race: a 'you chase, I run' and 'you are second, I am first' model, in which both nations will continue to thrive and compete regardless of the outcome."[9] Liu wanted the rules of engagement to change from conventional war to great nation competition on an economic and ideological field.

Allowing China to establish the rules of engagement may initially provide it with a competitive advantage. Liu explained how China draws on millenniums of war experience to inform its decisions. Historically, brute force has been the secondary option after it exhausted tricks and conspiracy. Some of these tactics have included the buildup of military might to frighten opponents, marrying the opposition to foster assimilation, and using trade to enrich the opponent and create dependency. One strategy Liu said China advocates is "conquering the unyielding with the yielding."[10]

If patience is a grand strategy to preserve strength and resources, then allowing an opponent, whose house is divided and weary, to collapse upon itself, as the French did, may prove most profitable. Liu said, "However much foreign policy elites may ignore or deplore it, the United States lacks the domestic political base to create a unipolar world."[11]

China's strategy of leveraging another's strength is most apparent in American corporations' economic models. Throughout this book we have seen how US MNCs have yielded political pressure to foster US policies that made it easier for them to do business with China and to lobby for China's inclusion in international agreements on Chinese favorable terms.

Leverage, or as the Chinese think of it, "killing with a borrowed sword," shows up in their use of nationalism and produces pressure on corporations and governments to acquiesce and practice self-censorship, kowtowing to Chinese desires. The Chinese government leverages its own people to lock their pocketbooks in boycotting products and places. China has unique levers of access in galvanizing its populace to turn against products and more broadly against nations. It operates the most sophisticated propaganda machine ever devised, coupled with institutionalized education with a baseline of humiliation at the hands of foreigners and cultural traits that are based on the collective rather than individual, where affiliation and status are motivation. Boycotts are a very powerful weapon.

In 2018 a group of associate professors at Cornell University published "Commercial Casualties: Political Boycotts and International Disputes." The paper's purpose was to assess how disputes between countries can be used to encourage consumers to harm the opponent's economy by boycotting products or countries. The paper argued that consumer boycotts effectively become commercial weapons, and how the target product or nation reacts gives insight into how resolved it is to fight or fold. As international tensions flare, if a country can change consumer behavior to boycott, even though that consumer may have sunk costs and harbor emotional brand attachments, this reaction sends a powerful signal. Further, even if the consumer does not agree with the political message being sent, they may participate in the boycott because owning or using the product could carry negative social consequences. China is a collectivist society, where standing out is not socially desirable.[12]

Chinese consumer boycotts have been very effective. Demonstrated within these pages are MNCs undertaking self-rectifications, apologies for hurting the feelings of the people, and contorting themselves to be embraced by the Chinese consumer.

For decades Michael Pillsbury was a well-known China dove or "panda hugger." His thinking changed in the mid-2000s, and today he is considered a stringent China hawk or "dragon slayer." In 2015, Pillsbury published *The Hundred-Year Marathon, China's Secret Strategy to Replace America as the Global Superpower*. In his book he outlined how China reaches back through its centuries of warfare to create and utilize what became the thirty-six stratagems, and they are still studied and applied today. He called out America's willful blindness and hubris in understanding who China really is, what it wants, and how it intends to get it. "For four decades now, my colleagues and I believed that 'engagement' with the Chinese would induce China to cooperate with the West on a wide range of policy problems. It hasn't. . . . [I]n our hubris, Americans love to believe that the aspiration of every other country is to be just like the United States."[13]

The dangers to America portrayed by Pillsbury and many other China hawks infiltrated and supported the policy moves and rhetoric espoused by the Trump Administration, furthering a war of words, the trade war, and bipartisan reaction in US domestic politics.

China's response has given us a clearer window into its true intentions. China's more aggressive stance in rhetoric through wolf-warrior diplomacy, reciprocal tariffs, and internal agitation propaganda has prompted many of its people to turn against the US and its corporations.

Following Trump, President Biden struck a similar tone in acknowledging our misreading of China's long-term trajectory but a dissimilar stance in the path forward. Biden's National Security Council advisor Jake Sullivan and Kurt Campbell, Indo-Pacific coordinator, penned for *Foreign Affairs* "Competition Without Catastrophe." Sullivan and Campbell echoed Pillsbury's thoughts on the failure of our collective wisdom in believing engagement with China would over time bring changes to China's administration of political and economic theory. However, they warned for the US to not make the same mistake by assuming that competition will in some way change the long-term trajectory of China's behavior. Their recommendation was "to achieve not a definitive end state akin to the Cold War's ultimate conclusion but a steady state of clear-eyed coexistence on terms favorable to US interest and values."[14]

As American enterprise seeks to "derisk" its supply chains and Wall Street moves to a risk-off stance for investments in China, realities of geopolitics and the strategic competitive race are well underway. Ryan Hass's *Stronger* book acknowledges not only the truth of our competition but also the layer of interdependence now embedded from our decades of economic ties. Hass noted that breaking free of the interdependence would incur prohibitive costs, and this competition is here for the foreseeable future. As Liu noted, the strategic competition was between only our two nations, Hass explained why. Our respective nations are currently and expected to remain far ahead of others in wealth, power, and prestige. Further, neither country can afford or risk trying to impose its will on the other. Hass saw us "at sharp odds with each other on fundamental issues, ranging from the balance between social stability vs individual liberties to the role of the state in the economy and the distribution of power in the international system."[15]

To be the tiger has been the goal of China's current regime. Helmed by Xi, it has rewritten the mindset of the populous. The reform and opening that we misread by framing the English words with our subjective connotations, and our steadfast belief that the arc of history would bend China to a more Westernized political and economic system, point to our folly in not really knowing who China is.

Under Mao's leadership, what we failed or were not allowed to see was the destruction of a way of life in China and the whipsaw changes that resulted from the economic reforms that Deng undertook in his race to modernize and lift people into a more prosperous life. The monumental changes to the people's means of livelihood shifted like loose sands through their fingers. The change's most vivid metaphor is the breaking of the iron rice bowl. The cradle-to-grave stewardship of Chinese lives by the party disappeared and with it the perceived equality for all their needs, including the social safety nets of health, education, lifetime employment, and pensions.

What Americans have seen is the astounding economic success, witnessed by the minting of hundreds of billionaires, unrivaled infrastructure, and a burgeoning middle class with an insatiable demand for the world's finest, representing 30 percent of luxury goods consumption. Americans saw this as the proof that our government and corporations had sold us out. We lost our jobs, our innovative edge, and US students' Ivy League seats to something called state capitalism that officially calls itself communist.

We did not see the millions of workers in China who lost their jobs or the millions of children who were left behind with relatives as the young parents made their way to urban areas for work. We did not see the ramifications of the psychic toll that to be rich is glorious in a country so vast that making the pie larger brought untold environmental toxicity and labor abuses.

Just as America's 1 percent create disdain yet are lauded as influencers, the Chinese feel the same way, questioning the riches of some yet following their key opinion leaders' every move. It is in this milieu that we see a rise in neo-Maoism. The party has wrapped itself in the red flag and embraces Mao Zedong's tactics to control the masses. The CPC is writing a new page, four-cornered by state-owned-enterprise, national champions housed within Made in China 2025, nationalist unity and patriotism housed under the banner of the Chinese Dream, and their desire for the world to applaud their theory of governance as testament to their superiority over the imperialists.

XJT outlines the six contradictions that the paramount leader Xi Jinping must solve. While the resolutions are vastly important, they are considered wicked problems. Beginning with the Chinese Dream through the public proclamations of XJT and Xi's declaration of an open-reign, China was on its front foot. As 2023 ended, China seemed to be on its back foot. During this time many impediments to contradiction resolution arose. US corporations woke up to their folly of Chinese dependence for revenue and production, exacerbated by the global pandemic emanating from China. There is quiet unrest among the Chinese people, who too experienced stability-shaking effects from the pandemic. They suffer from meaning-of-life questions and trust deficits. Their stores of wealth, mainly in property, turned into a mirage, unemployment skyrocketed, and their birth rate plummeted to a level not seen since the Great Famine that left millions of Mao's people dead.

China's leadership realizes it is in a precarious position. Its bellicose rhetoric has somewhat receded. At the 2024 Davos meeting, Reuters reported on Chinese premier Li Qiang speech where he said that China was open for business, open to foreign investment, and all should lower their barriers to trade, welcome competition, and take on the challenges the globe faces.[16] When President Biden and President Xi met face to face in November 2023 in California, as reported by *The Guardian*, Biden began his speech by acknowledging there was great tension between the nations but that we must guard against allowing this to lead to conflict. Xi responded that our nations must not turn our backs to one another. Xi seemed to be for the moment trying to strike a more conciliatory tone by stating, "Planet Earth is big enough for the two countries to succeed, and one country's success is an opportunity for the other."[17] Did Xi's reference of the planet being big enough for two superpowers mean China would settle for a bipolar world? Or once it regains its footing, will we be back to a race for the mountaintop and a unipolar world?

American enterprise has formed the front line in this strategic competition, but now a grand American strategy is needed to meet China's challenges, a strategy that can rise above our internal division and carry forward in a bipartisan way, spanning changes in presidential leadership.

An understanding of the competition the US faces is needed down to the American household level. We are entering a new industrial revolution, and if we are to weather it, we cannot be Luddites. When Joe Biden entered the White House, he installed a moon rock that was collected from the US moon landing in 1972. His thinking regarding the symbolism was to remind us of the ambition and accomplishments of the US and the power that results when we ask Americans to reach beyond themselves. Today the American Dream needs a reboot. We need great states people to articulate a grand vision, tell a great story, and mobilize a nation to rise to the competition. American enterprise will remain on the front line of the race for the mountaintop. A continuous learning stance about a complex and rapidly changing China will be paramount for our success, and a supportive, insightful, long-term US government-led strategy will be critical to get off the blocks. The starting gun has already been fired.

Summary

The US and China have reached a tipping point in our relationship. As both nations seek to be the leaders in the fourth industrial revolution that revolves around trade, technology, investment, and information, American enterprise has been drawn to the front line of this strategic competition. This competition includes more than economic supremacy; the background is ideological. Will the leader of the twenty-first century be the US, with capitalism and democracy at its core, or will it be China's vision utilizing state capitalism and digital authoritarianism?

Globalization has led to interdependency between nations as commerce sought efficiencies and cost reductions. However, in maintaining much leverage in key inputs of materials and manufacturing capacity, China was allowed to weaponize interdependence, awakening American enterprise to reduce and derisk this dependency. In this competition a new type of battle tactic emerged—economic coercion. Driven by the power and desire to obtain the Chinese yuan, American enterprise became complicit in Chinese demands and now faces new struggles to protect its markets and brands.

China's opacity in words and deeds as well as the West's belief that its embrace would lead China to operate differently has shown a light on how little we really know and understand the People's Republic of China.

Since the Chinese Communist Party's founding in 1921, China has seen three transformative leaders rise and shape China. Mao Zedong pulled the people together and marched them through life-changing campaigns. Millions died under his watch, and when he finished, the people were deemed sufficiently communists, but they were morally broken. Trust, meaning-of-life questions, and centuries of traditions and values that had held them together disappeared. Deng Xiaoping kept the country together but relied on economic incentives via reform and opening to pull the people into the twentieth century and modernity. His policies to achieve this left many critical issues China now faces.

Xi Jinping took the leadership mantle with a vision to obtain what all previous leaders had wanted: a respected, great nation, subservient to no one. He also inherited major contradictions within society that resulted from Mao's and Deng's leadership decisions. These contradictions have no easy answers and will be long and challenging.

Throughout this book, the steps China took to rectify the contradictions have had ramifications for US MNCs. You should be able to rip US news media headlines and tie them back to one of Xi's six stated contradictions.

1. Rectifying environmental issues: China found a way to unite and tie innovation and self-sufficiency to its plan known as Made in China 2025. The goals articulated in the plan go to the heart of the fourth industrial revolution.

2. Creating common prosperity, an original goal of socialism is proving very difficult. The positive economic changes for some resulting from reform and opening also left many behind, and wealth spread unevenly across the country with coastal regions benefitting from SEZs and interior provinces lagging. Managing migration and *hukou* status leaves many financially focused on covering basic needs. The issues were compounded by a near three-year

shutdown of the economy resulting from the pandemic and the ensuing high unemployment.

3. Issues of graft and corruption ensnared many high- and low-level officials and entrepreneurs. This ongoing campaign will serve to quell the masses' anger and allow the CCP to control and purge at will.

4. The demographic cliff and imbalance in gender will be ongoing as imploring the people to have more children is bumping up against a more developed nation mentality that weighs the trade-offs of career limits and financial burdens.

5. The facture of traditional values and spiritual yearning to accompany material gain, coupled with an incomplete and less than desired formal legal system, have led the CCP to attempt to inculcate sanctioned core values and to co-opt historical Confucian philosophy. The desired outcome is to create a self-regulating society that finds their decisions and actions subject to a techno-authoritarian system administered through a still-forming social credit system.

6. China saves its last contradiction for the strategic race of twenty-first-century dominance against the US. China seeks to mold this competition to its benefit and proclaims it does not seek physical war but a race in technological breakthroughs and ideological governance models.

China, recognizing it could no longer reach its goals simply operating as the world's factory floor, will need bold moves and face disruptive forces within. The people will have to push through the third industrial revolution and embrace innovation to reach the fourth.

As the CCP works to change mindsets internally, it has also sought to export infrastructure projects like ports, rail and manufacturing facilities, technology like mobile phones, surveillance equipment, and digital currency payment systems as well as governance models to developed and developing nations via their Belt and Road Initiative. Hence the statement that should MNCs search for new markets and outsourced production, they may find their Chinese competitors already there.

Armed with the six contradictions and the eight Ps—People, Party, Politics, Policy, Patriotism, Propaganda, Philosophy, Pandemic—my goal was to assist with some understanding of a fascinating country. As you venture forth in this economic competition, you will be a step ahead of the many barriers and pitfalls MNCs have experienced to date.

As a former corporate executive who worked both internationally and domestically, I understand the value of your time. My desire was to provide value-added knowledge. Your review of this book on whatever platform you purchased it would be most appreciated.

APPENDIX

Ford's Folly: A Cautionary Tail-Pipe

China made literal moonshot history by landing on the dark side of the moon in 2019. However, it is China's figurative moonshot of dominating new energy vehicles that may prove the success of the Made in China 2025 plan and support the country's drive for self-sufficiency.

The New York Times opinion columnist Thomas Friedman penned in 2010 "Their Moon Shot and Ours" five years before China officially disclosed Made in China 2025. Friedman's thoughts concerned China's designs on the auto industry.

> China is doing moon shots. Yes, that's plural. When I say "moon shots" I mean big, multibillion-dollar, 25-year-horizon, game-changing investments. . . . Beijing just announced that it was providing $15 billion in seed money for the country's leading auto and battery companies to create an electric car industry. . . . In essence, China Inc., . . . [plans] to move China off oil and into the next industrial growth engine: electric cars."[1] Friedman deducts from an interview with Shai Agassi the C.E.O. of Better Place, that there are three reasons the electric car industry is critical. "First, the auto industry was the foundation for America's manufacturing middle class. Second,

the country that replaces gasoline-powered vehicles with electric-powered vehicles—in an age
of steadily rising oil prices and steadily falling
battery prices—will have a huge cost advantage
and independence from imported oil. Third,
electric cars are full of power electronics and
software. Think of the applications industry that
will be spun out from electric cars,' says Agassi.[2]

Agassi's observation that the auto industry was a back-
bone in supporting a middle class was also recognized by
one enterprising Chinese businessman, Cao Dewang, CEO of
Fuyao Glass. In 2019 Fuyao Glass and its CEO were chroni-
cled in the Netflix film *American Factory*. Cao had purchased a
defunct auto supplier manufacturing plant in Dayton, Ohio.
The film focused on the disconnect between American and
Chinese coworkers as Cao retooled the plant to manufacture
auto glass and the resultant clash between the two culture's
work styles, expected pay, and general lack of understanding,
respect, and trust.

Not in the movie but relevant to the importance of the auto
industry is fostering far-ranging positive social and economic
assets, noted by Cao in a print interview. In the American tradition of pulling oneself up by the bootstraps, Cao had come
from a wealthy family only to see it all lost during the Chinese
Civil War. At age fourteen, leaving school to herd cattle, he set
his sights on regaining what had been lost. He created a glass
company that served China's domestic auto market, then he
discovered the opportunities of doing the same in the US for
the American auto industry. His reasoning for entering the US
was based on an analysis of the benefits: lower tax burdens,
lower labor costs once mandatory Chinese insurance payments were deducted, lower energy costs, and no shipping
necessary. But it was his trip to America in 1990 to ascertain

how he would construct his business that cut to the heart of the auto industry's social and economic power. Cao's US host took him to the Ford Motor Museum. He related his insights:

> Figuring out that this museum represents America's industrial history, I realized just how large the industrial and economic gap between the US and China really is. . . . Upon visiting the museum, I got the sense that the Chinese economy was 100 years behind America's. In 1900, the proportion of the US population working in agriculture was 60 percent, a similar percentage to that of China's in the 1990s. In the Ford Motor Museum, I saw that traditional industry was leading the way at that time. Steel, PPG glass, and home appliance glass all emerged during this period, and even today they are not obsolete. In times of economic change, traditional industries are required to provide building materials.[3]

There may be no other entrenched industry experiencing the level of complete economic disruption as the one faced by the American automobile industry. This hundred-plus-year-old industry is moving from a symbol of American freedom, individual self-expression, and fit for utility to potentially nothing more than a commodity fit for serving human mobility.

The speed and nature of change to the fundamental mechanics of what an automobile is continue to pull into its ecosystem disparate technologies, companies, and governmental policies and politics. We are seeing business models upended and traditional operations struggling to align portfolio product mixes, distribution channels, pricing and revenue stream strategies, and product uses.

Four main tranches are emerging to bucket how automakers must plan to move through this automobile transition: autonomous, connected, electric, and shared (ACES).

We have come a long way from the democratization of car ownership, attributed to Henry Ford and his success in mastering the assembly line during the second industrial revolution and his infamous quip, "You can have any car you like as long as it's black." The Chinese prescription may be "You can have any car you like as long as it meets our specifications."

Today, Bill Ford, Henry's great-grandson, is executive chairman of Ford Motor Company. In a 2014 interview with McKinsey & Co., a consultancy, he discussed the changing landscape and warned of what may come if Ford does not weather the transition:

> It used to be that the auto industry, and the car itself, were part of a self-contained ecosystem. If there were breakthroughs, they were developed within the industry. That's all been turned on its head; we now have disruption coming from every angle, from the potential ways we fuel our vehicles to the ownership model. The reality is that we will not own or develop, most of these technologies. So, we have to be a thoughtful integrator of other peoples' technologies and understand where we add value. Because if we're not careful, we could become like some mobile-handset makers, where all the value is added by someone else.[4]

China is the world's largest car market, selling nearly twenty-seven million vehicles in 2022. Historically, an American auto company has had two avenues for selling in the Chinese market: import the vehicle, subject to a 25 percent tariff, or establish a joint venture with a Chinese company that allows no more than a 50 percent equity stake and a transfer of technology to the manufacturing entity. In 1994, General Motors (GM) entered a joint venture with Shanghai Automotive Industry Corporation (SAIC). GM's Buick in China is a fascinating tale of a tarnished brand brought back to life. In America, Buick had become the symbol of an old person's car. This legacy had dogged the company since the 1980s, and its awareness of this negative connotation led it to restyle and attempt an American repositioning as a young, cool car. Buick's commercials acknowledged the throwback image by including grandmas riding along and expressing dismay at how it was no longer the Buick of their day.

In China Buick found a unique asset, and it picked up on an important Chinese brand attribute: the history or back-story of a brand. Fortuitously, there were two important historical Chinese figures associated with Buick.

China's last imperial ruler, Emperor Pu Yi, preferred Buicks. Sun Yat-sen, much more broadly acceptable and considered the founder of modern China, was a Buick man. In seeking regulatory permission in 1997 to open a Buick plant in Shanghai, GM leaned heavily on the Sun Yat-Sen association and carried it through to its in-market identity. The back-story of how Sun became a Buick man is a reminder to Ford of missed opportunities. In 2013 Ford Motor released correspondence from 1924 between Sun and Henry Ford. Sun's request was for Ford to create an industrial empire in China larger than its American counterpart. "But an assistant in Mr. Ford's office sent Dr. Sun a terse rejection, acknowledging receipt of the invitation but saying, 'We desire to advise, however, that Mr. Ford has made no plans for visiting China in the very near future.'"[5]

However, Ford Motor Company did follow GM in 2001, establishing a joint venture with Changan Automobile Group

Company. Joseph White, in *The Wall Street Journal*, succinctly explained both companies' thinking: "For the Chinese government, using joint ventures to develop competitive Chinese auto makers is a cornerstone of industrial policy and generates lots of cash besides. Of course, the global manufacturers will keep on investing in China regardless of the debate, and content themselves that half a loaf is better than none, especially when the loaf is so very, very big."[6]

Today the loaf may be big, but it's beginning to be sliced like finger sandwiches. So is Bill Ford's family dynasty poised to ensure its does not become the analogous mobile-handset shell, allowing others to ride to profits during this period of massive disruption?

Vision, strategy, and management play a key role, even before Bill Ford's "thoughtful" integration of partners is considered. Since the recession of 2008, Ford has pursued several strategic paths and been led by several senior executives.

In 2006 Bill Ford chose Alan Mulally, former president and CEO of Boeing Commercial Aircraft, to lead Ford Motors. Mulally inherited a portfolio of ninety-four unique name plates being manufactured around the world. Bryce Hoffman wrote in *Forbes*: "Ford had created this mammoth product portfolio out of desperation. When one product failed to achieve the desired increase in sales in a particular segment, Ford introduced another one. But it often kept producing the original model out of fear of losing existing customers and the market share they represented."[7]

Mulally used the same strategy he had executed at Boeing for a turnaround: streamline the product offering and create a best in class for each major market segment. The plan was known as One Ford, and it was a modern-day version of black. Reduce the complexity to gain efficiencies. One brand that did not survive the One Ford plan was Mercury, of the Lincoln-Mercury division. Mercury was positioned as the midpoint between the Ford line and the luxury line of Lincoln, with its counterpart in GM being the Buick, which sat between the Chevrolet and the Cadillac.

Waiting in the wings, while working closely with Mulally as his number two, was Mark Fields, a Ford employee since 1989. After Mulally's retirement in 2014, he assumed the role of CEO. Mark Fields was relieved of his post in May 2017. Bill Ford said of Fields's departure, "This is a time of unprecedented change. A time of great change requires a transformational leader."[8]

In the decade that Fields held key decision-making authority, he seemed to struggle with one foot in the core business and one foot in the future. To prepare for the future paradigm shift of mobility, Fields hired Jim Hackett in March 2016 to run the Ford Smart Mobility subsidiary that was formed to design, build, and grow emerging mobility services. Hackett ascended to CEO with Fields's departure.

Missteps seemed to come from divergent challenges. Significant investments were made in ACES technology through partnerships and acquisitions. Yet GM remained ahead in autonomous vehicles and ridesharing tie-ups.

As the Chinese market became the clear driver of demand, the streamlined One Ford plan hurt its China product mix. Ford found itself without the traditional marketing pull-through strategy of good, better, best in the auto lineup. Nowhere had the pure play idea of good, better, best in positioning and pricing held sway in the American marketplace like the automobile. In the 1960s and 70s heyday of US autos, you were either a Ford or a Chevy family. Climbing the success ladder meant progressing through an entry-level Ford to a Mercury to a Lincoln, or a Chevrolet, to a Buick/ Oldsmobile to a Cadillac. I came from a Ford family. At birth, coming home from the hospital in a Ford, matriculating to a Mercury, and learned to drive on a used but classic, 1965

Lincoln Continental with suicide doors—aka the tank—getting about ten miles to the gallon.

The sheer size and opportunity of China's auto demand makes paramount the holding and growing of market share, as China's sales accounted for 31 percent of global sales by mid-2023. While both Ford and Chevy had been achieving year over year growth, they achieved peak total Chinese market share between 2016 and 2017. The Chinese consumer was changing, and the realities of the marketplace, driven by the Chinese government, were too.

In 2017 a McKinsey survey led to projections that by 2022, 50 percent of sales in China would be SUVs and premium brands would increase at a 10.5 percent compound annual growth rate vs nonpremium at 4.1 percent. While Chinese domestic brands were big winners in the SUV segment, international brands held court in the premium segment. In the lower price tier, Chinese domestic brands captured 89 percent and by 2016 had 48 percent of the total SUV market. This segment's explosive growth led to a plethora of Chinese domestic SUV models being introduced, and pricing and margins fell substantially. The domestic auto industry's behavior was exhibiting what had been seen in many emerging Chinese owned industries—a chase to produce cheap, undifferentiated products.

Some domestic players were attempting to fight their way out of this race to the bottom and introduce more premium SUVs, and they were running into well-established international internal combustion engine brands. McKinsey found in 2017 that only 8 percent of consumers believed that domestic brands were aspirational.[9]

China's vehicle ownership in 2022 had reached 415 million out of a population of 1.4 billion. Brand loyalty, as American marketers typically think of it, is not yet as solidified across consumer goods in China. McKinsey's survey showed that about 70 percent were first time auto buyers, and of these about 30 percent purchased premium brands.[10] The race for the first-time buyer was still on. The good, better, best pull-through strategy had been the most efficient for generating brand loyalty and maximizing profits.

The growing importance of China's upwardly mobile middle class had left Ford with two gaps in its product mix. By eliminating the Mercury, Ford could not compete with GM's Buick, and Cadillac had established a foothold, but Lincoln was not there.

Under the One Ford plan, CEO Mulally had planned to kill the Lincoln brand, but Mark Fields saved it. He recognized that without Lincoln, Ford would be the only major global manufacturer without a premium brand. In a 2016 interview, Fields explained why Lincoln had to stay. While globally premium autos comprise only 9 percent of total sales, they contribute about 35 percent of total profits.[11]

In 2014 Ford officially introduced the Lincoln brand to China via imports, subject to 25 percent tariffs. The press release stated that for Chinese luxury brand sales, it would develop relationships with these consumers as opposed to transactional sales, and its design would be specifically targeted to these consumers.[12] Ford had identified several pain points in the traditional sales and service model and believed its "Lincoln Way" would address these.

In 2016 Ford said its Lincoln offerings would include a midsize luxury sedan, a small luxury utility vehicle, a midsize luxury SUV, a full-size luxury sedan, and a large luxury SUV. It appointed Amy Marentic as president of Lincoln, China.

Marentic had made a career at Ford, working in everything from engineering to product marketing, but she wanted a new challenge and asked for the China assignment, admitting she had never been there, knew little about the country, and did not speak Mandarin. In a 2017 interview, she shared insights on the consumer profile and Ford's marketing strategy. "About 64 percent of the luxury buyers are in a 'family life stage,' vs fewer than 20 percent in the US, Marentic said. Average luxury customers in China are in their mid-30s. And, unlike the US, a lot of first-time car buyers choose luxury vehicles. Chinese families often prefer cars and SUVs that can hold children, parents and grandparents at once. Car buyers frequently climb into back seats before getting behind the wheel."[13] Her observation on the importance of the rear seat holds true across all premium providers due to the 4-2-1 family unit, (that of four grandparents, two parents, one child) and the frequent use of private chauffeurs.

For China, Marentic said, "We have a clean slate where we can try things to see what works. We have a great heritage. When people in China think Lincoln, they think of JFK, Elvis, Marilyn Monroe and weddings. The Chinese consumer will tell you heritage is important, but the product has to deliver. It's ultracompetitive."[14]

Lincoln's challenges were coming from not only other premium automakers but also policies China was enacting. The invisible hand of the market met the visible hand of the government. In September 2017 the Chinese government, via Chinese Ministry of Industry and Information Technology, signaled the coming demise of the internal combustion engine. While the timeline on the ultimate ban was not given, nearer-term goals on auto efficiency and pollution control, including a cap-and-trade scheme, were set for 2030.

Echoing the realities Friedman had found in why US automakers acquiesced with noncontrolling joint ventures, the enormity of China's loaf of bread is just too big to ignore. Per *The Economist*: "William Russo of China's Gao Feng Advisory, a consultancy who was previously a senior executive at Chrysler, says China is simply far too big to lose out on. 'If China says no more fossil-fuel powered cars, global carmakers must follow.'"[15]

The power of the government to create regulations, such as dampening demand in congested tier-one cities by creating license tag lotteries to drive a car, coupled with state capitalism to build domestic champions, cannot be dismissed. *The Economist* said, "Western firms are not going to get things their own way, however. China's government is getting better at boosting its own EV manufactures after years of giving out ill-considered subsidies and setting unrealistic sales targets. Local manufacturers have not been able to match the quality and innovation of petrol-fueled cars produced by Western rivals. But China has advantages when it comes to electrification and connected cars. It has many inventive internet companies, is home to some of the world's biggest battery producers and is the center of electronics manufacturing."[16]

In 2018, as the American political machine was dismantling polices established to push fuel mileage standards upward, there was an unexpected pushback from American companies with sunk costs from the previously required investment and innovation to meet the US laws. The benefits of pushing an industry through policy to innovate may not have been lost on China, especially in the auto sector. Summarizing the value-add ecosystem that has sprung from decades of tightening US auto emissions, Greg Dotson, assistant professor of law at the University of Oregon and former senior energy congressional staffer, said, "I have learned that well-designed environmental standards can spur innovation and give our domestic companies a 'first-mover advantage.'"[17] Dotson cited suppliers' belief that reducing standards "could strand current investments and jeopardize new investments in domestic manufacturing of clean car technologies."[18] To support Dotson's statement, manufacturers listed the job growth that resulted from compliance and the more than $3 billion invested in the calendar year of 2017. The bottom line: "Under this virtuous cycle, the US leads with tougher standards that drive research, technology development, commercialization and manufacturing. That technology is then sold to the world. China, however, is leap-frogging the US policy. . . . It helps Chinese industry capture domestic market share while establishing Chinese automakers as global leaders in the technology; it also develops their domestic battery-making sector."[19]

Of strategic note, not only has China learned how to leverage its policies to support Made in China 2025 self-reliance objectives, but also it has steered its industries in going out to secure critical inputs to achieve those goals. As *The Economist* reported with rare-earth minerals: "Four-fifths of the cobalt sulphates and oxides used to make the all-important cathodes for lithium-ion batteries are refined in China."[20] About half the world's cobalt reserves and production come from the Democratic Republic of Congo. *The Economist* stated, "Concerns about China's grip on Congo's cobalt production deepened when GEM, a Chinese battery maker, said it would acquire a third of the cobalt shipped by Glencore, the world's biggest producer of the metal, between 2018 and 2020—equivalent to almost half of the world's 110,000-tonne production in 2017."[21]

By April 2017, Ford's stock price under Mark Fields had fallen more than 40 percent. Fields made one of his last appearances as CEO in Shanghai, stating, "The time is right for Ford to expand our EV lineup and investments in China."[22] To address the diverse needs of consumers in China, including the growing demand for electric vehicles, Ford announced a comprehensive range of electrified solutions by 2025—hybrids, plug-in hybrids, and fully battery-powered electric vehicles. By then, 70 percent of all Ford name plates would contain electrified power train options, including the full range of name plates produced by Changan Ford.

To end 2017, Bill Ford and Ford's latest CEO, Jim Hackett, announced they would introduce fifty new vehicles in China over the next eight years. Fifteen of those would be battery electrics or plug-in hybrids. Further, by the end of 2019, in China, Lincoln would begin manufacturing its lineup featuring more than a dozen electric vehicles and eight new SUVs.

With Ford's sales declining in China, by early 2019, it introduced a product reboot—the Ford China 2.0 plan. Ford's China plan was to focus on Chinese consumer needs and desires. Design, engineering, and innovation would be in China for China. Tim Slatter, Ford's executive director for product development in China, said, "We have for a long time been very proud about global design, making sure there is a very recognizable design language for Ford, but the reality is, times have changed."[23]

In Ford's 2019 quest to turn things around, it was making other changes. In order to develop efficiencies, it attempted to import its American model of a national distribution services division by combining sales, marketing, distribution, and services across its two Chinese auto joint ventures, Changan and Jiangling. The immediate on-the-ground blowback caused rapid retreat. In an interview with China Ford's third chief in two years, Anning Chen, a familiar refrain was uttered: "I would say there was a lack of deep understanding on how relationships work in China."[24] At issue? Trust. The Reuters report stated, "Chinese automakers, often in 50-50 partnerships with foreign car makers, are reluctant to lose control over sales decisions, rarely willing to trust each other and loyal to local provinces that are fiercely competitive in their quest for economic growth and tax revenues from vehicle sales."[25] Reuters surmised Ford's China dilemma: "Ford has publicly pinned the blame on an aging model lineup but company officials familiar with the matter said the breakdown in relationships with its joint venture partners and dealers as well as missteps by previous management teams were the bigger factors at play."[26] But at its Michigan headquarters, Joe

Hinrichs, president of Ford Automotive, remained sanguine. The goal was profitability in China. "You can be a profitable business in China with a relatively low market share because of . . . the size of the market."[27]

Bill Ford had said that China was "at the heart of electric vehicle and SUV growth and the mobility movement."[28] The press release announcing Hackett as CEO had said, "The company will modernize using new tools and techniques to unleash innovation, speed decision making and improve efficiency. This includes increasingly leveraging big data, artificial intelligence, advanced robotics, 3D printing and more."[29] These technologies are at the heart of Made in China 2025—Ford's transition to electric vehicles in China will be the beginning of the transformation it must manage, as predicted by Bill Ford in 2014. The disruption of ACES will take Bill Ford back to his original concern: Would Ford be a shell for others' technology, or would it remain in the driver's seat?

Friedman closed his 2010 op-ed stating that if the US adopted similar strategies as China, both countries could achieve a win-win but if only China took the necessary steps, "the industry will gravitate there."[30]

As 2023 ended, it was clear that the electric vehicle industry had gravitated to China. China emerged from a three-year pandemic-induced blackout that kept the world's prying eyes from the progress Chinese companies had made in auto electrification. From the dominance of battery manufacturing, rare-earth mineral monopolies to create them, original brands, and the features customers wanted in their next means of mobility, the world's automakers had a rude awakening.

The Chinese Communist Party and every layer of government had thrown their weight behind a key Made in China 2025 goal: the dominance of electrification. What had begun in 2010 with $15 billion government-provided seed money had ballooned to a cumulative $130 billion by 2023, as estimated by the Center for Strategic and International Studies. The support came from industrial policy, protectionism, provincial government land subsidies, rare earth mining and refining, a massive buildout of charging stations, tax breaks, and a proliferation of Chinese electric vehicle startups whose animal spirits had been awakened by Tesla and the simplicity of building electric vs combustion engine.[31]

By the end of 2023, China was flooding the world's market with inexpensive electric and combustion engine vehicles, displacing Japan as the world's largest exporter.[32] With legacy unused internal combustion engine factory capacity, China kept workers churning out inexpensive autos for export and frantically building car-carrier ships to push them offshore. American Warren Buffett had backed China's BYD (Build Your Dreams), and it had become the number one seller in China, with Tesla in the number two position, while Ford sat at number seventeen.

Not only had China's electric vehicle industry reaped the benefits of industrial policy sunk costs, but also greenfield opportunities were being capitalized on. Brand legacy no longer carried over from the combustion engine to electric vehicle switch. China was building new, ground-up brands, defined by narrow, limited product lineups that were not product focused. Like tech companies they competed and understood it was about cockpit innovation and user-oriented features. The near monopoly of battery technology and manufacturing of this plug-and-drive resource made getting to market simpler and faster.

The world needed electric vehicles to meet developed nations' mandated emission standards and the developing world needed inexpensive electric vehicles. The big Chinese electric vehicle makers were building factories in Brazil, Europe, and Thailand to meet their needs.[33] As China was going out, Ford was coming home. The US government, through the Department of Energy, granted Ford a conditional loan to work jointly with SK On Co., a South Korean battery maker, to build two battery manufacturing plants in the US. In addition to the federal loan, the states of Tennessee and Kentucky provided multimillion-dollar incentives for plant construction in their states.

One core tenant of the Made in China 2025 plan was to develop and hold the intellectual property for new technologies. CATL, China's largest maker of electric vehicle batteries, had licensed its intellectual property to Ford to be used in a to-be-built, wholly owned Ford battery factory in Michigan. Congressional lawmakers began to question the veracity of CATL's supply chain running through Xinjiang, a western province in China, whose majority population is historically Muslim but had for many years been run as a high-surveillance, reeducation camp that included forced labor.

In September 2023 the Michigan plant construction was paused. Ford CEO Farly said Ford wanted to ensure it could competitively operate the plant.[34] Furthermore, to better compete, Ford would bring more of its supply chain in-house by securing contracts for rare-earth battery materials to support production of two million electric vehicles by 2026. It would simplify its electric vehicle lineup with less customization options and rely on outside partners for its in-cockpit software. It seemed that Bill Ford's articulated concern in 2014 of becoming the analogous mobile phone handset maker, allowing others to ride to profits, was also coming home.

Made in China 2025 is the driving strategy for China's self-sufficiency. Its value-add supply chain upgrading and its ability to develop protected intellectual property technology and standards provides an engine to power its people past the middle-income trap. It creates soft power externally regarding climate change and points internally to environmental leadership. E^2—doing good for the ecology—can be a wind-fall for economic advantage. The electric vehicle industry, and the associated ecosystem to support it, may be China's first win in its Made in China 2025 plan.

Hollywood Hijacked: The Politics of Art

In the world of entertainment, one man became known as "a dragon from head to tail." Wang Jianlin, in 2016, at age sixty-one, was the king of the world—or at least the Middle Kingdom. He was considered China's richest man, coming in at number eighteen on *Forbes*'s richest person list. By 2018 he had fallen to number thirty-six.

Wang's backstory embodies much of what we see repeated in the unprecedented minting of billionaires in China since 1978 and the fate that befalls these highflyers as the CCP's priorities change and the internal recognition of the CCP's international power increases.

Wang's cautionary tale demonstrates being on the wrong side of the CCP's changing priorities. His downfall was not presenting himself in an understated manner, witnessed by his many candid remarks to the press.

Wang was the son of a revolutionary hero who, following the founding of new China, rose through the CCP's ranks. Wang Jianlin was not shy about using or later referring to his political connections to receive special benefits. His father's access allowed him to enter the People's Liberation Army at age fifteen, and he remained there until the mid-1980s. From there he joined the local government in Dalian. Seizing the opportunity to ride the wave of economic reform, he took over a failing property development. His knack for property development formed the basis of his fortune, and he named his conglomerate Dalian Wanda.

As his wealth mounted, he maintained close ties with the CCP, but his outspoken nature of the true reality of Chinese wealth and success was unusual. Wang was caught off guard when receiving an award in 2010. As reported by the UK *Telegraph*, the award presenter said, "I'm not sure everyone knows that Jianlin's father is a Red Army veteran. The Red Army wanted to subvert the rich entirely. Now his son has become the richest of people. . . . Does he detest you or like you?"[1] Wang, after listing the things he had done for his parents, said, "So later I asked my parents which is better: relying on the institution or relying on your son? They said it themselves: relying on their son was better. Although their goal in the past was to undermine the rich, now they wholly feel having money is better than not having it."[2]

In 2013 Wang made a realpolitik statement: "China is a government-oriented economy. No one can say he can run his business entirely without government connections. Anybody who says he or she can do things alone with [out] any connection with the government in China is a hypocrite."[3] A party man to the core, Wang tried to hold on to his empire by using it to serve CCP priorities. In 2012, as Xi was heavily pushing the building of Chinese soft power, Wang turned his funds toward the acquisition and sponsorship of soccer teams and events.

His gaze was also directed at Hollywood. Stating that Dalian Wanda would go abroad, "his ambition was to control 20 percent of the global film market by 2020."[4] In 2012 he bought AMC Entertainment Holdings for $2.6 billion. Per Lindsay Conner, an entertainment lawyer, "This deal satisfies Wanda's corporate goal and Wang's personal goal to be the No. 1 theater business in the US, as they are in China."[5] Wang continued to purchase other US theater chains, amassing a theater screen tally of over fifteen thousand in the US, nearly three thousand in Europe, and nearly five thousand in China.

Wang dug further into the vertical of the film industry. In 2013 he began constructing a "Chinese Hollywood" in Qingdao with an estimated price tag over $8 billion. The complex included twenty studios, an indoor amusement park, and a yacht club. For the groundbreaking ceremony, Wang co-opted Hollywood stars, including Leonardo DiCaprio and Nicole Kidman, to be in attendance.

In 2016 Wang purchased the US company Legendary Entertainment, a co-financier and producer of film and television, for $3.5 billion in cash. *The Economist* quoted Wang as saying, "There is no single company in the whole world that has a big-scale production base, and at the same time has screening and distribution channels. . . . Wanda Group is the first one in the world."[6]

The Economist looked at the state of the film industry in China, and in an interview with Yu Dong, head of a Chinese studio, he described it as, "In some ways China's movie industry resembles 1930s Hollywood, when studios controlled all business lines—from talent to production to theaters—before a 1948 Supreme Court ruling forced them to divest. In China this is called 'being a dragon from head to tail.'"[7] The referenced US Supreme Court decision came to be known as the Paramount decrees, which dismantled collusion among the major studies in areas of ticket price fixing, required distribution of competing studios' films into other studios' theater chains, and broke marketing and theater screen monopolies in certain geographic locations.

Wang's vocal inflammatory ambitions continued. In 2016, as Disney prepared to open Shanghai Disneyland, Dalian Wanda announced it would open a chain of theme parks across China. Wang stated, "Disney should not have come to China. . . . Shanghai has one Disney, while Wanda, across the nation, will open 15 to 20. . . . One tiger is no match for a pack of wolves."[8]

Amid all the bluster and Hollywood attention-getting acquisitions, the real issues confronting the film industry were coming into focus. While the American film industry has reached maturation, the Chinese film industry is in its relative infancy. PricewaterhouseCoopers (PwC) projected that China's box office would reach $15 billion by 2020 (figure 6).

Figure 6: China-US Box Office, 2011–2019

China's growth was coming not only from domestic production but also a frenzy of cinema screen construction, with an estimated twenty-six screens added daily in 2017, and by 2018 the country had amassed more than sixty thousand total screens.

With China set to become the world's largest box office and increasingly a lifeblood for Hollywood, long-term issues moved to the fore. In 2015 the US-China Economic and Security Review Commission published "Directed by Hollywood, Edited by China: How China's Censorship and Influence Affect Films Worldwide." The 2017 abstract stated that the WTO found China in violation of the import of foreign films. Further, "Hollywood relies on China's film market for revenue, but the process to get films into China is arduous due to strict and opaque regulation of film imports. China's regulations and processes for approving foreign films reflect the CCP's position that art, including film, is a method of social control. As a result of these regulations, Hollywood filmmakers are required to cut out any scenes, dialogue, and themes that may be perceived as a slight to the Chinese government. With an eye toward distribution in China, American filmmakers increasingly edit films in anticipation of Chinese censors' many potential sensitivities."[9]

After appeals, China lost the WTO case and was required to comply by March 2011. Their failure to do so led to a memorandum of understanding between the US and China in February 2012, requiring China to increase importation of foreign films and revenue sharing. This memo stipulated a minimum of thirty-four revenue sharing films and 25 percent of box-office receipts, up from twenty films and a 13 percent revenue share. It is important to note that these thirty-four films are not guaranteed to be American but simply foreign.

There had been two tracks for Hollywood films to compete for the thirty-four annual slots: distribute for a flat fee or take a 25 percent revenue share, or coproduce with a Chinese company outside of the thirty-four minimum film floor, requiring at least partial production in China to receive a fixed 50 percent total box office share. The memorandum of understanding expired in 2017, and as of early 2021, no new agreement had been reached to assure any US film would be exhibited.

In America, the film industry has often been a mirror of

American culture. From its aspirational golden age of glamour, the dark days of McCarthyism and blacklisting of actors as Communist sympathizers, its favorable and unfavorable depictions of war, and in contemporary times the uniquely US values of individualism and diversity.

In China the government holds Chinese movie business power. Per *The Hollywood Reporter*: "It wants people to see films that will inculcate Chinese values and culture. And it wants them to go voluntarily: the party used to force people to watch propaganda films."[10]

Xi's Chinese Dream is not to be infiltrated by the attributes of the American Dream. Film, as a form of art, is a pillar in the dream's construction. Speaking at an entertainment and arts symposium in October 2014, Xi said, "Art and culture . . . were indispensable to the Chinese dream of national rejuvenation."[11] Xi, quoted in *Global Times*, said, "Artists should not lose themselves in the tide of the market economy nor go astray while answering the question of 'whom to serve' . . . Socialist culture and art is, in essence, the culture and art of the people."[12] Xi continued with a directive of what the creative output should accomplish: "disseminate contemporary Chinese values, embody traditional Chinese culture, reflect the Chinese people's aesthetic pursuits and are of intellectual, artistic, and exhibitory importance. Art should also have patriotism as its main theme and foster 'correct viewpoints' of history, nationality and culture."[13]

Much of the press's coverage of this speech found a resemblance to Mao's edicts regarding art in 1942 as recalled by *The Hollywood Reporter*: "There is in fact no such thing as art for art's sake, art that stands above classes, art that is detached from or independent of politics."[14] Xi had included in his 2014 remarks that artists must learn from the masses. To ensure that they did, *The Guardian* reported, "Scriptwriters, directors, broadcasters and anchors will also be sent to work and live for at least 30 days in ethnic minority and border areas, and areas that made major contributions to the country's victory in the revolutionary war."[15] Xi may have been a sent-down youth, learning from the masses, hauling manure, and sleeping on a *kang* bed, but today it is the creatives who must embed themselves among the proletariat and haul the water of the CCP.

As Xi continued to erect a wall against foreign influence and infiltration, another destabilizing risk was mounting. To support Chinese domestic companies going global, debt was accumulating at dangerous levels. The money escaping China's shores was not feeding the larger beast that had become the priority—those industries housed within Made in China 2025 that supported self-sufficiency and value-chain ascension.

Mr. Wang was in the wrong business, and *The Economist* recognized this in 2015, writing, "Designer suits, luxury yachts, extravagant parties: Mr. Wang risks coming across as too much the playboy in an increasingly Cromwellian China. He deserves credit for building a mighty business empire and certainly has much to celebrate. But as his ambition grows, investors may come to see his enviable contacts as a growing vulnerability. The son of a Communist guerrilla hero should know that from time to time the party suddenly and unexpectedly devours its own."[16]

The government deemed Wang's foreign buying patterns as irrational. Throughout 2017 and 2018, Wang's far-reaching empire was dismantled. A specialist on China, University of Southern California professor Stanley Rosen summarized the issues best to *Deadline*:

> They allowed Wang Jianlin to build a company using publicly owned land and then make it private for the betterment of the Chinese people. The problem was that he took the government's

money and then began funneling it outside the country, including the very public purchase of Legendary. . . . The first move (by the Chinese government) was to tell China's main bank to constrain him. . . . Wanda needs to stabilize and reduce their exposure to debt and speak much more softly in terms of such things as driving Disney out of China, buying a Hollywood studio to promote China's message to the world, etc. China is trying to present a benign image of a peaceful rise, But Wang Jianlin is making China seem aggressive and that China's rise will come at the expense of the US, at least in terms of cultural expansion.[17]

As of mid-2019, Wang's holdings in Legendary had been sold and 50 percent of his movie theater holdings divested.

Wang Jianlin had sought to serve the desires of the CCP when he proclaimed how he would use his US cinema screens to distribute Chinese movies to better tell China's story in service of Xi's directive for soft power. What was unforeseen in this strategy were changes in US-China relations. The power was shifting to China through a growing domestic box office compared to a plateau in the US. There was great improvement in the quality of Chinese films through production learning with US studio coproductions and most importantly the power of Chinese censorship and financing to hijack US productions in service of CCP propaganda. American studios would too carry the water for the CCP to reap the yuan.

US movie studios' acquiescence to the CCP's narrative edicts are mostly unnoticed by the American moviegoing public. However, China's influence on Hollywood films has implications for US free speech and the types of stories that will be told. This influence has far-reaching ramifications, as disclosed in a report by PEN America, a nonprofit organization whose objective is to protect free expression through all creative literature forms. PEN America's paper "Made in Hollywood Censored by Beijing" points out stories can affect change. "They can galvanize people. And they can speak truth to power. But not when they are censored, sanitized, or hijacked for a specific political purpose. And certainly not if they never get told in the first place."[18]

PEN America was sounding an alarm and pointing out that the current trajectory of China's political interference would only increase. "It is our hope that filmmakers and studios will take seriously the implications for how they respond to both overt and indirect influence from the Chinese government and choose to stand firmly in defense of creative freedom."[19] As PEN America asked the movie industry to stand in defense of creative freedom, there could be fewer clear-cut examples of American enterprise on the front line. But it is Hollywood's bottom line that is truly driving creative decisions. In a single decade, the growing financial heft of China's marketplace made it clear where filmed entertainment's center of gravity had shifted.

In the decade of shifting leverage from Hollywood studios to the CCP, several key elements appeared increasingly embedded. First, as film production costs continued to increase, cost recoupment and profit potential hinged further on Chinese box office receipts. As the big US studios sought to reduce sunk-cost risks and gain access to the Chinese market, coproductions with Chinese companies, both state-owned and private studios, offered financial burden sharing.

Second, with years of US companies and expats on the ground in China producing movies there, state-of-the-art storytelling and technical knowledge was increasing among the Chinese. How much longer would the Chinese industry really need US knowhow?

Third, with the memorandum of understanding expiring in 2017 and no formal agreement or enforceable recourse to get solely owned movies into Chinese theaters, how much longer could US studios expect to get any revenue out of the mainland?

Fourth, filmmakers want to see their work on the big screen. The 2020 pandemic may have altered the US cinema business forever. New distribution models were rolling out. Would the public ever return to the theater in a sustainable way?

Early in Xi's tenure, he made clear some of the objectives China has for its film industry. Movie control through censorship is an excellent way to service the Chinese axiom of "borrow a boat to go abroad" and achieve those objectives. Simply stated, get the US film industry to carry the Chinese message internationally. As relayed by PEN America, stories told through film can change hearts and minds. Films provide an excellent platform for nationalism, patriotism, and propaganda. Done cleverly, film offers the perfect vehicle for the pure definition of propaganda: one-way communication to eliminate dissent. It is designed to serve the sender and manipulate the receiver's response and behavior. Done properly, a propagandist message based on lies and deception can subconsciously seed ideas forcefully as opposed to its gentler cousin, public relations, which done honestly should rely on persuasion utilizing truth, facts, and two-way communication.

As Xi articulated what the art of cinema is expected to support, in 2018, the regulation of film censorship was moved from the State Administration of Press, Publication, Radio, Film and Television and put under the purview of the Publicity Department of the CCP, which had recently received a whitewashing and renamed from the Central Propaganda Department.

With the Publicity/Propaganda Department firmly in

service of the state, the industry becomes a ready vehicle to carry both nationalistic and patriotic messages in a more palatable manner to domestic audiences and internationally couched in a less suspect Trojan horse, that being the US studios' film banners. Xi's aim of soft power projection gets the patina of US soft power. His message control desires are satisfied through overt censorship and increasing self-censorship. And China can continue to avoid forced WTO rules of fair market access by allowing foreign coproduced movies screen time and in return keeps more of the revenue within Chinese coffers.

How successful has the Publicity/Propaganda Department been in achieving Xi's objectives? To date, mixed. First, let's look at two films that emanated from China, then we'll turn to two examples of Hollywood executive decisions before filming to increase odds for China screenings.

By year end 2020, China's top two box office Chinese-centric films were 2017's *Wolf Warrior II* and 2019's *The Wandering Earth*. The former had some US industry personnel participation; the latter was wholly Chinese.

The action-adventure picture *Wolf Warrior II* grossed $854 million in China and $5.9 million in North America. (The movie industry combines US and Canadian box office receipts.) While few Americans may have seen the movie, the term *wolf warrior* got a lot of media play during the Trump Administration. As the trade war accelerated in heated rhetoric, Chinese officials began labeling their own US facing discourse as Wolf Warrior diplomacy.

The movie is about a former Chinese special-forces operative who battles Western mercenaries (spoiler alert—he's an American) as the Wolf seeks to protect Chinese caught up in an African civil war. The tagline for the film was "Whoever offends China will be hunted down no matter how far away they are."

The film's success was attributed to Hollywood-caliber action matched with a story of unrestrained pride in China's national identity. Americans Joe and Anthony Russo, directors of Marvel's Captain America franchise, provided the Hollywood-style action. The Russos consulted and provided the stuntmen and recommended American actor Frank Grillo as the antagonist.

The movie made Frank Grillo a star in China. *The Hollywood Reporter* interviewed Grillo about his newfound Chinese fame, and his answers were giddy and very honest. Grillo said Joe Russo had recommended him, "And frankly, I was intrigued because it was Chinese. Everyone in Hollywood is trying to get into the Chinese market, or has tried and failed, or is already in co-productions. I think this is good business."[20] Asked why he thought the film had done so well in China, he said, "Not to be a jerky overblown actor guy, but I think it goes back to what we do as storytellers—how we continue legacies and pass on our history through storytelling. . . . People say this movie is nationalistic and it's propaganda—and in a sense, it is. But this pride in China is real, and the audience wants to believe that being Chinese means something special."[21] *The Hollywood Reporter*'s Patrick Brzeski noted that *Wolf Warrior II* had outperformed any Hollywood movie ever shown in China, and should US studios be concerned about their competitive edge? Grillo said, "What should really worry Hollywood is when the next iteration of Chinese films starts showing signs of crossing over. *Wolf Warrior II* is amazing, and it's done some business overseas, but it's mostly a Chinese film for China. When directors like Joe Russo, who understand story from a very global perspective, start working more and more with Chinese filmmakers, you'll start seeing Chinese films that connect with audiences all over Asia, Europe and South America—maybe even North America. That's what will break China out of the home market and make them a big threat to Hollywood's dominance."[22] And that is exactly what worries PEN America.

China's homegrown, big-budget sci-fi film *The Wandering Earth* showed no signs of crossing over in the US. The movie was eviscerated in the American press.

The Wandering Earth is classic future-set sci-fi. The sun is expected to explode; the earth is in peril and must be saved. The twist? It is not Americans or the US government that has the answers. The rescue is led by the Chinese, and the world is run by the United Earth Government. Patrick Brzeski of *The Hollywood Reporter*, interviewed the film's director, Frank Gwo. Keeping in mind Xi's directive of film's purpose—to serve the Chinese socialist culture—it was clear that Gwo sought to achieve Xi's objectives. Gwo's interview opened with a very nationalistic statement regarding the premise of the film—the world is in danger and the Chinese rally all people to pull together only to be led by the Chinese in victory. "[T]his central conceit (China leading) is what anchored the film thematically for the local audience."[23] Gwo continued to elaborate on elements of patriotism and nationalism that parroted the CCP's desires. Gwo said,

> When the Earth experiences this kind of crisis in Hollywood films, the hero always ventures out into space to find a new home, which is a very American approach—adventure, individualism. . . . But in my film, we work as a team to take the whole Earth with us. This comes from Chinese cultural values—homeland, history, and continuity. . . . We had to create something aesthetically different from Hollywood science fiction, because aesthetics are based in culture—and Chinese culture has a very different history and

trajectory. . . . The challenge was to develop an aesthetic system that doesn't give you this feeling of incompatibility—we had to look for elements that Chinese audiences would feel comfortable with. . . . [W]e also had to think about China's national background as a country. . . . If China were not far along enough in its development, we wouldn't be able to produce a science fiction film that has huge visual effects . . . if the country is not at a state of growth—or powerful enough—then it wouldn't be plausible for the country to play an important role in helping to solve a global crisis. . . . We had to design our plot according to the actual competencies and direction of the country.[24]

Both *Wolf Warrior II* and *The Wandering Earth* played in the US's AMC Theaters without US censor, then migrated to American streaming services.

Turning the lens back to China and its censorship power of imported US movies, we find two examples of preproduction self-censorship in anticipation of potential red flags. A CCP issue is "potentially" censorable because there are no written rules. Nothing is black and white. This lack of knowing forces a dependency on Chinese officials and Chinese go-betweens who nudge and suggest and leave the filmmaker forever in doubt. The stakes are high, and the fear of misstep is deep. The annals of recent Hollywood to China shortcomings in treating the Chinese people and nation with disrespect is replete with apologies and blacklisting. The ambiguity of what the CCP wants creates a reinforcing loop of self-censorship, spiraling decision-makers to the lowest common denominator that they can point to for their reasoning. Even if the filmmaker gets through all the compromises, they are still on eggshells as distribution timing and placement are not yet assured. Chinese government officials also determine the movie's opening date, number of screens, maximum advertising spend, and how long the film may play in-market. Hollywood has long used the day and date release of films, a strategy that allows a film to be released internationally on the same day to maximize worldwide marketing support. This support can be hampered if China forces a movie to wait a few weeks past said plan.

All this additional leverage the CCP wields by injecting ambiguity throughout the system drives Hollywood further into the arms of a solution of Chinese-based coproductions, some Chinese private companies and some state sponsored, but all censored in Beijing. This results in movies made for worldwide audiences watching films peppered with CCP propaganda Easter eggs that present China in the fashion it desires.

Two US films cited in the PEN America report show just how pervasive and how long Hollywood executives have been covertly considering and altering their content before the first take of production begins.

After North Korea hacked and dumped Sony Hollywood studio's executive emails, it was discovered that there had been internal discussions about the 2013 film *Captain Phillips*. The movie featured Tom Hanks as a captain whose ship was overtaken by Somali pirates. The top brass's concerns revolved around the lengths the US government would extend to save one man. Sony's head of worldwide distribution was concerned that the film would not make it into China because it "might clash with Beijing's rhetoric on the importance of the collective over any single individual."[25]

The other movie, also from 2013, by Paramount Studios, was the zombie thriller, *World War Z*, starring Brad Pitt. Its storyline provides ominous foreshadowing for the year 2020.

Pitt had already been banned from China for starring in the 1997 movie *Seven Years in Tibet*. While censorship rules are not formalized, the industry insider knows today to avoid the "three Ts" in China: Tibet, Taiwan, Tiananmen. Nevertheless, *World War Z* was meant to be an international blockbuster, and Pitt was not only the star but also a coproducer. Paramount wanted a Chinese release and hoped that Pitt's Chinese banishment was far enough in the rearview mirror. But there was a troubling bug in the script. The zombie outbreak Pitt fought was from a virus that had originated in China. Paramount proactively removed the reference of China being the source of the virus. Few in Hollywood will discuss on the record decisions that are made to appease China for fear of future retaliation, but the book author of *World War Z*, Max Brooks, went on the record.

In 2020, Brooks explained why he set the virus origin in China. "I was modeling *World War Z* on the first SARS outbreak, in the early 2000s. . . . I needed an authoritarian regime with strong control over the press. Smothering public awareness would give my plague time to spread, first along the local population, then into other nations. . . . Because it's not enough to have a large population and a rapid transportation network, so the virus can spread like wildfire. You also needed a government that is willing to suppress the truth, which is what happened with the SARS outbreak, where the World Health Organization knew there was something going on and China was doing its impression of Eddie Murphy in *Raw*, going 'hey, it wasn't me.'"[26]

As the CCP holds the theatrical power in China, and the preemptive self-censorship becomes ingrained in Hollywood's creative decision making, China can simply say, "Hey, it isn't us."

PEN America believes that if Hollywood decision makers don't stand in defense of their own values, in the future they will lose their creative freedom to "a government that sees all forms of storytelling as subsidiary to their specific political agenda."[27]

Dalian Wanda didn't need to own US cinema screens to get Chinese movies and messages into the US. The CCP has co-opted Hollywood to do the work for it.

NBA Netizens: The Tweet Heard
Around the World

In mid-2019, China's president Xi had two goals for Hong Kong—exercising control and generating growth—and these had come under tremendous pressure. The situation that evolved may be the loudest 3:00 a.m. wake-up call American enterprise has received. Hong Kong, the storied port, a historic gateway to greater mainland China with 7.5 million inhabitants, turned into a petri dish of conflicting values and power dynamics.

Since reform and opening, Hong Kong had become a harbor for many American businesses. It's a place where English is widely spoken, its internet is open, and its legal system is highly developed and familiar. But in the early summer of 2019, Hong Kong became a flash point as its administrative government sought to enact an extradition agreement reached with the mainland. For Hong Kongers, it was a bridge too far. The Hong Kong people had witnessed Chinese dissidents removed from their purview under cover of night and returned to the mainland to face charges, only to be "disappeared," the code word for hidden trials and verdicts, with many defendants never again seen.

Hong Kongers, fearful of the continuing erosion of their laws and a desire to maintain separation from the mainland's form of justice, began mass protests. As the frequency, size, and severity of the protests grew, with weeks turning into months, Hong Kong's free press brought to bear international awareness and scrutiny. The protestors targeted economically important infrastructure and retail outlets. Disruptors brought Hong Kong's airport and ground transportation links to the mainland to a halt, narrowing the funnel of human and commerce flow. Global luxury goods' brand flagship stores were unable to conduct business.

China began staging the People's Liberation Army, both cadre and military equipment, on the border of Hong Kong, poised to enter at a moment's notice. With media images circling the globe, the commentary quickly drew analogies to the protests and subsequent military crackdown during the Tiananmen Square crisis of 1989. Foreign nations chastised China not to repeat the mistakes of the past, and China bristled at the questioning of its sovereign right to administer its country according to its methods. As some in the US Congress were warning of sanctions should the People's Liberation Army enter the city, admonitions against China and international support of the Hong Kong protestors increased.

A geopolitical tsunami arose. The crux of the matter for American enterprise is best represented by a Nike campaign tagline: "Believe in something. Even if it means sacrificing everything." This marketing campaign was associated with American NFL player Colin Kaepernick. Nike had secured him as a celebrity endorser, and the brand positioning was that Kaepernick was a living demonstration of deeply embedded US values of free speech and peaceful protest after Kaepernick knelt during the national anthem to bring awareness to the need for justice reform regarding people of color in the US.

What the Hong Kong protestors brought to the fore was a discussion about the trade-offs between American values and economic gains. Had American enterprise been put in the position of propagating US values worldwide? Were they expected to do the work of the US government, or was their job to propagate capitalism? Were they beholden to stockholders in their search for new markets and market share? Or were they being subjected to an American values tariff by acquiescing to self-censorship?

A new type of prairie fire was ignited and with it an awareness of China's power to bend American enterprise to its will, the degree to which was not previously realized by the American public. The match that lit the flame was a tweet. Before the flames were doused, much had burned, and from the hot center concentric circles emanated, pulling in copious numbers of behemoth organizations, high-profile personalities, politicians, and basketball fans on both sides of the Pacific.

The inflammatory tweet came courtesy of the NBA's Houston Rockets' general manager, Daryl Morey. On the eve of exhibition games in Japan, with much attention globally focused on Hong Kong protests, a hashtag of support was trending in the free world. #FightforFreedom. Stand with Hong Kong. Morey, from his personal Twitter account, had furthered the propagation of the tweet with support.

What came next is a most egregious example of the CCP's selective information dissemination on the mainland. Twitter is banned in China proper, but China closely monitors America's free media. China's propaganda department plucked Morey's tweet from the many thousands echoing this hashtag and raised it to spectacular heights.

Why this man's tweet at this time? To date, the West has yet to offer a definitive answer. Hence, I will engage in speculation. American politicians were threatening Chinese sovereignty over China's territory of Hong Kong. The Trump Administration had reached an impasse in trade negotiations. Prior Chinese protests against US companies for hurting the feelings of the Chinese people had invariably elicited apologies and promises to correct their knowledge and endeavors. Numerous recent missteps by US businesses had largely gone unnoticed to the American public. The NBA as a target was bound to draw in many high-profile people and companies that resonated on both sides of the Pacific. The CCP had learned from previous experience that to pressure powerful US enterprises was to wield leverage with US politicians, as US companies would lobby in favor of their own interest to continue expansion into China.

The NBA, its star players, and its most associated consumer brand, Nike, were beloved by the Chinese public, and all three entities were well known as outspoken guardians of American free speech, equality, and individual freedom. Did the CCP fear its power of voice and ideals would spill into the internal discussions of the rights of Hong Kongers? No matter the CCP's reasoning, from a business and marketing perspective it was a disheartening development.

The NBA, the players, and Nike had played a long game in China. Their respective histories over decades of immersion into China, learning, understanding, cultivating, and nurturing their businesses, had been textbook examples of how to get the brand and the product right for the Chinese market.

For the NBA, basketball as a sport in China could be traced back to the 1890s when the game was brought there by US missionaries. The sport had taken hold well enough that China had sent its own team to the 1936 Olympics. China, without a history of organized sports as is familiar to the West, found unique assets in basketball to serve several purposes. First was the space required to play the game. In densely populated urban areas, the ability to carve out court space was easier. In rural areas, the simplicity and low cost to stand up a court helped the game spread widely throughout the countryside. Even Mao was a fan. Helen Gao said in *The Atlantic*, "During the Long March (the Red Army's storied yearlong retreat in the 1930s to evade the nationalist army), Communist soldiers and officers played basketball to lift their spirits and boost solidarity. The party continued to support the sport after it took power in 1949. During the Cultural Revolution, Mao declared war against almost all Western bourgeois affections . . . but he never wavered in support of basketball." [1]

The NBA began harnessing China's organic growth and love of basketball in the 1980s when then NBA commissioner David Stern met with officials of China's state-run television network, CCTV. To bring awareness to China of the US's version of professional basketball, he offered TV rights for free of the 1994 NBA Finals.

In 1992, the future and now current NBA commissioner, Adam Silver, had joined the executive ranks of the NBA and recognized a key attribute in increasing the appeal of basketball internationally—the star player. The insight of personality over game to cultivate and adhere the audience was proven in China in 2002. That year the Houston Rockets used its number-one draft pick to choose Yao Ming from Shanghai. His first game was aired in China to an audience of two hundred million. The Houston Rockets became the de facto favorite NBA team in China.

Concurrently to Commissioner Stern's 1980s trips to China, Nike founder Phil Knight made his own pilgrimage to the Middle Kingdom. Knight began moving his manufacturing from South Korea and Taiwan to China. *Time* magazine said, "But he saw China as more than a workshop. 'There are 2 billion feet out there. . . . Go get them!'"[2]

One of those charged with getting the iconic Nike swoosh logo on feet was the Chinese-speaking Terry Rhoads, then Nike's director of sports marketing in China. Rhoads played a long, community-based strategy to seed the brand tied to a game already familiar to his target audience. He worked with high schools, donating equipment, establishing a league, and piping in recorded music and cheers to heighten spectator enthusiasm, and he got CCTV to broadcast high school league finals. He paid high schools to open their courts after school to allow anyone to play. Today it is estimated that approximately three hundred million amateur players play across China today. In 1999 Rhoads discovered and signed Yao Ming to a four-year endorsement contract for US $200,000 dollars.

Rhoads was leveraging Nike's US ties with the NBA as more games began to be broadcast and star players such as Michael Jordan were being sent to China as basketball ambassadors. *Time* magazine noted Rhoads was building the holy grail of a brand's desire for cradle to grave loyalty: "Our goal was to hook kids into Nike early and hold them for life."[3]

The growth for both organizations was phenomenal, and the perceptive strategies and tactics to foster this growth were unique. In 2009, the NBA teamed up with Tencent, one of China's largest and most successful internet streaming entertainment and technology companies. From 2015 to 2020 Tencent paid the NBA $500 million for exclusive game-streaming rights and in 2019 renewed the contract for another five years for $1.5 billion. Per *South China Morning Post*, during the 2018–2019 season, 490 million Chinese watched streaming games, "three times the number for the 2014–2015 season."[4] The NBA's revenue was further enhanced by all the attendant sponsorships and merchandising. The NBA didn't stop there. It studied its market and sought to tailor its product to the sensibilities of the marketplace. It embraced the technologically forward-leaning Chinese and created content and broadcast strategies to draw fans deeper into the elements that would hold the audience's attention, even when games were not in play. It understood China was a mobile-first society, and everything served this platform first. It customized a plethora of in-market ancillary content for China's approved social media outlets. It made viral-ready highlight clips for fans to post. It encouraged players during the US offseason to play in the Chinese Basketball Association under its federation president Yao Ming, who had left the Rockets in 2011. It also supported players taking Chinese brand endorsements and to develop a robust social media presence.

The NBA is not a public company and does not disclose a breakdown of revenue and its sources, but estimates show approximately $8 billion annually, with this gross remaining steady from the 2015–2016 season through the 2019–2020 season. It is estimated that the NBA's annual revenue from China is at least $500 million. *Sports Business Journal* values NBA China, a separate business arm of the NBA, at $5 billion. With gross revenue bumping against a ceiling in the US for several seasons, China represented a potential growth engine.

Encouraged by the NBA and through exposure to China, many superstar players embraced the Chinese people and the financial opportunities available from the world's largest NBA fanbase. Kobe Bryant was the NBA superstar pioneer in China. He created the template for players to follow in developing and maintaining a relationship with Chinese basketball fans. Part of his success was timing good fortune, coupled with a sincere desire to reach out, connect, and help the Chinese. Bryant's first China visit was in 1998 to host a basketball clinic. From 2006 through 2015, he participated annually in Nike promotional tours of China. He played on the gold medal–winning US team at the 2008 Beijing Olympics. As Bryant's star was rising from his LA Lakers play, social media platforms were proliferating in the US and China. He embraced these platforms to create country-specific content and connections. He acted as a goodwill ambassador and created a charitable foundation to assist children in China and utilized his US charity to promote Chinese culture in the US. His revenue associated with China is undisclosed, but per the China-based consultancy Mailman, which produces the annual REDCARD NBA that tracks Chinese public sentiment of US NBA teams and players, Kobe Bryant is the number-one legend of the NBA. His Chinese acuity and legacy are best described by Patrick Rishe of *Forbes*: "His vision, intelligence and willingness to engage the people of China offered a great lesson in how those who invest their time into fan engagement will produce the most loyal followings."[5]

As many NBA players followed Kobe's footprints to lucrative endorsement deals, Nike tours, and fan adulation, another giant emerged—LeBron James. As a Nike athlete, James enjoys one of the most valuable NBA deals. To date, James has not pursued the custom, China-centric digital content on a Kobe Bryant scale, but he traveled to China and participated in exhibition games and promotional tours.

What James did embrace was the very progressive stance the NBA has taken on social issues in the US. He is on track to be one of the greatest players of all time, and he is also acquiring the mantle of a leading social activist. His focus has been on social and police justice, voting rights, and assisting underprivileged children in the US.

Nike is a common thread throughout basketball's association and success in China. Basketball may have gotten Nike in the door, but it has extended its brand to enter other sports and leisurewear, with China representing their greatest year-over-year percentage growth worldwide. During the 2020 pandemic, Nike sales worldwide without China declined for the first time in the most recent decade—but not in China, where it continued to grow at 8 percent (figure 7). [6]

Figure 7: Year Over Year Revenue Growth, Nike, 2015–2020

With so much right about basketball in China, a trip over a loose shoelace began to unravel an intricately constructed financial ecosystem. Houston Rockets general manager Morey's tweet appeared the evening of October 4, 2019, three days after China's National Day, an annual celebration of the founding of the People's Republic of China (PRC). This celebration had been extraordinary, for it commemorated the seventieth anniversary and was accompanied by numerous ceremonial events and a grand military parade, with China's President, Xi Jinping taking center stage throughout.

China's press and propaganda had been on high alert for weeks to ensure that the images and coverage of this important day were viewed domestically and internationally as proof of a strong and rising China. Morey's tweet was seen to feed the narrative that the CCP was propagating—it was Western forces who were fomenting the instability and the demands emanating from the Hong Kong populous.

Backlash to Morey's tweet came from many viewpoints, some surprising, concerning, opportunistic, and some seeming to indicating that the NBA's positioning was inauthentic and laden with hypocrisy.

Within hours of the infamous tweet, Morey's boss and owner of the Houston Rockets, Tilman Fertitta, tweeted that Morey was not speaking for his organization and that it was not a political organization. Morey deleted his tweet and quickly apologized to Chinese Rocket fans and friends. The Chinese Basketball Association, led by Yao, immediately halted cooperation with the Rockets. Chinese social media lit up with calls to fire Morey.

Commissioner Silver and the NBA were in a delicate position. Because the firestorm had ignited in both countries (the Chinese felt that their sovereignty over Hong Kong was questioned, while Americans saw Morey as expressing his American free speech rights), Silver sought to bifurcate his messaging—one for the US and the one for China, widely panned in the US as pandering to the Chinese. Silver found himself at the center of a circular firing squad. In trying to clear up the distinction between the NBA's two statements, Silver tried to find a way back to the brand values he had for so long fostered with the NBA in the US. In acknowledgement of the confusion, Silver said, "Our initial statement left people angered, confused or unclear on who we are or what the NBA stands for. . . . It is inevitable that people around the world—including from America and China—will have different viewpoints over different issues. It is not the role of the NBA to adjudicate those differences. . . . However, the NBA will not put itself in a position of regulating what players, employees and team owners say or will not say on these issues. We simply could not operate that way."[7]

American politicians piled on in a surprisingly united bipartisan voice with Senator Elizabeth Warren's statement indicative of the sentiment, summed up simply as the NBA had chosen "its pocketbook over principles."[8] Donald Trump, mired in a stalled trade war with China, accused the NBA of pandering to China but took no true stance, remarking that "They have to work out their own situation. The NBAs—they know what they're doing."[9]

While Fertitta somewhat walked back his distancing from Morey, another NBA owner emerged with skin in the game in both countries. Joe Tsai, cofounder of Alibaba, China's behemoth online storefront, had purchased the Brooklyn Nets for $2.35 billion in September 2019. Tsai, writing an open letter on Facebook, made clear where his allegiance lay and parroted the often-heard protestations of the CCP. Tsai said,

> A student of history will understand that the Chinese psyche has heavy baggage when it comes to any threat, foreign or domestic, to carve up Chinese territories. . . . By now I hope you can begin to understand why the Daryl Morey tweet is so damaging to the relationship with our fans in China. I don't know Daryl personally. I am sure he is a fine NBA general manager, and I will take at face value this subsequent apology that he was not as well informed as he should have been. But the hurt that this incident has caused will take a long time to repair.[10]

Silver acknowledged the significant loss of revenue expected from the fallout. Dominos quickly fell. First, Rockets games were pulled from Tencent's streaming service, soon to be followed by a blackout of all NBA games meant for broadcast in China. Chinese sponsors pulled out, and Chinese e-commerce giants removed Rocket merchandise. Nike, as the official on-court apparel sponsor for the NBA, was concerned that Chinese consumers might turn against its brand across the board. It immediately pulled Rockets merchandise from in-country stores and online. With a progressive social positioning like the NBA's, Nike came out with statements separating its US positioning from its Chinese-focused brand. The official line was that Nike in

China was a China brand for China, and its financial success in China was proof.

Several high-profile NBA players receive considerable remuneration from their Chinese business activities and actively express their social activism in the US. The one player who had the most on the line from an authentic brand positioning associated with social activism was LeBron James of the LA Lakers.

James, straight from high school to the pros in 2003, signed on with Nike. In an Associated Press interview in 2005, James said: "In the next 15 or 20 years, I hope I'll be the richest man in the world. . . . That's one of my goals. I want to be a billionaire. I want to get to a position where generation on generation don't have to worry about nothing. I don't want family members from my kids to my son's kids to never have to worry. And I can't do that now just playing basketball."[11] In the coming years, Nike and China were an important cornerstone for reaching his goal. The LeBron-Nike player-product tie-up was determined to be so successful that in 2015 Nike inked a lifetime deal with James believed to be the single largest guarantee in company history, estimated at more than $1 billion.[12]

James in 2005 not only explicitly stated grand financial goals for his life early in his career but also embraced the idea that his superstar status could be a large megaphone for social issues he cared about. In an Associated Press interview it was noted,

> On a promotional trip to China this summer, James was welcomed like a conquering hero by a nation that has fallen in love with the NBA. . . . And, like his experience playing for the US Olympic team, the overseas visit broadened James' world view and his place in it. . . . James:

"I've moved in my life and my first day in a new school I was always able to make new friends. That's difficult for some people. So someday being an ambassador to the world and not just the NBA would be great. I want to be the face of a lot of things."[13]

James's superstar status only increased over the next decade, and during the Trump Administration, the turmoil in America's streets regarding social and criminal justice led to much on and off the court protestations by NBA players, with James often in the forefront. As America's conservative media weighed in on the social concerns raised by NBA players such as James, a commentator on Fox News said of James that he should "shut up and dribble."[14] Of the chide to know his place, it seemed to further inflame the player's ambitions to be a larger voice in the discussion. "'I don't think the companies are afraid anymore,' James told ESPN's Mina Kimes. 'The companies are realizing and understanding that the athletes, that they have a voice . . . And their voice carries more than dribbling a basketball or swinging a racket. I think these athletes have so much more power than their respective sport and what we see of them in their uniform. Because we are educated, and we do have feelings and we do have passion about things that go on.'"[15]

The power of these beloved NBA players beyond their on-court acumen may have been what most concerned the CCP. Could the superstars' social activism and fearless willingness to use their words become a rallying cry of support both in the US and China for Hong Kong protestors?

As the league found itself in a defensive position with the Chinese government over the Morey tweet, James used his voice again, saying of Morey that he "wasn't educated on the situation at hand . . . so many people could have been

harmed . . . financially, physically, emotionally [and] spiritual-
ly."[16] The incongruence of James's US outspokenness with his
unwillingness to support Morey quickly raised questions and
cries of hypocrisy in Hong Kong and the US. Hong Kongers
burned James's jersey, and many in the US questioned his
loyalties to American values. Bill Bishop, author of a China-
focused newsletter distributed through his website Sincosim.
com, brought business reality to the conversation.

> People say they're a bunch of hypocrites because
> they (won't) talk about China . . . but at the end
> of the day, they are human and we have to really
> wonder is it fair to expect them to sacrifice their
> careers and earnings. . . . It's the genius—and I
> don't mean this in a positive way—of how the
> communist party has set up this global censor-
> ship mechanism. NBA players have learned the
> cost of speaking out (about China) . . . These are
> individuals who have a lot of money on the line,
> and you have major corporations with billions
> of dollars of revenue assets who are unwilling to
> take a stand.[17]

By early 2020, with NBA games still blacked out in China,
the US was moving on. Rumblings of a deadly virus in China
emerged, and then China's most beloved NBA player, Kobe
Bryant, was killed in a helicopter crash on January 26.

Two days before his death, Bryant posted on his Chinese
Weibo (China's version of Twitter) account a happy Chinese
New Year greeting. His legacy in China had been one of a
sports ambassador between our respective nations. It was a
role he seemed to cherish, and his philanthropic work was
viewed as authentic. He had remained above the fray of the
Morey fallout, never making public comments on the issue.

Bryant's daughter Gianna perished with him in the crash on the way to her basketball game. His wife, at their memorial service, had said of Gianna that she had embraced Kobe's love of China, taking up Mandarin with the ability to speak, read, and write China's official language.[18] It seemed he was teaching her the Kobe Bryant playbook on how to be a cultural bridge.

While the icy relations between the NBA and the CCP remained, the significant outpouring of Chinese public mourning and adoration led to an acknowledgement of Bryant beyond someone who simply dribbled. The CCP-controlled media outlet *People's Daily* wrote, "His fearless spirit of fighting, both on the court and in real life, is worth remembering."[19]

Throughout, Adam Silver had worked to restore the NBA in China, walking a tightrope between our respective governments, business interests, fans, and conflicting values. A first test had been his assertion, denied by the Chinese that, "We were being asked to fire him [Daryl Morey] by the Chinese government. . . . We said, there's no chance that's happening—there's no chance we'll even discipline him."[20] But by mid-October, Morey announced he would resign on November 1, 2020, telling ESPN in an interview, "For me, it was just a great run . . . just the right time to see what's next with family and other potential things in the future. It just felt like the right time."[21]

Silver needed to get the US games back on air in China. "In May [2020], the NBA announced a new head of its Chinese operations, Michael Ma, the son of the founder of CCTV Sports, Ma Guoli. It was thought that connection could help the league but at the time CCTV released a statement 'reiterating its consistent stance on national sovereignty' and continued its position."[22]

Silver's Chinese outreach had included financial and medical equipment donations by the league to support China's fight against COVID-19. In early October 2020, one year after the infamous Morey tweet, CCTV announced it would broadcast live game five of the NBA Finals. In the announcement CCTV said, "During the recent Chinese National Day and Mid-Autumn Festival celebrations, the NBA sent their well wishes to fans in China.... We also took note of the league has been continuously delivering goodwill (to China), particularly making positive contributions to Chinese people's fight against COVID-19 pandemic."[23]

In late September 2020, after a year of attacks from all angles, Silver did an interview with US sports journalist Bob Costas. He reflected on the value of sports diplomacy, officially under the purview of the US State Department: "There was a decision that it was good for the world to build these relationships through sports. . . . The thought was, these cultural exchanges were critically important especially at times when normal channels weren't operating for diplomatic conversations."[24]

Costas pressed further. Should the NBA be doing business in a country that America was accusing of gross human rights violations? Silver's reply: "There are definitely trade-offs there, and somebody could say given the system of government in China, you the NBA should make a decision not to operate there. I would only say that at the end of the day, I think those are decisions for our government in terms of where American businesses should operate."[25]

Endnotes

Introduction

[1]Bruce D. Henderson, "The Origins of Strategy," *Harvard Business Review* (November–December 1989), https://hbr.org/1989/11/the-origin-of-strategy.

[2]Henderson, "The Origins of Strategy."

[3]Carl Crow, *400 Million Customers*, (United Kingdom: Eastbridge Books, 2017), 197

[4]Jean-Pierre Lehmann, "Why the world has to study Chinese history, and how China views history," *South China Morning Post*, August 8, 2017 https://www.scmp.com/comment/insight-opinion/article/2105912/why-world-has-study-chinese-history-and-how-china-views

Part 1

CHAPTER 1: Xi Jinping and His Thoughts for a New Era

[1]Mingfu, Liu (2015-05-05). *The China Dream: Great Power Thinking and Strategic Posture in the Post-American Era*, (CN Times Books), Kindle Edition.

[2]Mingfu, Liu (2015-05-05). *The China Dream: Great Power Thinking and Strategic Posture in the Post-American Era* (Kindle Locations 513-514), (CN Times Books) Kindle Edition.

[3]Mingfu, Liu (2015-05-05). *The China Dream: Great Power Thinking and Strategic Posture in the Post-American Era* (Kindle Locations 5301-5305). CN Times Books. Kindle Edition.

[4]Evan Osnos, "Born Red," *The New Yorker*, April 6, 2015, https://www.newyorker.com/magazine/2015/04/06/born-red

[5]Evan Osnos, "Born Red," *The New Yorker*, April 6, 2015, https://www. newyorker.com/magazine/2015/04/06/born-red

[6]Evan Osnos, "Born Red," *The New Yorker*, April 6, 2015, https://www. newyorker.com/magazine/2015/04/06/born-red

[7]Evan Osnos, "Born Red," *The New Yorker*, April 6, 2015, https://www. newyorker.com/magazine/2015/04/06/born-red

[8]Ryan Mitchell, "China's Crown Theorist," *Foreign Affairs*, December 4, 2017

[9]Ryan Mitchell, "China's Crown Theorist," *Foreign Affairs*, December 4, 2017

[10]Ryan Mitchell, "China's Crown Theorist," *Foreign Affairs*, December 4, 2017

[11]Liu Mingfu, Wang Zhongyuan, *The Thoughts of Xi Jinping*, (USA: American Academic Press, 2017) 297

[12]Liu Mingfu, Wang Zhongyuan, *The Thoughts of Xi Jinping*, (USA: American Academic Press, 2017) viii

[13]Jon Huntsman, "Xi Jinping China's leading man," *Time Magazine*, April 23, 2014, http://time.com/collection-post/70857/xi-Jinping-2014-time-100

[14]Liu Mingfu, Wang Zhongyuan, *The Thoughts of Xi Jinping*, (USA: American Academic Press, 2017) 299

[15]Liu Mingfu, Wang Zhongyuan, *The Thoughts of Xi Jinping*, (USA: American Academic Press, 2017) 296

[16]"Xi Jingping millionaire relations reveal fortunes of elite", Bloomberg News, June 29, 2012, https://bloomberg.com/news/articles/2012-06-29/xi-Jinping-millionaire-relations-reveal-fortunes-of-elite.

[17]Edward Wong, "At Bloomberg, Special Code Keeps Some Articles Out of China", *New York Times*, November 13, 2013, http://sinosphere. blogs nytimes.com/2013/11/13/at-bloomberg-special-code-keeps-some-articles-out-of-china/

[18]Eleanor Randolph, *The Many Lives of Michael Bloomberg*, (New York: Simon & Schuster, 2019), 316-317

[19]Eleanor Randolph, *The Many Lives of Michael Bloomberg*, (New York: Simon & Schuster, 2019), 317

[20]Stephen McDonell, "Why China censors banned Winnie the Pooh," BBC News, July 17, 2017, https://www.bbc.com/news/blogs-china-blog-40627855

CHAPTER 2: **Chinese Dream**

[1]Thomas L. Friedman, "China Needs Its Own Dream," *The New York Times*, October 2, 2012, https://www.nytimes.com/2012/10/03/opinion/friedman-china-needs-its-own-dream.html

[2]Thomas L. Friedman, "China Needs Its Own Dream," *The New York Times*, October 2, 2012, https://www.nytimes.com/2012/10/03/opinion/friedman-china-needs-its-own-dream.html

[3]*Xi Jinping: The Governance of China Volume I* [English Language Version], (Beijing: Foreign Languages Press, 2014), 38

[4]"Chasing the Chinese dream," *The Economist*, May 4, 2013, https://www.economist.com/briefing/2013/05/04/chasing-the-chinese-dream

[5]*Xi Jinping: The Governance of China Volume I* [English Language Version], (Beijing: Foreign Languages Press, 2014), 48-49

[6]Brenda Geren, "Motivation: Chinese theoretical perspectives", New York Institute of Technology Bahrain, *Journal of Behavioral Studies in Business*, https://www.aabri.com/manuscripts/10692.pdf

[7]Brenda Geren, "Motivation: Chinese theoretical perspectives", New York Institute of Technology Bahrain, *Journal of Behavioral Studies in Business*, https://www.aabri.com/manuscripts/10692.pdf

[8]Brenda Geren, "Motivation: Chinese theoretical perspectives", New York Institute of Technology Bahrain, *Journal of Behavioral Studies in Business*, https://www.aabri.com/manuscripts/10692.pdf

[9]"Beijing Olympics showcase harmony concept," *Peoples World*, August 16, 2008, https://www.peoplesworld.org/article/beijing-olympics-showcase-harmony-concept/

[10]"Beijing Olympics showcase harmony concept," *Peoples World*, August 16, 2008, https://www.peoplesworld.org/article/beijing-olympics-showcase-harmony-concept/

[11]"The Philosophy of Harmony," ChinaDaily.com.cn, August 8, 2008, http://www.chinadaily.com.cn/olympics/2008-08/09/content_6920168.htm

[12]*Xi Jinping: The Governance of China Volume I* [English Language Version], (Beijing: Foreign Languages Press, 2014), 189

[13]Howard W. French, *Everything Under the Heavens, How the Past Helps Shape China's Push for Global Power*, (New York: Knoph, 2017), 8

[14]*Xi Jinping: The Governance of China Volume I* [English Language Version], (Beijing: Foreign Languages Press, 2014), 189

[15]"In Box Office Hit, American Dream Is Still Alive—In a Maturing China," ChinaFile.com, June 13, 2013, https://www.chinafile.com/reporting-opinion/media/box-office-hit-american-dream-still-alive-maturing-china

Part 2

CHAPTER 3: The People of Qing

[1]Howard W. French, *Everything Under the Heavens, How the Past Helps Shape China's Push for Global Power*, (New York: Knoph, 2017), 37

[2]Howard W. French, *Everything Under the Heavens, How the Past Helps Shape China's Push for Global Power*, (New York: Knoph, 2017), 38

[3]Howard W. French, *Everything Under the Heavens, How the Past Helps Shape China's Push for Global Power*, (New York: Knoph, 2017), 39

[4]Liu Mingfu, Wang Zhongyuan, *The Thoughts of Xi Jinping*, (USA: American Academic Press, 2017), 229

[5]"How is China Feeding its Population of 1.4 billion?" China Power, January 25, 2017, http://chinapower.csis.org/china-food-security/#toc-2

[6]Bella Huang, Amy Qin, "Xi Declares War on Food Waste, and China Races to Tighten Its Belt", *New York Times*, August 21, 2020, https://www.nytimes.com/2020/08/21/world/asia/china-food-waste-xi.html

[7]The Opium Wars still shape China's view of the West", *The Economist*, December 19, 2017, https://www.economist.com/christmas-specials/2017/12/19/the-opium-wars-still-shape-chinas-view-of-the-west

[8]The Opium Wars still shape China's view of the West", *The Economist*, December 19, 2017, https://www.economist.com/christmas-spe-

cials/2017/12/19/the-opium-wars-still-shape-chinas-view-of-the-west

[9]Howard W. French, *Everything Under the Heavens, How the Past Helps Shape China's Push for Global Power*, (New York: Knoph, 2017), 69

[10]Howard W. French, *Everything Under the Heavens, How the Past Helps Shape China's Push for Global Power*, (New York: Knoph, 2017), 70

[11]Frank Dikotter, *The Tragedy of Liberation: A History of the Chinese Revolution 1945-1957*, (United Kingdom: Bloomsbury, 2013), 24

[12]Howard W. French, *Everything Under the Heavens, How the Past Helps Shape China's Push for Global Power*, (New York: Knoph, 2017), 72

[13]Henry Kissinger, *On China*, (England: Penguin, 2012), 6

[14]Theodore White, "Life Looks at China", *Theodore H. White at Large*, (New York: Random House, 1992), 98

[15]Theodore White, "Life Looks at China", *Theodore H. White at Large*, (New York: Random House, 1992), 98

[16]Theodore White, "Life Looks at China", *Theodore H. White at Large*, (New York: Random House, 1992), 98

[17]Theodore White, "Life Looks at China", *Theodore H. White at Large*, (New York: Random House, 1992), 99

Chapter 4: The People of Mao

[1]Henry Kissinger, *On China*, (England: Penguin, 2012), 90

[2]Frank Dikotter, *The Tragedy of Liberation: A History of the Chinese Revolution 1945-1957*, (United Kingdom: Bloomsbury, 2013), 26-27

[3]Frank Dikotter, *The Tragedy of Liberation: A History of the Chinese Revolution 1945-1957*, (United Kingdom: Bloomsbury, 2013), 47

[4]Brian Anse Patrick, *The Ten Commandments Of Propaganda*, (Arktos Media, Ltd., 2013), 57

[5]Frank Dikotter, *The Tragedy of Liberation: A History of the Chinese Revolution 1945-1957*, (United Kingdom: Bloomsbury, 2013), 49

[6]Frank Dikotter, *The Tragedy of Liberation: A History of the Chinese Revolution 1945-1957*, (United Kingdom: Bloomsbury, 2013), 67

[7] Frank Dikotter, *The Tragedy of Liberation: A History of the Chinese Revolution 1945-1957*, (United Kingdom: Bloomsbury, 2013), 75

[8] Frank Dikotter, *The Tragedy of Liberation: A History of the Chinese Revolution 1945-1957*, (United Kingdom: Bloomsbury, 2013), 75

[9] Frank Dikotter, *Mao's Great Famine: The History of China's Most Devastating Catastrophe, 1958-1962*, (USA: Bloomsbury, 2010), 21

[10] Frank Dikotter, *Mao's Great Famine: The History of China's Most Devastating Catastrophe, 1958-1962*, (USA: Bloomsbury, 2010), 34

[11] Frank Dikotter, *Mao's Great Famine: The History of China's Most Devastating Catastrophe, 1958-1962*, (USA: Bloomsbury, 2010), 57-59

[12] Frank Dikotter, *Mao's Great Famine: The History of China's Most Devastating Catastrophe, 1958-1962*, (USA: Bloomsbury, 2010), xiii

[13] Frank Dikotter, *Mao's Great Famine: The History of China's Most Devastating Catastrophe, 1958-1962*, (USA: Bloomsbury, 2010), xvii

[14] Frank Dikotter, *Mao's Great Famine: The History of China's Most Devastating Catastrophe, 1958-1962*, (USA: Bloomsbury, 2010), 79

[15] Frank Dikotter, *Mao's Great Famine: The History of China's Most Devastating Catastrophe, 1958-1962*, (USA: Bloomsbury, 2010), 79

[16] Chris Buckley, Steven Lee Myers, "As New Coronavirus Spread, China's Old Habits Delayed Fight", *The New York Times*, February 1, 2020, https://www.nytimes.com/2020/02/01/world/asia/china-coronavirus.html

[17] Raymond Zhong, Paul Mozur, Jeff Kao, Aaron Krolik, "No 'Negative' News: How China Censored the Coronavirus", *The New York Times*, December 19, 2020, https://www.nytimes.com/2020/12/19/technology/china-coronavirus-censorship.html

[18] Raymond Zhong, Paul Mozur, Jeff Kao, Aaron Krolik, "No 'Negative' News: How China Censored the Coronavirus", *The New York Times*, December 19, 2020, https://www.nytimes.com/2020/12/19/technology/china-coronavirus-censorship.html

[19] Raymond Zhong, Paul Mozur, Jeff Kao, Aaron Krolik, "No 'Negative' News: How China Censored the Coronavirus", *The New York Times*, December 19, 2020, https://www.nytimes.com/2020/12/19/technology/china-coronavirus-censorship.html

[20]Raymond Zhong, Paul Mozur, Jeff Kao, Aaron Krolik, "No 'Negative' News: How China Censored the Coronavirus", *The New York Times*, December 19, 2020, https://www.nytimes.com/2020/12/19/technology/china-coronavirus-censorship.html

[21]Frank Dikotter, *Mao's Great Famine: The History of China's Most Devastating Catastrophe, 1958-1962*, (USA: Bloomsbury, 2010), 7

[22]Frank Dikotter, *Mao's Great Famine: The History of China's Most Devastating Catastrophe, 1958-1962*, (USA: Bloomsbury, 2010), 228-229

[23]Frank Dikotter, *The Cultural Revolution: A People's History 1962-1976*, (United Kingdom: Bloomsbury), 2016, xii

[24]Frank Dikotter, *The Cultural Revolution: A People's History 1962-1976*, (United Kingdom: Bloomsbury), 2016, 27

[25]Frank Dikotter, *The Cultural Revolution: A People's History 1962-1976*, (United Kingdom: Bloomsbury), 2016, 19-20

[26]Frank Dikotter, *The Cultural Revolution: A People's History 1962-1976*, (United Kingdom: Bloomsbury), 2016, 18

[27]Frank Dikotter, *The Cultural Revolution: A People's History 1962-1976*, (United Kingdom: Bloomsbury), 2016, 34

[28]James Griffiths, "Chinese KFC restaurant dedicated to Communist hero Lei Feng", CNN, March 5, 2019, https://www.cnn.com/2019/03/05/asia/kfc-china-lei-feng-intl/index.html

[29]Anna Fifield, "China's Communist Party tries to create a new hero for the masses", *Washington Post*, November 3, 2019, https://www.washingtonpost.com/world/asia-pacific/chinas-communist-party-tries-to-create-a-new-hero-for-the-masses/2019/11/02/09851ac6-fb1d-11e9-9e02-1d45cb3dfa8f_story.html

[30]Brian Anse Patrick, *The Ten Commandments Of Propaganda*, (Arktos Media, Ltd., 2013), 142

[31]Brian Anse Patrick, *The Ten Commandments Of Propaganda*, (Arktos Media, Ltd., 2013), 149

[32]Anna Fifield, "China's Communist Party tries to create a new hero for the masses", *Washington Post*, November 3, 2019, https://www.washingtonpost.com/world/asia-pacific/chinas-communist-party-

tries-to-create-a-new-hero-for-the-masses/2019/11/02/09851ac6-fb1d-11e9-9e02-1d45cb3dfa8f_story.html

[33] Anna Fifield, "China's Communist Party tries to create a new hero for the masses", *Washington Post*, November 3, 2019, https://www. washingtonpost.com/world/asia-pacific/chinas-communist-party-tries-to-create-a-new-hero-for-the-masses/2019/11/02/09851ac6-fb1d-11e9-9e02-1d45cb3dfa8f_story.html

[34] Frank Dikotter, *The Cultural Revolution: A People's History 1962-1976*, (United Kingdom: Bloomsbury), 2016, 36

[35] Jun Mai, "Mao Zedong's 'little red book' gets modern twist with mobile app for studying 'Xi Jinping Thought'", *South China Morning Post*, March 31, 2019

[36] Frank Dikotter, *The Cultural Revolution: A People's History 1962-1976*, (United Kingdom: Bloomsbury), 2016, 74

[37] Frank Dikotter, *The Cultural Revolution: A People's History 1962-1976*, (United Kingdom: Bloomsbury), 2016, 81

[38] Frank Dikotter, *The Cultural Revolution: A People's History 1962-1976*, (United Kingdom: Bloomsbury), 2016, 94

[39] Frank Dikotter, *The Cultural Revolution: A People's History 1962-1976*, (United Kingdom: Bloomsbury), 2016, 105

[40] Frank Dikotter, *The Cultural Revolution: A People's History 1962-1976*, (United Kingdom: Bloomsbury), 2016, 204

[41] Henry Kissinger, *On China*, (England: Penguin, 2012), 194

[42] Frank Dikotter, *The Cultural Revolution: A People's History 1962-1976*, (United Kingdom: Bloomsbury), 2016, 266

[43] Frank Dikotter, *The Cultural Revolution: A People's History 1962-1976*, (United Kingdom: Bloomsbury), 2016, 207

[44] Theodore White, "Journey Back To Another China", *Theodore H. White at Large,* (New York: Random House, 1992), July 17, 1972, 127

[45] Theodore White, "Journey Back To Another China", *Theodore H. White at Large,* (New York: Random House, 1992), July 17, 1972, 127-128

[46] Henry Kissinger, *On China*, (England: Penguin, 2012), 268

[47]Theodore White, "Journey Back To Another China", *Theodore H. White at Large,* (New York: Random House, 1992), July 17, 1972, 133

[48]Theodore White, "Journey Back To Another China", *Theodore H. White at Large,* (New York: Random House, 1992), July 17, 1972, 134

[49]Richard Solomon, "Chinese Political Negotiating Behavior, 1967-1984", Rand, 1995, https://www.rand.org/pubs/monograph_reports/MR663.html

[50]Nick Torrens, *China's 3Dreams*, 2014, Nick Torrens Films and Screen Australia

[51]Nick Torrens, *China's 3Dreams*, Synopsis, nicktorrensfilms.com

CHAPTER 5: The People of Deng

[1]Ezra F. Vogel, *Deng Xiaoping and the Transformation of China*, (USA: Harvard University Press, 2011), 17

[2]Ezra F. Vogel, *Deng Xiaoping and the Transformation of China*, (USA: Harvard University Press, 2011), 218

[3]Ezra F. Vogel, *Deng Xiaoping and the Transformation of China*, (USA: Harvard University Press, 2011), 223

[4]Ezra F. Vogel, *Deng Xiaoping and the Transformation of China*, (USA: Harvard University Press, 2011), 226

[5]Ezra F. Vogel, *Deng Xiaoping and the Transformation of China*, (USA: Harvard University Press, 2011), 241

[6]Henry Kissinger, *On China*, (England: Penguin, 2012), 334

[7]Ezra F. Vogel, *Deng Xiaoping and the Transformation of China*, (USA: Harvard University Press, 2011), 2-3

[8]*Xi Jinping: The Governance of China Volume I* [English Language Version], (Beijing: Foreign Languages Press, 2014), 25

[9]Ezra F. Vogel, *Deng Xiaoping and the Transformation of China*, (USA: Harvard University Press, 2011), 164

[10]Ezra F. Vogel, *Deng Xiaoping and the Transformation of China*, (USA: Harvard University Press, 2011), 227

[11]Xi Jinping, *Up and Out of Poverty*, (Beijing: Foreign Languages Press, 2016), p 2

[12]Ezra F. Vogel, *Deng Xiaoping and the Transformation of China*, (USA: Harvard University Press, 2011), 77

[13]Ezra F. Vogel, *Deng Xiaoping and the Transformation of China*, (USA: Harvard University Press, 2011), 85

[14]Ezra F. Vogel, *Deng Xiaoping and the Transformation of China*, (USA: Harvard University Press, 2011), 478

[15]Ezra F. Vogel, *Deng Xiaoping and the Transformation of China*, (USA: Harvard University Press, 2011), 495

[16]Xi Jinping, *The Governance of China Volume II*, (Beijing: Foreign Languages Press, 2017), 475

[17]Xi Jinping, *The Governance of China Volume II*, (Beijing: Foreign Languages Press, 2017), 461-462

[18]ERS Report: "Interdependence of China, United States, and Brazil in Soybean Trade", Farm Policy News, June 19, 2019, https://farmpolicynews.illinois.edu/2019/06/ers-report-interdependence-of-china-united-states-and-brazil-in-soybean-trade/

[19]

[20]Jim Jones, "Trump's trade war China is fueling Amazon rainforest destruction", *Des Moines Register*, September 3, 2019, https://www.desmoinesregister.com/story/opinion/columnists/2019/09/03/trumps-trade-war-china-fueling-amazon-rainforest-fires/2201495001/

[21]Jay Sjerven, "Despite huge purchases of US soybeans, China may not meet commitments", Food Business News, September 20, 2020 https://www.foodbusinessnews.net/articles/16958-despite-huge-purchases-of-us-soybeans-china-may-not-meet-commitments

[22]Xi Jinping, *The Governance of China Volume II*, (Beijing: Foreign Languages Press, 2017), 468

[23]https://foreignpolicy.com/2021/02/16/semiconductors-us-china-tai...mail&utm_campaign=30797&utm_term=China%20Brief%20OC&?tpcc=30797#

[24]https://foreignpolicy.com/2021/02/16/semiconductors-us-china-tai...mail&utm_campaign=30797&utm_term=China%20Brief%20OC&?tpcc=30797#

[25]https://foreignpolicy.com/2021/02/16/semiconductors-us-china-tai...
mail&utm_campaign=30797&utm_term=China%20Brief%20
OC&?tpcc=30797#

[26]https://foreignpolicy.com/2021/02/16/semiconductors-us-china-tai...
mail&utm_campaign=30797&utm_term=China%20Brief%20
OC&?tpcc=30797#

[27]Jeongmin Seong, et. al., "Global flows: The ties that bind in an inter-
connected world", McKinsey Global Institute, November 2022, 14

[28]Jeremy Goldkorn, "Another Foreign Company In Trouble With China for Geographical Sins", TheChinaProject.com, January 31, 2018,
https://thechinaproject.com/2018/01/31/another-foreign-compa-
ny-trouble-china-geographical-sins/

[29]Jennifer Lo, "Marriott gets a boost in Asia-Pacific after Starwood deal",
Nikkei Asian Review, September 24, 2016, https://asia.nikkei.com/
Business/Marriott-gets-a-boost-in-Asia-Pacific-after-Starwood-deal

[30]Daniel Ren, "Delta Air Lines, Zara join Marriott in China's bad books
over Tibet, Taiwan gaffes", *South China Morning Post*, January 12,
2018

[31]Daniel Ren, Delta Air Lines, *Zara join Marriott in China's bad books
over Tibet, Taiwan gaffes*, South China Morning Post, 1/12/18 https://
www.scmp.com/news/china/society/article/2128046/delta-air-lines-
zara-join-marriott-chinas-bad-books-over-tibet

[32]"China shuts Marriott's website over Tibet and Taiwan error",
BBC.com, January 12, 2018, https://www.bbc.com/news/busi-
ness-42658070

[33]Alanna Petroff & Steven Jiang, "China blocks Marriott for listing Tibet
and Taiwan as countries", CNN Business, January 11, 2018, https://
money.cnn.com/2018/01/11/news/companies/marriott-china-web-
site-app-blocked-tibet-taiwan/index.html

[34]Kris Cheng, "Hotelier Marriott unveils 'eight-point rectification plan'
after Tibet and Hong Kong geography "gaffe", *Hong Kong Free Press*,
January 19, 2018, https://hongkongfp.com/2018/01/19/hotelier-mar-
riott-unveils-eight-point-rectification-plan-tibet-hong-kong-geogra-
phy-gaffe/

[35]Wayne Ma, "Marriott Employee Roy Jones Hit 'Like.' Then China Got Mad," *The Wall Street Journal*, March 3, 2018, https://www.wsj.com/articles/marriott-employee-roy-jones-hit-like-then-china-got-mad-1520094910

[36]Ben Schlapping, "Dear Marriott: Does The Way You Fired This Employee Reflect Your Core Values?" https://onemileatatime.com/marriott-fires-employee-over-tibet-tweet/

[37]Geremie R Barme, "Spiritual Pollution Thirty Years On," The China Story, Journal, 17, November 2013, https://chinaheritage.net/archive/spiritual-pollution-thirty-years-on/

[38]Andrew J. Nathan, "The New Tiananmen Papers," Foreign Affairs, May 30, 2019, https://www.foreignaffairs.com/articles/china/2019-05-30/new-tiananmen-papers

[39]Kirk A. Denton, "1989 Democratic Movement and The May Fourth," Journal of Chinese Philosophy 20, 1993, 392

[40]Kirk A. Denton, "1989 Democratic Movement and The May Fourth," Journal of Chinese Philosophy 20, 1993, 395

[41]Deb Riechman, AP, "Document Gives New View of Tiananmen," *The Washington Post*, December 4, 2018, https://www.chinafile.com/conversation/did-president-george-hw-bush-mishandle-china

[42]Jonathan Cohn, "Decisive Moments," *Mother Jones*, Jan/Feb 1997, https://www.motherjones.com/politics/1997/01/decisive-moments/

[43]"Full Text of Clinton's Speech on China Trade Bill", *The New York Times*, March 9, 2000, https://archive.nytimes.com/www.nytimes.com/library/world/asia/030900clinton-china-text.html

[44]Full Text of Clinton's Speech on China Trade Bill", *The New York Times*, March 9, 2000, https://archive.nytimes.com/www.nytimes.com/library/world/asia/030900clinton-china-text.html

[45]Full Text of Clinton's Speech on China Trade Bill", *The New York Times*, March 9, 2000, https://archive.nytimes.com/www.nytimes.com/library/world/asia/030900clinton-china-text.html

[46]Brian Anse Patrick, *The Ten Commandments Of Propaganda*, (Arktos Media, Ltd., 2013), 30

[47]Andrew J. Nathan, "The New Tiananmen Papers," Foreign Affairs, May

30, 2019, https://www.foreignaffairs.com/articles/china/2019-05-30/new-tiananmen-papers

[48]Orville Schell, "China's Cover-Up," *Foreign Affairs*, Jan/Feb 2018, 24

[49]Brian Anse Patrick, *The Ten Commandments Of Propaganda*, (Arktos Media, Ltd., 2013), 30

[50]K. Kris Hirst, "'Who Controls the Past Controls the Future', Quote Meaning", ThoughtCo.com, Hune 11, 2019, https://www.thoughtco.com/what-does-that-quote-mean-archaeology-172300

[51]Andrew J. Nathan, "The New Tiananmen Papers," Foreign Affairs, May 30, 2019, https://www.foreignaffairs.com/articles/china/2019-05-30/new-tiananmen-papers

Chapter 6: The People of Xi

[1]"Xi Story: The weight of Chinese 'rice bowl'", Xinhuanet.com, October 16, 2021, http://www.news.cn/english/2021-10/16/c_1310249871.htm

[2]James Palmer, "The balinghou", Aeon.co, https://aeon.co/essays/chinas-generation-gap-has-never-yawned-wider

[3]"China's super rich population drops as tech crackdown, global factors hurt wealth", Reuters, March 23, 2023, https://www.reuters.com/world/china/chinas-super-rich-population-drops-tech-crackdown-global-factors-hurt-wealth-2023-03-23/

[4]Louise Keely, et. al., "No More Tiers Navigating The Future Of Consumer Demand Across China's Cities," Demand Institute, December 1, 2015, https://www.conference-board.org/publications/Navigating-Future-Consumer-Demand-China-CFO

[5]Carl Crow, *400 Million Customers*, (United Kingdom: Eastbridge Books, 2017), 304

[6]Millward Brown, *The Power and Potential of the Chinese Dream*, February 2014, https://www.wpp.com/-/media/Project/WPP/Files/Imported-News/chinese-dream_feb14.pdf

[7]Helen Wang, *The Chinese Dream: The Rise of the World's Largest Middle Class and What It Means to You*, (USA: Best Seller Press, 2010)

[8]Helen Wang, *The Chinese Dream: The Rise of the World's Largest Middle Class and What It Means to You*, (USA: Best Seller Press, 2010)

[9]Helen Wang, *The Chinese Dream: The Rise of the World's Largest Middle Class and What It Means to You*, (USA: Best Seller Press, 2010)

[10]Helen Wang, *The Chinese Dream: The Rise of the World's Largest Middle Class and What It Means to You*, (USA: Best Seller Press, 2010), 153

[11]Millward Brown, *The Power and Potential of the Chinese Dream*, February 2014, https://www.wpp.com/-/media/Project/WPP/Files/Imported-News/chinese-dream_feb14.pdf

[12]Helen Wang, *The Chinese Dream: The Rise of the World's Largest Middle Class and What It Means to You*, (USA: Best Seller Press, 2010), 58

[13]Helen Wang, *The Chinese Dream: The Rise of the World's Largest Middle Class and What It Means to You*, (USA: Best Seller Press, 2010), 98

[14]Carl Crow, *400 Million Customers*, (United Kingdom: Eastbridge Books, 2017), 307

[15]Lola Woetzel, et. al., "China and the World", McKinsey Global Institute, July 2019, https://www.mckinsey.com/featured-insights/china/china-and-the-world-inside-the-dynamics-of-a-changing-relationship

[16]Lola Woetzel, et. al., "China and the World", McKinsey Global Institute, July 2019, https://www.mckinsey.com/featured-insights/china/china-and-the-world-inside-the-dynamics-of-a-changing-relationship

[17]China Power Team, "How Well-off is China's Middle Class?" CSIS, September 30, 2021, https://chinapower.csis.org/china-middle-class/#:~:text=The%20Rise%20of%20China's%20Middle%20Class,-Decades%20of%20economic&text=China's%20Gross%20National%20Income%20(GNI,end%20among%20fellow%20BRICS%20countries.

[18]Chad Bray, 'Breakneck growth in China's credit-card debt since 2012 raises worries about a potential bust, says ratings agency S&P', *South China Morning Post*, July 5, 2019, https://www.scmp.com/business/banking-finance/article/3017371/breakneck-growth-chinas-credit-card-debt-2012-raises

[19]Lola Woetzel, et. al., "China and the World", McKinsey Global Insti-

tute, July 2019, https://www.mckinsey.com/featured-insights/china/china-and-the-world-inside-the-dynamics-of-a-changing-relationship

[20]Frank Tang, Doug Palmer, "US-China trade war deal could be too late for the likes of Mastercard, American Express and Visa", *South China Morning Post*, April 2, 2019, https://www.scmp.com/economy/china-economy/article/3004180/us-china-trade-war-deal-could-be-too-late-likes-mastercard

[21]Frank Tang, Doug Palmer, "US-China trade war deal could be too late for the likes of Mastercard, American Express and Visa", *South China Morning Post*, April 2, 2019, https://www.scmp.com/economy/china-economy/article/3004180/us-china-trade-war-deal-could-be-too-late-likes-mastercard

[22]Jiang Xueqing, "UnionPay holds all the cards", ChinaDaily.com.cn, February 24, 2018, http://www.chinadaily.com.cn/cndy/2018-12/24/content_37418036.htm

[23]Frank Tang, Doug Palmer, "US-China trade war deal could be too late for the likes of Mastercard, American Express and Visa", *South China Morning Post*, April 2, 2019, https://www.scmp.com/economy/china-economy/article/3004180/us-china-trade-war-deal-could-be-too-late-likes-mastercard

[24]'Counter-flow', The Economist, 7/6/19 pg. 10

[25]Lola Woetzel, et. al., "China and the World", McKinsey Global Institute, July 2019, https://www.mckinsey.com/featured-insights/china/china-and-the-world-inside-the-dynamics-of-a-changing-relationship

[26]"Foreign financiers look pat trade war and ramp up in China", The Economist, July 6, 2019, https://www.economist.com/finance-and-economics/2019/07/06/foreign-financiers-look-past-the-trade-war-and-ramp-up-in-china

[27]"Far from home", *The Economist*, June 1, 2019, 59

[28]Jodi Xu Klein, 'A year into trade war, Wall Street is the latest front for US suspicions about China', South China Morning Post, 7/16/19

[29]"Counter-flow", *The Economist*, July 6, 2019,10

[30]Jing Yang, Goldman Sachs to Acquire 100% of China Securities Joint Venture, *The Wall Street Journal*, December 8, 2020, https://www.

wsj.com/articles/goldman-sachs-moves-to-acquire-100-of-china-securities-joint-venture-11607402421

[31]Billy Wong, "China's Middle-Class Consumers: Preferences and Spending Trends", Hong Kong Trade Development Council, July 18, 2017

[32]Billy Wong, "China's Middle-Class Consumers: Preferences and Spending Trends", Hong Kong Trade Development Council, July 18, 2017

[33]Ana Swanson, "The Contentious U.S.-China Relationship, by the Numbers", *The New York Times*, July 7, 2023, https://www.nytimes.com/2023/07/07/business/economy/us-china-relationship-facts.html

[34]"Profiles of International Transactions in US Residential Real Estate 2018", National Association of Realtors

[35]Laura He, "Evergrande posts losses of $81 billion over two years as it reports long-delayed results", July 18, 2023, https://www.cnn.com/2023/07/18/investing/china-evergrande-losses-intl-hnk/index.html

[36]Jacky Wang, "Don't Bet on Strong Medicine for Chinese Housing", *Wall Street Journal*, June 6, 2023, https://www.wsj.com/articles/dont-bet-on-strong-medicine-for-chinese-housing-e89bf272

[37]Lola Woetzel, et. al., "China and the World", McKinsey Global Institute, July 2019, https://www.mckinsey.com/featured-insights/china/china-and-the-world-inside-the-dynamics-of-a-changing-relationship

[38]"The Future of Chinese International Travel", Resonance and China Luxury Advisors, November 2018

[39]Avery Booker and Yang Gu, "What Do Chinese Tourists Care About in New York?", CLA Insight, November 9, 2015

[40]"China's high-spending tourists bring political clout", *The Economist*, February 23, 2019, https://www.economist.com/china/2019/02/23/chinas-high-spending-tourists-bring-political-clout

[41]"China's high-spending tourists bring political clout", *The Economist*, February 23, 2019, https://www.economist.com/china/2019/02/23/chinas-high-spending-tourists-bring-political-clout

[42]"The Future of Chinese International Travel", Resonance and China Luxury Advisors, November 2018

[43]"The Future of Chinese International Travel", Resonance and China Luxury Advisors, November 2018

[44]Martha C. White, 'Chinese Tourists' US Spending Has Plunged. The Trade War May Be to Blame', *The New York Times*, June 12, 2019, https://www.nytimes.com/2019/06/12/business/trade-war-us-china-tourism.html

[45]Ana Swanson, "The Contentious U.S.-China Relationship, by the Numbers", *The New York Times*, July 7, 2023, https://www.nytimes.com/2023/07/07/business/economy/us-china-relationship-facts.html

[46]https://www.pwccn.com/en/press-room/press-releases/pr-230622.html

[47]Dominic Barton, Yougang Chen, and Amy Jin, "Mapping China's middle class", McKinsey Quarterly, June 2013

[48]Zak Dychtwald, *Young China*, (USA: St. Martin Press, 2018), 31

[49]Doug Saunders, "China's millennials are unique, assertive—and potentially destabilizing", *The Globe And Mail*, May 16, 2018, https://www.theglobeandmail.com/opinion/chinas-millennials-are-unique-assertive-and-potentially-destabilizing/article28612450/

[50] Li Xueshi, "Buying to Survive: Why China Isn't Ready to Abandon Consumerism", Sixth Tone, November 15, 2018, https://www.sixthtone.com/news/1003193

[51]Li Xueshi, "Buying to Survive: Why China Isn't Ready to Abandon Consumerism", Sixth Tone, November 15, 2018, https://www.sixthtone.com/news/1003193

[52]"A dose of Sang", Newschinamag.com, October 1, 2018

[53]Helen Wang , *The Chinese Dream: The Rise of the World's Largest Middle Class and What It Means to You*, (USA: Best Seller Press, 2010), 196

[54]Alice Su, "'Just spend' and 'just borrow,' Jack Ma told China's youth. Then came the bill", *Los Angeles Times*, March 8, 2021, https://www.latimes.com/world-nation/story/2021-03-08/china-youth-jack-ma-ant-financial-credit-debt

[55]Alice Su, "'Just spend' and 'just borrow,' Jack Ma told China's youth. Then came the bill", *Los Angeles Times*, March 8, 2021, https://www.latimes.com/world-nation/story/2021-03-08/china-youth-jack-ma-ant-financial-credit-debt

[56]Daniel Zipser, Daniel Hui, Jia Zhou, Cherie Zhang, "2023 McKinsey China Consumer Report", December 2022, 5

[57]Daniel Zipser, Daniel Hui, Jia Zhou, Cherie Zhang, "2023 McKinsey China Consumer Report", December 2022, 1

[58]"How far can 'revenge spending' consumers carry China's economic rebound?", Fidelity International, February 17, 2023, https://www.fidelity.com.hk/en/articles/investment-spotlight/2023-02-17-how-far-can-revenge-spending-consumers-carry-chinas-economic-rebound-1676540870273

PART 3

CHAPTER 7: E²: Ecology and Economy

[1]Liu Mingfu, Wang Zhongyuan, *The Thoughts of Xi Jinping*, (USA: American Academic Press, 2017), 49

[2]Liu Mingfu, Wang Zhongyuan, *The Thoughts of Xi Jinping*, (USA: American Academic Press, 2017), 49

[3]Liu Mingfu, Wang Zhongyuan, *The Thoughts of Xi Jinping*, (USA: American Academic Press, 2017), 236

[4]Liu Mingfu, Wang Zhongyuan, *The Thoughts of Xi Jinping*, (USA: American Academic Press, 2017), 237

[5]Liu Mingfu, Wang Zhongyuan, *The Thoughts of Xi Jinping*, (USA: American Academic Press, 2017), 234

[6]Xi Jinping, *The Governance of China Volume II*, (Beijing: Foreign Languages Press, 2017), 217

[7]Xi Jinping, *The Governance of China Volume II*, (Beijing: Foreign Languages Press, 2017), 218

[8]Xi Jinping, *The Governance of China Volume II*, (Beijing: Foreign Languages Press, 2017), 430

[9]Xi Jinping, *The Governance of China Volume II*, (Beijing: Foreign Languages Press, 2017), 218

[10]*Xi Jinping: The Governance of China Volume I* [English Language Version], (Beijing: Foreign Languages Press, 2014), 55

[11]*Xi Jinping: The Governance of China Volume I* [English Language Version], (Beijing: Foreign Languages Press, 2014), 132

[12]*Xi Jinping: The Governance of China Volume I* [English Language Version], (Beijing: Foreign Languages Press, 2014), 132

[13]*Xi Jinping: The Governance of China Volume I* [English Language Version], (Beijing: Foreign Languages Press, 2014), 133

[14]*Xi Jinping: The Governance of China Volume I* [English Language Version], (Beijing: Foreign Languages Press, 2014), 134

[15]*Xi Jinping: The Governance of China Volume I* [English Language Version], (Beijing: Foreign Languages Press, 2014), 136

[16]Ezra F. Vogel, *Deng Xiaoping and the Transformation of China*, (USA: Harvard University Press, 2011), 307

[17]Ezra F. Vogel, *Deng Xiaoping and the Transformation of China*, (USA: Harvard University Press, 2011), 671

[18]Ezra F. Vogel, *Deng Xiaoping and the Transformation of China*, (USA: Harvard University Press, 2011), 674

[19]Xi Jinping, *The Governance of China Volume II*, (Beijing: Foreign Languages Press, 2017), 227

[20]Lui He. "A Comparative Study of Two Global Crises." Discussion Paper, Belfer Center for Science and International Affairs, Harvard Kennedy School. June 2014

[21]Lui He, "A Comparative Study of Two Global Crises." Discussion Paper, Belfer Center for Science and International Affairs, Harvard Kennedy School. June 2014

[22]Xi Jinping, *The Governance of China Volume II*, (Beijing: Foreign Languages Press, 2017), 56

[23]Scott Kennedy, "Made in China 2025," Center for Strategic and International Studies, June 1, 2015

[24]Jost Wübbeke, Mirjam Meissner, Max J. Zenglein, Jaqueline Ives, and Björn Conrad, "Made in China 2025: The making of a high-tech superpower and consequences for industrial companies" (Mercator Institute for China Studies, December 2016)

[25]Jost Wübbeke, Mirjam Meissner, Max J. Zenglein, Jaqueline Ives, and Björn Conrad, "Made in China 2025: The making of a high-tech

superpower and consequences for industrial companies" (Mercator Institute for China Studies, December 2016)

[26] Jost Wübbeke, Mirjam Meissner, Max J. Zenglein, Jaqueline Ives, and Björn Conrad, "Made in China 2025: The making of a high-tech superpower and consequences for industrial companies" (Mercator Institute for China Studies, December 2016)

[27] "Made in China 2025: Global Ambitions Built on Local Protections", US Chamber of Commerce, 2017

[28] "The battle for digital supremacy," *The Economist*, March 17, 2018, 11

[29] Jost Wübbeke, Mirjam Meissner, Max J. Zenglein, Jaqueline Ives, and Björn Conrad, "Made in China 2025: The making of a high-tech superpower and consequences for industrial companies" (Mercator Institute for China Studies, December 2016)

[30] Peter Martin, Keith Zhai, "Is Xia Threat to Foreign Businesses in China?", *Bloomberg*, October 16, 2017, https://www.bloomberg.com/news/articles/2017-10-12/is-xi-a-threat-to-foreign-businesses-in-china?embedded-checkout=true

[31] Joshua Green, "Bannon's Back and Targeting China", *Bloomberg*, September 28, 2017, https://www.bloomberg.com/news/articles/2017-09-28/bannon-s-back-and-targeting-china

[32] Joshua Green, "Bannon's Back and Targeting China", *Bloomberg*, September 28, 2017, https://www.bloomberg.com/news/articles/2017-09-28/bannon-s-back-and-targeting-china

[33] Thilo Hanemann, et. al., "Two-Way Street-US-China Investment Trends-2021 Update", Rhodium Group, May 19, 2021, https://rhg.com/research/twowaystreet-2021/

[34] Jost Wübbeke, Mirjam Meissner, Max J. Zenglein, Jaqueline Ives, and Björn Conrad, "Made in China 2025: The making of a high-tech superpower and consequences for industrial companies", (Mercator Institute for China Studies, December 2016)

[35] Jost Wübbeke, Mirjam Meissner, Max J. Zenglein, Jaqueline Ives, and Björn Conrad, "Made in China 2025: The making of a high-tech superpower and consequences for industrial companies", (Mercator Institute for China Studies, December 2016)

[36]Jost Wübbeke, Mirjam Meissner, Max J. Zenglein, Jaqueline Ives, and Björn Conrad, "Made in China 2025: The making of a high-tech superpower and consequences for industrial companies", (Mercator Institute for China Studies, December 2016)

[37]Xi Jinping, *The Governance of China Volume II*, (Beijing: Foreign Languages Press, 2017), 222

[38]*Xi Jinping: The Governance of China Volume I* [English Language Version], (Beijing: Foreign Languages Press, 2014), 137

[39]Jost Wübbeke, Mirjam Meissner, Max J. Zenglein, Jaqueline Ives, and Björn Conrad, "Made in China 2025: The making of a high-tech superpower and consequences for industrial companies" (Mercator Institute for China Studies, December 2016)

[40]Jost Wübbeke, Mirjam Meissner, Max J. Zenglein, Jaqueline Ives, and Björn Conrad, "Made in China 2025: The making of a high-tech superpower and consequences for industrial companies", (Mercator Institute for China Studies, December 2016)

[41]Jost Wübbeke, Mirjam Meissner, Max J. Zenglein, Jaqueline Ives, and Björn Conrad, "Made in China 2025: The making of a high-tech superpower and consequences for industrial companies", (Mercator Institute for China Studies, December 2016)

CHAPTER 8: Creating a Moderately Prosperous Society

[1]Liu Mingfu, Wang Zhongyuan, *The Thoughts of Xi Jinping*, (USA: American Academic Press, 2017), 50

[2]Liu Mingfu, Wang Zhongyuan, *The Thoughts of Xi Jinping*, (USA: American Academic Press, 2017), 50

[3]Liu Mingfu, Wang Zhongyuan, *The Thoughts of Xi Jinping*, (USA: American Academic Press, 2017), 50

[4]Liu Mingfu, Wang Zhongyuan, *The Thoughts of Xi Jinping*, (USA: American Academic Press, 2017), 53

[5]Richard Wide and Bridget Parker, "Corruption, Pollution, Inequality Are Top Concerns in China", Pew Research, September 24, 2015, https://www.pewresearch.org/global/2015/09/24/corruption-pollution-inequality-are-top-concerns-in-china/

[6]China Power Team, "How well off is China's middle class?" April 26,2017, https://chinapower.csis.org/china-middle-class

[7]Liu Mingfu, Wang Zhongyuan, *The Thoughts of Xi Jinping*, (USA: American Academic Press, 2017), 221

[8]Liu Mingfu, Wang Zhongyuan, *The Thoughts of Xi Jinping*, (USA: American Academic Press, 2017), 221

[9]Liu Mingfu, Wang Zhongyuan, *The Thoughts of Xi Jinping*, (USA: American Academic Press, 2017), 219

[10]Yuwa Hedrick-Wong, "The Reality of China's Economic Slowdown", *Forbes*, August 23, 2018, https://www.forbes.com/sites/yuwahedrickwong/2018/08/23/the-reality-of-chinas-economic-slowdown/?sh=686d6fc14d86

[11]Liu Mingfu, Wang Zhongyuan, *The Thoughts of Xi Jinping*, (USA: American Academic Press, 2017), 222

[12]"The great sprawl of China," *The Economist*, January 24, 2015, 37

[13]"China approves Plan to Increase Urban Population," *The Wall Street Journal*, March 18, 2014, A9

[14]Liu Mingfu, Wang Zhongyuan, *The Thoughts of Xi Jinping*, (USA: American Academic Press, 2017), 224

[15]Liu Mingfu, Wang Zhongyuan, *The Thoughts of Xi Jinping*, (USA: American Academic Press, 2017), 224

[16]Liu Mingfu, Wang Zhongyuan, *The Thoughts of Xi Jinping*, (USA: American Academic Press, 2017), 225

[17]Elaine Chan, "Can China's emerging cities help counter the economic slowdown and US-China trade war?" *South China Morning Post*, February 19, 2019, https://www.scmp.com/economy/china-economy/article/2186740/can-chinas-emerging-cities-help-counter-economic-slowdown-and

[18]Elaine Chan, "Can China's emerging cities help counter the economic slowdown and US-China trade war?" *South China Morning Post,* February 19, 2019, https://www.scmp.com/economy/china-economy/article/2186740/can-chinas-emerging-cities-help-counter-economic-slowdown-and

[19]Elaine Chan, "Can China's emerging cities help counter the economic slowdown and US-China trade war?" *South China Morning Post*, February 19, 2019, https://www.scmp.com/economy/china-economy/article/2186740/can-chinas-emerging-cities-help-counter-economic-slowdown-and

[20]Liu Mingfu, Wang Zhongyuan, *The Thoughts of Xi Jinping*, (USA: American Academic Press, 2017), 229

[21]Orange Wang, "China's wealth gap widens as more than half of its provinces missed growth targets last year," *South China Morning Post*, February 12, 2019, https://www.scmp.com/economy/china-economy/article/2185738/chinas-wealth-gap-widens-more-half-its-provinces-missed-growth

[22]Orange Wang, "China's wealth gap widens as more than half of its provinces missed growth targets last year," *South China Morning Post*, February 12, 2019, https://www.scmp.com/economy/china-economy/article/2185738/chinas-wealth-gap-widens-more-half-its-provinces-missed-growth

[23]Jonathan Cheng, "China Is the Only Major Economy to Report Economic Growth for 2020", *Wall Street Journal*, January 18, 2021, https://www.wsj.com/articles/china-is-the-only-major-economy-to-report-economic-growth-for-2020-11610936187

[24]China Power Team, "Is China Succeeding at Eradicating Poverty", October 23, 2020, https://chinapower.csis.org/poverty/

[25]Chaguan, "China's anti-poverty drive is not disinterested charity", *The Economist*, https://www.economist.com/china/2020/01/19/chinas-anti-poverty-drive-is-not-disinterest-charity

[26]Chaguan, "China's anti-poverty drive is not disinterested charity", *The Economist*, https://www.economist.com/china/2020/01/19/chinas-anti-poverty-drive-is-not-disinterest-charity

Chapter 9: The Antigraft Campaign

[1]Liu Mingfu, Wang Zhongyuan, *The Thoughts of Xi Jinping*, (USA: American Academic Press, 2017), 51

[2]"Global Attitudes & Trends", Pew Research Center, , September 19, 2013; September 24, 2015

[3]Anthony Goh, Matthew Sullivan, "The Most Misunderstood Business Concept in China," *Business Insider*, September 24, 2011, https://www.businessinsider.com/the-most-misunderstood-business-concept-in-china-2011-2

[4]Anthony Goh, Matthew Sullivan, "The Most Misunderstood Business Concept in China," *Business Insider*, September 24, 2011, https://www.businessinsider.com/the-most-misunderstood-business-concept-in-china-2011-2

[5]Jin Guan, "Guanxi: The Key to Achieving Success in China", Sino-Platonic Papers, Univ. of Pa, No. 217, December 2011, https://sino-platonic.org/complete/spp217_guanxi.pdf

[6]Jin Guan, "Guanxi: The Key to Achieving Success in China", Sino-Platonic Papers, Univ. of Pa, No. 217, December 2011, https://sino-platonic.org/complete/spp217_guanxi.pdf

[7]Jin Guan, "Guanxi: The Key to Achieving Success in China", Sino-Platonic Papers, Univ. of Pa, No. 217, December 2011, https://sino-platonic.org/complete/spp217_guanxi.pdf

[8]Jin Guan, "Guanxi: The Key to Achieving Success in China", Sino-Platonic Papers, Univ. of Pa, No. 217, December 2011, https://sino-platonic.org/complete/spp217_guanxi.pdf

[9]Anthony Goh, Matthew Sullivan, "The Most Misunderstood Business Concept in China," *Business Insider*, September 24, 2011, https://www.businessinsider.com/the-most-misunderstood-business-concept-in-china-2011-2

[10]Carl Crow, *400 Million Customers*, (United Kingdom: Eastbridge Books, 2017), 80

[11]Carl Crow, *400 Million Customers*, (United Kingdom: Eastbridge Books, 2017), 84

[12]Liu Mingfu, Wang Zhongyuan, *The Thoughts of Xi Jinping*, (USA: American Academic Press, 2017), 148

[13]"Corruption Perceptions Index, Transparency International, 2023, https://www.transparency.org/en/cpi/2023/index/chn

¹⁴Liu Mingfu, Wang Zhongyuan, *The Thoughts of Xi Jinping*, (USA: American Academic Press, 2017), 149

¹⁵Liu Mingfu, Wang Zhongyuan, *The Thoughts of Xi Jinping*, (USA: American Academic Press, 2017), 158-159

¹⁶Liu Mingfu, Wang Zhongyuan, *The Thoughts of Xi Jinping*, (USA: American Academic Press, 2017), 391

¹⁷Liu Mingfu, Wang Zhongyuan, *The Thoughts of Xi Jinping*, (USA: American Academic Press, 2017), 156

¹⁸Liu Mingfu, Wang Zhongyuan, *The Thoughts of Xi Jinping*, (USA: American Academic Press, 2017), 156

¹⁹"Xi Jinping Millionaire Relations Reveal Elite Chinese Fortunes", *Bloomberg News*, June 29, 2012, https://bloomberg.com/news/articles/2012-06-29/xi-Jinping-millionaire-relations-reveal-fortunes-of-elite

²⁰Xi Jinping, *Up and Out of Poverty*, (Beijing: Foreign Languages Press, 2016), 9

²¹Xi Jinping, *Up and Out of Poverty*, (Beijing: Foreign Languages Press, 2016), 271

²²Theodore White, Life Looks at China, *Theodore H. White at Large*, (New York: Random House, 1992), 102

²³Theodore White, "Life Looks at China," *Theodore H. White at Large*, (New York: Random House, 1992), 102

²⁴Liu Mingfu, Wang Zhongyuan, *The Thoughts of Xi Jinping*, (USA: American Academic Press, 2017), 199

²⁵Liu Mingfu, Wang Zhongyuan, *The Thoughts of Xi Jinping*, (USA: American Academic Press, 2017), 175

²⁶Xi Jinping, *Up and Out of Poverty*, (Beijing: Foreign Languages Press, 2016), 31

²⁷Liu Mingfu, Wang Zhongyuan, *The Thoughts of Xi Jinping*, (USA: American Academic Press, 2017), 179

²⁸Liu Mingfu, Wang Zhongyuan, *The Thoughts of Xi Jinping*, (USA: American Academic Press, 2017), 179

²⁹Jun Mai, "Xi Jinping's anti-corruption drive brings down more generals than 20th century warfare", *South China Morning Post*, Novem-

ber 17, 2017, https://www.scmp.com/news/china/policies-politics/article/2120430/xi-jinpings-anti-corruption-drive-brings-down-more

[30]Visualizing China's Anti-Corruption Campaign, ChinaFile.com, August 15, 2018, https://www.chinafile.com/infographics/visualizing-chinas-anti-corruption-campaign

[31]Zak Dychtwald, *Young China*, (USA: St. Martin Press, 2018), 263

[32]Tania Branigan, "Politburo, army, casinos: China's corruption crackdown spreads," *The Guardian*, February 14, 2015, https://www.theguardian.com/world/2015/feb/14/china-corruption-crackdown-spreads-xi-jinping

[33]Weijing Zhu, "The side effects of the Anti-Corruption Campaign," theworldofchinese.com, May 2, 2014

[34]"Cheers to Uncle Sam," *The Economist*, November 27, 2014, https://www.economist.com/business/2014/11/27/cheers-to-uncle-sam

[35]Ruth Bender, "China Chills Remy," *The Wall Street Journal*, November 27, 2013

[36]"Priority Recommendations for US-China Trade Negotiations," US Chamber of Commerce, January 16, 2019

Chapter 10: Offspring: Nature vs Demand

[1]Liu Mingfu, Wang Zhongyuan, *The Thoughts of Xi Jinping*, (USA: American Academic Press, 2017), 52

[2]Chinese Sociology & Anthropology, Taylor & Francis Online, Vol. 24, 1992—issue 3, p. 11-16, published online, December 20, 2014

[3]"China's demographic divisions are getting deeper", *The Economist*, September 21, 2017, https://www.economist.com/china/2017/09/21/chinas-demographic-divisions-are-getting-deeper

[4]Ezra F. Vogel, *Deng Xiaoping and the Transformation of China*, (USA: Harvard University Press, 2011), 435

[5]"China's demographic divisions are getting deeper", *The Economist*, September 21, 2017, https://www.economist.com/china/2017/09/21/chinas-demographic-divisions-are-getting-deeper

[6]Sidney Leng, "An inconvenient truth? China omits key figures that may have highlighted its demographic time bomb from official statistics",

South China Morning Post, October 27, 2017, https://www.scmp.com/news/china/economy/article/2117167/inconvenient-truth-china-omits-key-figures-may-have-highlighted#!

[7]"Bare branches, redundant males," *The Economist*, April 18, 2015, https://www.economist.com/asia/2015/04/18/bare-branches-redundant-males#

[8]"From too few girls to too many men", *The Economist*, January 19, 2017, https://www.economist.com/leaders/2017/01/19/from-too-few-girls-to-too-many-men

[9]"Bare and profligate," *The Economist*, 11/7/15

[10]"From too few girls to too many men", *The Economist*, January 19, 2017, https://www.economist.com/leaders/2017/01/19/from-too-few-girls-to-too-many-men

[11]"Wedding vows," *The Economist*, February 26, 2015, https://www.economist.com/china/2015/02/26/wedding-wows

[12]Bob Davis, "China's One-Child Shift Will First Drain Workforce", *The Wall Street Journal*, 11/22/13

[13]Laurie Burkitt, "China Eases Limits on Births as Labor Shortage Looms," *The Wall Street Journal*, November 22, 2013, https://www.wsj.com/articles/SB10001424052702304607104579211351308910382

[14]Liyan Qi, Shen Lu, "China is pressing women to have more babies. Many are saying no," *The Wall Street Journal*, January 2, 2024, https://www.wsj.com/articles/china-population-births-decline-womens-rights-5af9937b

[15]James Ellis, "China Needs Help Having Babies," *Bloomberg Businessweek*, July 17, 2017

[16]James Ellis, "China Needs Help Having Babies," *Bloomberg Businessweek*, July 17, 2017

[17]"Two little, too late," *The Economist,* November 5, 2015, https://www.economist.com/leaders/2015/11/05/two-little-too-late

[18]Nicholas Eberstadt, "China's Coming One-Child Crisis," *The Wall Street Journal*, November 26, 2013, https://www.wsj.com/articles/SB10001424052702304791704579216630468814424

[19]Leta Hong Fincher, "China Dropped Its One-Child Policy. So Why Aren't Chinese Women Having More Babies?", *The New York Times*, February 20, 2018, https://www.nytimes.com/2018/02/20/opinion/china-women-birthrate-rights.html

[20]"Can China become a scientific superpower?", *The Economist*, January 12, 2019, https://www.economist.com/science-and-technology/2019/01/12/can-china-become-a-scientific-superpower

[21]Liu Yanfei, Coco Feng, "Infant-Formula Makers Milk Chinese Consumers' Wallets," *Caixin Global*, November 2, 2017, https://www.caixinglobal.com/2017-11-02/infant-formula-makers-milk-chinese-consumers-wallets-101164893.html

[22]James Ellis, "China Needs Help Having Babies," *Bloomberg Businessweek*, July 17, 2017

CHAPTER 11: Spiritual Wealth and Values

[1]Liu Mingfu, Wang Zhongyuan, *The Thoughts of Xi Jinping*, (USA: American Academic Press, 2017), 53

[2]Liu Mingfu, Wang Zhongyuan, *The Thoughts of Xi Jinping*, (USA: American Academic Press, 2017), 53

[3]Ian Johnson, "China's Great Awakening," *Foreign Affairs*, March/April 2017, Vol. 96 No.2, 83

[4]Ian Johnson, "China's Great Awakening," *Foreign Affairs*, March/April 2017, Vol. 96 No.2, 83

[5]Ian Johnson, "China's Great Awakening," Foreign Affairs, March/April 2017, Vol. 96 No.2, 95

[6]*Xi Jinping: The Governance of China Volume I* [English Language Version], (Beijing: Foreign Languages Press, 2014), 7

[7]*Xi Jinping: The Governance of China Volume I* [English Language Version], (Beijing: Foreign Languages Press, 2014), 20

[8]Ezra F. Vogel, *Deng Xiaoping and the Transformation of China*, (USA: Harvard University Press, 2011), 466

[9]Ezra F. Vogel, *Deng Xiaoping and the Transformation of China*, (USA: Harvard University Press, 2011), 684

[10]*Xi Jinping: The Governance of China Volume I* [English Language Version], (Beijing: Foreign Languages Press, 2014), 118

[11]*Xi Jinping: The Governance of China Volume I* [English Language Version], (Beijing: Foreign Languages Press, 2014), 118

[12]Samuel P. Huntington, *The Clash Of Civilizations and the Remaking of World Order*, (USA: Simon & Schuster, 1996), 19

[13]Samuel P. Huntington, The Clash Of Civilizations and the Remaking of World Order, (USA: Simon & Schuster, 1996), 21

[14]Samuel P. Huntington, *The Clash Of Civilizations and the Remaking of World Order*, (USA: Simon & Schuster, 1996), 20

[15]Samuel P. Huntington, *The Clash Of Civilizations and the Remaking of World Order*, (USA: Simon & Schuster, 1996), 21

[16]Samuel P. Huntington, *The Clash Of Civilizations and the Remaking of World Order*, (USA: Simon & Schuster, 1996), 41

[17]Samuel P. Huntington, *The Clash Of Civilizations and the Remaking of World Order*, (USA: Simon & Schuster, 1996), 42

[18]Samuel P. Huntington, *The Clash Of Civilizations and the Remaking of World Order*, (USA: Simon & Schuster, 1996), 47

[19]Document No. 19, Central Committee Of CPC, March 31, 1982, 2

[20]Document No. 19, Central Committee Of CPC March 31, 1982, 5-6

[21]Henry Kissinger, *On China*, (England: Penguin, 2012), 307

[22]Document No. 19, Central Committee Of CPC March 31, 1982, 9-10

[23]"The Story of Propaganda", American Historical Association, 1944, https://www.historians.org/about-aha-and-membership/aha-history-and-archives/gi-roundtable-series/pamphlets/em-2-what-is-propaganda-(1944)/the-story-of-propaganda

[24]Document No. 19, Central Committee Of CPC March 31, 1982, 14

[25]Document No. 19, Central Committee Of CPC March 31, 1982, 2

[26]Document No. 19, Central Committee Of CPC March 31, 1982, 12

[27]Ian Johnson, "Vatican Eager for Chinese Ties, Asks 'Underground' Bishops to Step Aside", *The New York Times*, January 29, 2018, https://www.nytimes.com/2018/01/29/world/asia/china-catholics-vatican.html

[28] Amy B Wang, "Bowing to pressure from China, Mercedes-Benz apologizes for quoting the Dalai Lama in ad," *The Washington Post*, February 6, 2018, https://www.washingtonpost.com/news/worldviews/wp/2018/02/06/bowing-to-pressure-from-china-mercedes-benz-apologizes-for-quoting-the-dalai-lama-in-ad/

[29] Howard W. French, "A Sage for All Seasons," *The Wall Street Journal*, April 11, 2015

[30] Howard W. French, "A Sage for All Seasons," *The Wall Street Journal*, April 11, 2015

[31] "Confucius says, Xi does," *The Economist*, July 25, 2015, https://www.economist.com/china/2015/07/25/confucius-says-xi-does

[32] Huijie Cher, "The Political Utility of Morality: A discourse analysis of China's 'Core Socialist Values' campaign" Leiden University, July 2018, 7, https://studenttheses.universiteitleiden.nl/handle/1887/64225?solr_nav%5Bid%5D=d6c492f14869a01877fe&solr_nav%5Bpage%5D=0&solr_nav%5Boffset%5D=1

[33] Aris Teon, "Law In Imperial China—Confucianism and Legalism," China Journal, May 7, 2016, https://china-journal.org/2016/05/07/law-in-imperial-china-confucianism-legalism/

[34] Aris Teon, "Law In Imperial China—Confucianism and Legalism," China Journal, May 7, 2016, https://china-journal.org/2016/05/07/law-in-imperial-china-confucianism-legalism/

[35] Aris Teon, "Law In Imperial China—Confucianism and Legalism," China Journal, May 7, 2016, https://china-journal.org/2016/05/07/law-in-imperial-china-confucianism-legalism/

[36] Aris Teon, "Law In Imperial China—Confucianism and Legalism," China Journal, May 7, 2016, https://china-journal.org/2016/05/07/law-in-imperial-china-confucianism-legalism/

[37] Aris Teon, "Law In Imperial China—Confucianism and Legalism," China Journal, May 7, 2016, https://china-journal.org/2016/05/07/law-in-imperial-china-confucianism-legalism/

[38] "A hit TV series in China skewers cranky old parents", *The Economist*, March 23, 2019, https://www.economist.com/china/2019/03/21/a-hit-tv-series-in-china-skewers-cranky-old-parents

[39]Aris Teon, "Law In Imperial China—Confucianism and Legalism," China Journal, May 7, 2016, https://china-journal.org/2016/05/07/law-in-imperial-china-confucianism-legalism/

[40]Aris Teon, "Law In Imperial China—Confucianism and Legalism," China Journal, May 7, 2016, https://china-journal.org/2016/05/07/law-in-imperial-china-confucianism-legalism/

[41]Huijie Cher, "The Political Utility of Morality: A discourse analysis of China's 'Core Socialist Values' campaign" Leiden University, July 2018, 15-17, https://studenttheses.universiteitleiden.nl/handle/1887/64225?solr_nav%5Bid%5D=d6c-492f14869a01877fe&solr_nav%5Bpage%5D=0&solr_nav%5Boffset%5D=11

[42]Huijie Cher, Huijie Cher, "The Political Utility of Morality: A discourse analysis of China's 'Core Socialist Values' campaign" Leiden University, July 2018, 15-17, https://studenttheses.universiteitleiden.nl/handle/1887/64225?solr_nav%5Bid%5D=d6c-492f14869a01877fe&solr_nav%5Bpage%5D=0&solr_nav%5Boffset%5D=1

[43]Huijie Cher, "The Political Utility of Morality: A discourse analysis of China's 'Core Socialist Values' campaign" Leiden University, July 2018, 15-17, https://studenttheses.universiteitleiden.nl/handle/1887/64225?solr_nav%5Bid%5D=d6c-492f14869a01877fe&solr_nav%5Bpage%5D=0&solr_nav%5Boffset%5D=1

[44]Huijie Cher, "The Political Utility of Morality: A discourse analysis of China's 'Core Socialist Values' campaign" Leiden University, July 2018, 17-18, https://studenttheses.universiteitleiden.nl/handle/1887/64225?solr_nav%5Bid%5D=d6c-492f14869a01877fe&solr_nav%5Bpage%5D=0&solr_nav%5Boffset%5D=1

[45]Brian Anse Patrick, *The Ten Commandments Of Propaganda*, (Arktos Media, Ltd., 2013), 46

[46]*Xi Jinping: The Governance of China Volume I* [English Language Version], (Beijing: Foreign Languages Press, 2014), 187

[47]*Xi Jinping: The Governance of China Volume I* [English Language Version], (Beijing: Foreign Languages Press, 2014), 188

[48]Huijie Cher, "The Political Utility of Morality: A discourse analysis of China's 'Core Socialist Values' campaign" Leiden University, July 2018, 20-22, https://studenttheses.universiteitleiden.nl/handle/1887/64225?solr_nav%5Bid%5D=d6c-492f14869a01877fe&solr_nav%5Bpage%5D=0&solr_nav%5Boffset%5D=1

[49]Mareike Ohlberg, Shazeda Ahmed, Bertram Lang, "Central Planning, local experiments The complex implementation of China's Social Credit System", Merics.org, December 12, 2017, https://merics.org/en/report/central-planning-local-experiments

[50]Rogier Creemers, "China's Social Credit System: An Evolving Practice of Control," University of Leiden, May 9, 2018, https://papers.ssrn.com/sol3/papers.cfm?abstract_id=3175792

[51]Rogier Creemers, "China's Social Credit System: An Evolving Practice of Control," University of Leiden, May 9, 2018, https://papers.ssrn.com/sol3/papers.cfm?abstract_id=3175792

[52]Rogier Creemers, "China's Social Credit System: An Evolving Practice of Control," University of Leiden, May 9, 2018, https://papers.ssrn.com/sol3/papers.cfm?abstract_id=3175792

[53]Rogier Creemers, "China's Social Credit System: An Evolving Practice of Control," University of Leiden, May 9, 2018, https://papers.ssrn.com/sol3/papers.cfm?abstract_id=3175792

[54]Mareike Ohlberg, Shazeda Ahmed, Bertram Lang, "Central Planning, local experiments The complex implementation of China's Social Credit System", Merics.org, December 12, 2017, https://merics.org/en/report/central-planning-local-experiments

[55]Rogier Creemers, "China's Social Credit System: An Evolving Practice of Control," University of Leiden, May 9, 2018, https://papers.ssrn.com/sol3/papers.cfm?abstract_id=3175792

[56]Rogier Creemers, "China's Social Credit System: An Evolving Practice of Control," University of Leiden, May 9, 2018, https://papers.ssrn.com/sol3/papers.cfm?abstract_id=3175792

[57]Mareike Ohlberg, Shazeda Ahmed, Bertram Lang, "Central Planning, local experiments The complex implementation of China's Social Credit System", Merics.org, December 12, 2017, https://merics.org/en/report/central-planning-local-experiments

[58]Mareike Ohlberg, Shazeda Ahmed, Bertram Lang, "Central Planning, local experiments The complex implementation of China's Social Credit System", Merics.org, December 12, 2017, https://merics.org/en/report/central-planning-local-experiments

[59]Rogier Creemers, "China's Social Credit System: An Evolving Practice of Control," University of Leiden, May 9, 2018, https://papers.ssrn.com/sol3/papers.cfm?abstract_id=3175792

[60]Mareike Ohlberg, Shazeda Ahmed, Bertram Lang, "Central Planning, local experiments The complex implementation of China's Social Credit System", Merics.org, December 12, 2017, https://merics.org/en/report/central-planning-local-experiments

[61]Rogier Creemers, "China's Social Credit System: An Evolving Practice of Control," University of Leiden, May 9, 2018, https://papers.ssrn.com/sol3/papers.cfm?abstract_id=3175792

[62]Tugba Sabanoglu, "Top personal protective products exporting nations worldwide in 2019", Statista, July 12, 2021, https://www.statista.com/statistics/1121545/top-exporters-of-personal-protective-products-worldwide/

[63]Meng Jing, "This small team is building a social credit system app for China's youth to determine who's naughty or nice," *South China Morning Post*, March 25, 2019, https://www.scmp.com/tech/apps-social/article/3003158/small-team-building-social-credit-system-app-chinas-youth

[64]Meng Jing, "This small team is building a social credit system app for China's youth to determine who's naughty or nice," *South China Morning Post,* March 25, 2019, https://www.scmp.com/tech/apps-social/article/3003158/small-team-building-social-credit-system-app-chinas-youth

[65]Meng Jing, "This small team is building a social credit system app for China's youth to determine who's naughty or nice," *South China*

Morning Post, March 25, 2019, https://www.scmp.com/tech/apps-social/article/3003158/small-team-building-social-credit-system-app-chinas-youth

[66]"The Digital Hand How China's Social Credit System Conditions Market Actors", European Union Chamber of Commerce in China, 2019, https://www.europeanchamber.com.cn/en/publications-corporate-social-credit-system

CHAPTER 12: One Mountain, Two Tigers

[1]Liu Mingfu, Wang Zhongyuan, *The Thoughts of Xi Jinping*, (USA: American Academic Press, 2017), 139

[2]Ayyappa Nagubandi, "The Different Kinds of Leaders—the Lion, the Tiger, and the Cheetah" May 30, 2014, https://yourstory.com/2014/05/leaders

[3]https://www.griffith.edu.au/__data/assets/pdf_file/0025/292930/Griffith-Tsinghua-WP-no-2-final.pdf

[4]Liu Mingfu, Wang Zhongyuan, *The Thoughts of Xi Jinping*, (USA: American Academic Press, 2017), 141

[5]Liu, Mingfu, (2015-05-05). The China Dream: Great Power Thinking and Strategic Posture in the Post-American Era (Kindle Locations 545). CN Times Books. Kindle Edition

[6]Mingfu, Liu (2015-05-05). The China Dream: Great Power Thinking and Strategic Posture in the Post-American Era (Kindle Locations 710). CN Times Books. Kindle Edition

[7]Mingfu, Liu (2015-05-05). The China Dream: Great Power Thinking and Strategic Posture in the Post-American Era (Kindle Locations 4752). CN Times Books. Kindle Edition

[8]Mingfu, Liu (2015-05-05). The China Dream: Great Power Thinking and Strategic Posture in the Post-American Era (Kindle Locations 2905). CN Times Books. Kindle Edition

[9]Mingfu, Liu (2015-05-05). The China Dream: Great Power Thinking and Strategic Posture in the Post-American Era (Kindle Locations 1046). CN Times Books. Kindle Edition

[10]Mingfu, Liu (2015-05-05). The China Dream: Great Power Thinking

and Strategic Posture in the Post-American Era (Kindle Locations 3913). CN Times Books. Kindle Edition

[11]Mingfu, Liu (2015-05-05). The China Dream: Great Power Thinking and Strategic Posture in the Post-American Era (Kindle Locations 1569). CN Times Books. Kindle Edition

[12]Panle Jia Barwick, Shanjun Li, Jeremy Wallace, Jessica Chen Weiss, "Commercial Casualties: Political Boycotts and International Disputes", *Cambridge University Press*, October 23, 2023, https://www.cambridge.org/core/journals/journal-of-east-asian-studies/article/commercial-casualties-political-boycotts-and-international-disputes/DB7DFB64EF409B361E6863B6C8B0FF0B

[13]Michael Pillsbury, *The Hundred-Year Marathon: China's Secret Strategy to Replace America as the Global Superpower*, (USA: St Martin's Griffin, 2016), 7, 10

[14]Kurt Campbell, Jake Sullivan, "Competition with Catastrophe" *Foreign Affairs*, August 1, 2019, https://www.foreignaffairs.com/articles/china/competition-with-china-without-catastrophe

[15]Ryan Hass, *Stronger: Adapting America's China Strategy in an Age of Competitive Interdependence*, (Yale University Press, 2021), 4-5

[16]Antoni Slodkowski, "Chinese Premier Li calls for global cooperation, says China open for business," *Reuters*, January 16, 2024, https://www.reuters.com/world/asia-pacific/chinas-premier-li-address-davos-its-economy-struggles-2024-01-16/

[17]Amy Hawkins, "'Planet Earth is big enough for two': Biden and Xi meet for first time in a year", *The Guardian*, November 15, 2023, https://www.theguardian.com/us-news/2023/nov/15/joe-biden-xi-jin-ping-san-francisco-china-apec

Appendix

Case Study: Ford's Folly

[1]Thomas Friedman, "Their Moon Shot and Ours," *The New York Times*, September 25, 2010, https://www.nytimes.com/2010/09/26/opinion/26friedman.html

[2]Thomas Friedman, "Their Moon Shot and Ours," *The New York Times*, September 25, 2010, https://www.nytimes.com/2010/09/26/opinion/26friedman.html

[3]Jordan Schneider, 'The 'American Factory' Chinese Boss on Why He Invested in the US', ChinaTalk.media, September 3, 2019, https://www.chinatalk.media/p/an-interview-with-the-american-factory

[4]Hans-Werner Kaas, Thomas Fleming, "Bill Ford charts a course for the future," McKinsey & Co., October 1, 2014, https://www.mckinsey.com/industries/automotive-and-assembly/our-insights/bill-ford-charts-a-course-for-the-future

[5]Keith Bradsher, "After Nearly 90 Years, Ford Wants China to Give It a Second Chance," *The New York Times*, October 20, 2013, https://www.nytimes.com/2013/10/21/business/international/after-89-years-ford-wants-a-second-chance-in-china.html

[6]Joseph B. White, "China Lures More Investment," *The Wall Street Journal*, April 24, 2014, https://www.wsj.com/articles/SB10001424052702304788404579521510670705136

[7]Bryce Hoffman, "Here's What's Wrong With Ford's China Plan—And What's Right," *Forbes*, December 10, 2017, https://www.forbes.com/sites/brycehoffman/2017/12/10/blog-heres-whats-wrong-with-fords-china-plan-and-whats-right/?sh=7ce8d4c49454

[8]Ryan Felton, "Why Mark Fields Was Fired," Jalopnik.com, May 22, 2017, https://jalopnik.com/why-mark-fields-was-fired-1795431562

[9]Wouter Baan, Paul Gao, Arthur Wang, Daniel Zipser, "Savvy and sophisticated: Meet China's new car buyers," McKinsey & Company, September 21, 2017, https://www.mckinsey.com/industries/automotive-and-assembly/our-insights/savvy-and-sophisticated-meet-chinas-evolving-car-buyers

[10]Wouter Baan, Paul Gao, Arthur Wang, Daniel Zipser, "Savvy and sophisticated: Meet China's new car buyers," McKinsey & Company, September 21, 2017, https://www.mckinsey.com/industries/automotive-and-assembly/our-insights/savvy-and-sophisticated-meet-chinas-evolving-car-buyers

[11]Matthew DeBord, "How Lincoln returned from the brink of death

and put Ford back on the luxury map," *Business Insider*, October 24, 2016, https://www.businessinsider.com/how-lincoln-came-back-from-dead-put-ford-back-on-luxury-map-2016-9

[12]"Lincoln Launches in China; Unique Offering for Today's Chinese Luxury Auto Customers," Lincoln Media Center, April 17, 2014, https://media.lincoln.com/content/lincolnmedia/lna/us/en/news/2014/04/17/lincoln-launches-in-china--unique-offering-for-todays-chinese-lu.html

[13]Phoebe Wall Howard, "Ford executive finds China market laps up luxury, including Lincoln cars," *Detroit Free Press,* December 24, 2017, https://www.seattletimes.com/business/ford-executive-finds-china-market-laps-up-luxury-including-lincoln-cars/

[14]Phoebe Wall Howard, "Ford executive finds China market laps up luxury, including Lincoln cars," *Detroit Free Press*, 12/24/17, https://www.seattletimes.com/business/ford-executive-finds-china-market-laps-up-luxury-including-lincoln-cars/

[15]"China moves toward banning the internal combustion engine," *The Economist*, September 14, 2017, https://www.economist.com/business/2017/09/14/china-moves-towards-banning-the-internal-combustion-engine

[16]"China moves toward banning the internal combustion engine," *The Economist*, September 14, 2017, https://www.economist.com/business/2017/09/14/china-moves-towards-banning-the-internal-combustion-engine

[17]Greg Dotson, "Why EPS's U-turn on auto efficiency rules gives China the upper hand," The Conversation, March 29, 2018, https://theconversation.com/why-epas-u-turn-on-auto-efficiency-rules-gives-china-the-upper-hand-93840

[18]Greg Dotson, "Why EPS's U-turn on auto efficiency rules gives China the upper han," The Conversation, March 29, 2018, https://theconversation.com/why-epas-u-turn-on-auto-efficiency-rules-gives-china-the-upper-hand-93840

[19]Greg Dotson, "Why EPS's U-turn on auto efficiency rules gives China the upper hand," The Conversation, March 29, 2018, https://thecon-

versation.com/why-epas-u-turn-on-auto-efficiency-rules-gives-china-the-upper-hand-93840

[20]"What if China corners the cobalt market? *The Economist*, March 24, 2018, https://www.economist.com/finance-and-economics/2018/03/24/what-if-china-corners-the-cobalt-market

[21]"Goblin metals," *The Economist*, March 24, 2018, https://www.economist.com/finance-and-economics/2018/03/24/what-if-china-corners-the-cobalt-market

[22]"Ford announces ambitions electrification strategy," Ford Media Center, April 4, 2017, https://media.lincoln.com/content/fordmedia/fap/cn/en/news/2017/04/06/ford-announces-ambitious-china-electrification-strategy.html

[23]Hans Greimel, "Ford reboots in China, with deeper intel," *Automotive News China*, April 23, 2019, https://www.linkedin.com/pulse/ford-reboots-china-deeper-intel-hans-greimel-2019423-d-angelo?trk=public_post

[24]Norihiko Shirouzu, Ben Klayman, "Exclusive: In U-turn, Ford ditches plan to unify China sales system after partners push back," *Reuters*, September 4, 2019, https://www.reuters.com/article/idUSKCN-1VQ023/#:~:text=SHANGHAI%2FDETROIT%20(Reuters)%20%2D,the%20world's%20biggest%20car%20market

[25]Norihiko Shirouzu, Ben Klayman, "Exclusive: In U-turn, Ford ditches plan to unify China sales system after partners push back," *Reuters,* September 4, 2019, https://www.reuters.com/article/idUSKCN-1VQ023/#:~:text=SHANGHAI%2FDETROIT%20(Reuters)%20%2D,the%20world's%20biggest%20car%20market

[26]Norihiko Shirouzu, Ben Klayman, "Exclusive: In U-turn, Ford ditches plan to unify China sales system after partners push back," *Reuters,* September 4, 2019, https://www.reuters.com/article/idUSKCN-1VQ023/#:~:text=SHANGHAI%2FDETROIT%20(Reuters)%20%2D,the%20world's%20biggest%20car%20market

[27]Norihiko Shirouzu, Ben Klayman, "Exclusive: In U-turn, Ford ditches plan to unify China sales system after partners push back," *Reuters*, September 4, 2019, https://www.reuters.com/article/idUSKCN-

1VQ023/#:~:text=SHANGHAI%2FDETROIT%20(Reuters)%20
%2D,the%20world's%20biggest%20car%20market

[28]Aparna Narayanan, "This is Ford's Plan For The Market That's Driving EV, SUV Growth, Investors.com, December 5, 2017, https://www. investors.com/news/this-is-fords-plan-for-the-market-thats-driving-ev-suv-growth/

[29]"Ford intensifies China growth plan," Ford Media Center, December 5, 2017, https://media.ford.com/content/fordmedia/fna/us/en/ news/2017/12/05/ford-intensifies-china-growth-plan--more-smart-vehicles--expande.html

[30]Thomas Friedman, "Their Moon Shot and Ours," *The New York Times*, December 25, 2010, https://www.nytimes.com/2010/09/26/opinion/ 26friedman.html

[31]Akshat Rathi, Ari Natter and Keith Naughton, "Ford gets $9.2 Billion to Help US Catch Up With China's EV Dominance," *Bloomberg*, June 22, 2023, https://www.bloomberg.com/graphics/2023-ford-ev-battery-plant-funding-biden-green-technology/#:~:text=The%20 enormous%20loan%20—%20by%20far,to%20China%20in%20 green%20technologies.

[32]Keith Bradsher, "China Is Flooding the World With Cars," *The New York Times*, September 6, 2023, https://www.nytimes.com/2023/09/06/ business/china-car-exports.html

[33]Yoko Kubota, Selina Cheng, "In China, the Era of Western Carmakers Is Over" *The Wall Street Journal*, July 10, 2023, https://www.wsj. com/articles/rise-of-chinas-ev-makers-puts-end-to-wests-local-dominance-775d0811#

[34]Jack Ewing, "Ford Halts Work on E.V. Battery Plant in Michigan," *The New York Times*, September 25, 2023, https://www. nytimes.com/2023/09/25/business/energy-environment/ford-battery-plant-michigan.html

CASE STUDY: Hollywood Hijacked

[1]Malcolm Moore, "The rise and rise of Wang Jianlin, China's richest man", *Telegraph*, September 21, 2013, https://www.telegraph.co.uk/

news/worldnews/asia/china/10325019/The-rise-and-rise-of-Wang-Jianlin-Chinas-richest-man.html#:~:text=Malcolm%20Moore%20looks%20at%20the%20rise%20of%20China's%20richest%20man.&text=When%20he%20was%20a%20skinny,on%20any-thing%20but%20red%20carpet.

[2]Malcolm Moore, "The rise and rise of Wang Jianlin, China's richest man", *Telegraph*, September 21, 2013, https://www.telegraph.co.uk/news/worldnews/asia/china/10325019/The-rise-and-rise-of-Wang-Jianlin-Chinas-richest-man.html#:~:text=Malcolm%20Moore%20looks%20at%20the%20rise%20of%20China's%20richest%20man.&text=When%20he%20was%20a%20skinny,on%20any-thing%20but%20red%20carpet.

[3]Malcolm Moore, The rise and rise of Wang Jianlin, China's richest man, *Telegraph*, September 21, 2013, https://www.telegraph.co.uk/news/worldnews/asia/china/10325019/The-rise-and-rise-of-Wang-Jianlin-Chinas-richest-man.html#:~:text=Malcolm%20Moore%20looks%20at%20the%20rise%20of%20China's%20richest%20man.&text=When%20he%20was%20a%20skinny,on%20anything%20but%20red%20carpet.

[4]Jonathan Kaiman, "How Chinese tycoon Wang Jianlin is turning hard cash into soft power", *The Guardian*, December 9, 2014, https://www.theguardian.com/world/2014/dec/09/how-chinese-tycoon-wang-jianlin-is-turning-hard-cash-into-soft-power

[5]Ryan Faughnder, "AMC's Carmike bid extends Hollywood influence of China's richest man, Wang Jianlin. *Los Angeles Times*, 3/5/16, https://www.latimes.com/entertainment/envelope/cotown/la-et-ct-amc-carmike-deal-wang-jianlin-20160305-story.html

[6]"Leading man", *The Economist*, September 28, 2013, https://www.economist.com/business/2013/09/28/leading-man

[7]"The red carpet", *The Economist*, December 21, 2013

[8]"Billionaire Wang says Disney is no match for Wanda's 'wolf pack'", *South China Morning Post*, May 24, 2016, https://www.scmp.com/news/china/money-wealth/article/1952779/billionaire-wang-says-disney-no-match-wandas-wolf-pack

[9]Sean O'Connor, Nicholas Armstrong, "Directed by Hollywood, Edited by China: How China's Censorship and Influence Affect Films Worldwide." US-China Economic and Security Review Commission, October 28, 2015, https://www.uscc.gov/research/directed-hollywood-edited-china-how-chinas-censorship-and-influence-affect-films-worldwide

[10]"China's film industry The red carpet", *The Economist,* December 21, 2013, https://www.economist.com/christmas-specials/2013/12/21/the-red-carpet

[11]Clifford Coonan, "China's President Says Art Must Serve The People, Not The Market", *Hollywood Reporter*, October 17, 2014, https://www.hollywoodreporter.com/news/general-news/chinas-president-says-art-serve-741614/

[12]Jiang Jie, "Art should serve the people: Xi", *Global Times*, October 16, 2014, https://www.globaltimes.cn/content/886632.shtml

[13]Jiang Jie, "Art should serve the people: Xi", *Global Times*, October 16, 2014, https://www.globaltimes.cn/content/886632.shtml

[14]Clifford Coonan, "China's President Says Art Must Serve The People, Not The Market", *Hollywood Reporter*, October 17, 2014, https://www.hollywoodreporter.com/news/general-news/chinas-president-says-art-serve-741614/

[15]"China sends artists to the countryside in Mao-style cultural campaign", Agence France-Presse in Beijing, *The Guardian*, December 2, 2014,

[16]"It's a Wanda-ful life", *The Economist*, February 12, 2015, https://www.economist.com/business/2015/02/12/its-a-wanda-ful-life

[17]Anita Busch, "China Crackdown Hitting Hollywood: Where Do China Investments Stand?", *Deadline*, August 2, 2017, https://deadline.com/2017/08/china-crackdown-hollywood-where-investment-stands-1202140391/

[18]James Tager, "Made in Hollywood Censored by Beijing: The US Film Industry and Chinese Government Influence", PEN America, August 2020, https://pen.org/wp-content/uploads/2020/09/Made_in_Hollywood_Censored_by_Beiing_Report_FINAL.pdf

[19] James Tager, "Made in Hollywood Censored by Beijing: The US Film Industry and Chinese Government Influence", PEN America, August 2020, https://pen.org/wp-content/uploads/2020/09/Made_in_Hollywood_Censored_by_Beiing_Report_FINAL.pdf

[20] Patrick Brzeski, "Wolf Warrior II' Star Frank Grillo on How China's $780M Blockbuster Was Made (Q&A)", *The Hollywood Reporter*, August 22, 2017, https://www.hollywoodreporter.com/news/general-news/wolf-warrior-2-star-frank-grillo-how-chinas-780m-blockbuster-was-made-1031929/

[21] Patrick Brzeski, "Wolf Warrior II' Star Frank Grillo on How China's $780M Blockbuster Was Made (Q&A)", *The Hollywood Reporter*, August 22, 2017, https://www.hollywoodreporter.com/news/general-news/wolf-warrior-2-star-frank-grillo-how-chinas-780m-blockbuster-was-made-1031929/

[22] Patrick Brzeski, "Wolf Warrior II' Star Frank Grillo on How China's $780M Blockbuster Was Made (Q&A)", *The Hollywood Reporter*, August 22, 2017, https://www.hollywoodreporter.com/news/general-news/wolf-warrior-2-star-frank-grillo-how-chinas-780m-blockbuster-was-made-1031929/

[23] Patrick Brzeski, "Wandering Earth' Director Frank Gwo on Making China's First Sci-Fi Blockbuster", *The Hollywood Reporter*, February 20, 2019, https://www.hollywoodreporter.com/movies/movie-news/wandering-earth-director-making-chinas-first-sci-fi-blockbuster-1187681/

[24] Patrick Brzeski, "Wandering Earth' Director Frank Gwo on Making China's First Sci-Fi Blockbuster", *The Hollywood Reporter*, February 20, 2019, https://www.hollywoodreporter.com/movies/movie-news/wandering-earth-director-making-chinas-first-sci-fi-blockbuster-1187681/

[25] James Tager, "Made in Hollywood Censored by Beijing: The US Film Industry and Chinese Government Influence", PEN America, August 2020, https://pen.org/wp-content/uploads/2020/09/Made_in_Hollywood_Censored_by_Beiing_Report_FINAL.pdf

[26] James Tager, "Made in Hollywood Censored by Beijing: The US Film

Industry and Chinese Government Influence", PEN America, August 2020, https://pen.org/wp-content/uploads/2020/09/Made_in_Holly-wood_Censored_by_Beiing_Report_FINAL.pdf

[27]James Tager, "Made in Hollywood Censored by Beijing: The US Film Industry and Chinese Government Influence", PEN America, August 2020, https://pen.org/wp-content/uploads/2020/09/Made_in_Holly-wood_Censored_by_Beiing_Report_FINAL.pdf

Case Study: NBA Netizens

[1]Helen Gao, "From Mao Zedong to Jeremy Lin: Why Basketball Is China's Biggest Sport," *The Atlantic*, February 22, 2012, https://www.theatlantic.com/international/archive/2012/02/from-mao-zedong-to-jeremy-lin-why-basketball-is-chinas-biggest-sport/253427/

[2]Matthew Forney, "How Nike Figured Out China", *TIME*, October 17, 2004, https://content.time.com/time/magazine/article/0,9171,725113,00.html

[3]Matthew Forney, "How Nike Figured Out China", *TIME*, October 17, 2004, https://content.time.com/time/magazine/article/0,9171,725113,00.html

[4]Zhuang Pinghui, "NBA games return to China screens but Houston Rockets not included", *South China Morning Post*, October 14, 2019, https://www.scmp.com/news/china/society/article/3032849/nba-games-return-china-screens-houston-rockets-not-included#

[5]Patrick Rishe, "Kobe Bryant's Pioneering Impact On NBA Stars Building Lucrative Brands in China" *Forbes*, January 27, 2020, https://www.forbes.com/sites/prishe/2020/01/27/kobe-bryants-pioneering-impact-on-nba-stars-building-lucrative-brands-in-china/?sh=4e6b5de839f1

[6]Statista

[7]Jacob Pramuk, "Trump rips NBA players, officials for 'pandering to China,' but says league has to work out dispute on its own," CNBC, October 9, 2019, https://www.cnbc.com/2019/10/09/trump-rips-nba-players-officials-for-pandering-to-china-but-says-league-has-to-work-out-dispute-out-on-its-own.html

8Jemele Hill, "The NBA Is Going to Have to Choose", *The Atlantic*, October 8, 2019, https://www.theatlantic.com/ideas/archive/2019/10/nba-must-choose-its-own-values-over-chinas/599626/#

9Jacob Pramuk, "Trump rips NBA players, officials for 'pandering to China,' but says league has to work out dispute on its own", CNBC, October 9, 2019, https://www.cnbc.com/2019/10/09/trump-rips-nba-players-officials-for-pandering-to-china-but-says-league-has-to-work-out-dispute-out-on-its-own.html

10SCMP Reporter, "Brooklyn Nets owner Joe Tsai weighs in on Houston Rockets storm while James harden says team 'loves China'", *South China Morning Post*, October 7, 2019, https://www.scmp.com/sport/basketball/article/3031842/brooklyn-nets-owner-joe-tsai-weighs-houston-rockets-storm-saying

11Associated Press, ESPN, "Lebron James-beyond his years, beyond the hype", December 10, 2005, http://www.espn.com/espn/wire/_/section/nba/id/2254792

12Emmett Knowlton, "Lebron James business partner confirms lifetime deal with Nike is worth over $1 billion", *Business Insider*, May 17, 2016, https://www.businessinsider.com/lebron-james-nike-deal-exceeds-1-billion-maverick-carter-says-2016-5https://www.businessinsider.com/lebron-james-nike-deal-exceeds-1-billion-maverick-carter-says-2016-5

13Associated Press, ESPN, "Lebron James-beyond his years, beyond the hype", December 10, 2005, http://www.espn.com/espn/wire/_/section/nba/id/2254792

14Jerry Brembry, "Lebron James is the most powerful voice in his profession", Andscape, February 18, 2018, https://theundefeated.com/features/lebron-james-to-take-floor-for-nba-all-star-game-as-the-most-powerful-voice-in-his-profession/

15Jerry Brembry, "Lebron James is the most powerful voice in his profession", Andscape, February 18, 2018, https://theundefeated.com/features/lebron-james-to-take-floor-for-nba-all-star-game-as-the-most-powerful-voice-in-his-profession/

16Micheal Mccann, "Lebron's China comments and the financial fallout for NBA, US", SI.com, October 15, 2019, https://www.si.com/nba/2019/10/15/lebron-james-nba-china-financial-fallout

[17]Jeff Zillgitt, Mark Medina, "Lebron James' controversial comments 'furthers his brand power in China", *USA Today*, October 17, 2019, https://www.usatoday.com/story/sports/nba/2019/10/17/lebron-james-nike-china-revenue/3989915002/

[18]Cheng Li, Qiuyang Wang, "Kobe Bryant and his enduring impact on the Sino-American Friendship", China US Focus, May 4, 2020, https://www.chinausfocus.com/society-culture/kobe-bryant-and-his-enduring-impact-on-the-sino-american-friendship

[19]Lauren Teixeira, "Kobe Bryant was the United States' Best Ambassador in China", *Foreign Policy*, January 30, 2020, https://foreignpolicy.com/2020/01/30/china-basketball-kobe-bryant-nba-united-states/

[20]Sarah Zheng, "China denies it pressured NBA to sack Houston Rockets Daryl Morey, *South China Morning Post*, October 18, 2019, https://www.scmp.com/news/china/diplomacy/article/3033590/china-denies-it-pressured-nba-sack-houston-rockets-daryl-morey

[21]Tim MacMahon, "Daryl Morey stepping down as Houston Rockets GM", ESPN, October 15, 2020, https://www.espn.com/nba/story/_/id/30120824/daryl-morey-stepping-houston-rockets-gm-sources-say

[22]Brian Windhorst, "China's CCTV to air NBA finals Game 5 live; first broadcast in country in more than a year", ABC News, October 9, 2020, https://abcnews.go.com/Sports/chinas-cctv-air-nba-finals-game-live-broadcast/story?id=73521241

[23]Brian Windhorst, "China's CCTV to air NBA finals Game 5 live; first broadcast in country in more than a year", ABC News, October 9, 2020, https://abcnews.go.com/Sports/chinas-cctv-air-nba-finals-game-live-broadcast/story?id=73521241

[24]Johnathon White, "NBA existing China 'should be for US government to decide', says Adam Silver, *South China Morning Post*, September 23, 2020, https://www.scmp.com/print/sport/china/article/3102664/nba-exiting-china-should-be-us-government-decide-says-adam-silver

[25]Johnathon White, "NBA existing China 'should be for US government to decide', says Adam Silver, *South China Morning Post*, September 23, 2020, https://www.scmp.com/print/sport/china/article/3102664/nba-exiting-china-should-be-us-government-decide-says-adam-silver

Milton Keynes UK
Ingram Content Group UK Ltd.
UKHW020154291024
450401UK00008B/160